Forgotten Revolution

The Limerick Soviet 1919

[The Centenary Edition]

Liam Cahill

KELLY
PUBLISHING

Orla Kelly Publishing,
27 Kilbrody, Mount Oval,
Rochestown, Cork.

'History is a common meadow where everyone can make hay'.
– *Spanish Proverb*

The Author

Photo Credit: Philip O'Neill Photography, Swords, county Dublin

Liam Cahill is a historian and writer. He has researched and studied the Limerick Soviet for many years and has written, lectured and broadcast on it widely – in Irish and English.

A lifelong trade unionist, he has held many representative positions in the Labour movement from branch to national level and is a former Political Correspondent and Economics Correspondent with RTÉ, Ireland's public broadcaster. He has worked as a public servant and as an adviser in government, politics, the private sector and with campaign groups. For many years, he edited a popular web site *'An Fear Rua – The GAA Unplugged!'*.

Praise for the 1990 edition of 'Forgotten Revolution'

Liam Cahill has chronicled the Limerick Soviet with skill and balance, driven neither by blind enthusiasm for its memory or by heavy-handed pedantry. Unlike the soviet, his book is a success.

— *Seán Dunne, The Irish Examiner*

The story of the Limerick Soviet is told for the first time in this entertaining book. It is a fine addition to the now considerable volume of work of Labour historians and brings the Soviet justifiably back into the centre stage of our history.

— *Patrick Smyth, The Irish Times*

A very readable narrative. Cahill, an experienced journalist and himself a good union man, looks as though he has produced a story that anyone could find interesting and the historians won't sniff at. Excellent notes, bibliography and index and quite a few photos.

— *Books Ireland*

The establishment, maintenance and demise of the Limerick 'Soviet' is a good story and Liam Cahill tells it very well. Of interest to a wide audience.

— *Peter Cassells, former General Secretary, Irish Congress of Trade Unions*

Based on a wide range of primary and secondary sources in Ireland and Britain as well as local interviews, the book is meticulously researched and constitutes a valuable addition to local and national labour history studies in Ireland. The work is one of accurate scholarship and sound judgement.

— *Fergus D'Arcy, Professor Emeritus in modern history at University College Dublin*

A scholarly and well-written volume.

— *The Limerick Chronicle*

Very few people in Limerick are aware of this historic period and it is good that it has been documented so well by Liam Cahill.

— *The Limerick Leader*

The story of the Soviet deserves to be brought to a new and wider audience. Liam Cahill has written a well-researched and balanced account of the strike and its historical context.

— *The late Jim Kemmy TD*

The author's account of the contemporary Irish scene is brilliantly researched and outlined. This scholarly work, by an acknowledged expert on Irish labour history of the period 1916 to 1923, is an enduring and valuable commentary for the historian and student of that era.

— *The late Frank Prendergast, former TD and Mayor of Limerick*

Forgotten Revolution was an important book, and one that we were very proud to publish here at O'Brien Press.

– Michael O'Brien

Cahill's book is extremely well researched and is invaluable as an insight into the 1919 period in general.

– An Phoblacht

Books such as Liam Cahill's *'Forgotten Revolution, Limerick Soviet 1919'* were a great stimulus to my own.

– Conor Kostick, author of 'Revolution in Ireland', Research Associate in Medieval History, Trinity College Dublin

It was good to hear that this book was published at last, good to see it in the shops, good to see it among the top five titles in hardback sales. It is almost as good to read it. Cahill has researched his subject diligently. Nearly every detail of the events that led to the Limerick Soviet has been uncovered and revealed. As a local history of the Limerick Soviet this is unlikely to be bettered.

– D R O'Connor Lysaght 'Saothar 16', Journal of the Irish Labour History Society

Liam describes with great passion the events in Limerick at that time, when ordinary people displayed courage, humour and the kind of resourcefulness almost unparalleled in in Irish history.

– RTÉ Guide

Cahill's book, in a thorough and accessible fashion, brings the Soviet to life, locates the struggle in the broader political context of the time, and attempts to assess its ultimate success or failure and its longer-term impact for Irish Labour.

– SIPTU Newsline

The story of the Limerick Soviet is excellently told by Liam Cahill.

– Dónal Ó Drisceoil and Fintan Lane, Editors, 'Politics and the Irish Working Class, 1830– 1945'

Based on a wide range of primary and secondary sources in Ireland and Britain as well as on local interviews, the work is meticulously researched and constitutes a valuable addition to local and national history.

– Irish Economic and Social History: Journal of the Economic and Social History Society of Ireland, 1991

This book is obviously a labour of love. It describes the progress of the strike through interviews, memoirs, union minutes and official documents. Cahill beautifully tells a story that deserves a wide audience.

– Socialist Worker Review (UK)

Well worth reading and studying.
— *The News Line (UK)*

This is the definitive account of an unsung but important moment in Ireland's history.
— *The Communications Worker*

Liam Cahill brilliantly analyses the Limerick Soviet which produced its own newspapers and currency during 1919 in an attempt to thwart British rule.
— *Post News The Journal of An Post*

'*Forgotten Revolution*' is something else – a telling by Liam Cahill of the fascinating story of how, in 1919, nationalist forces and trade unionists fused into the Limerick Soviet which for two weeks controlled the city.
— *The Irish Post (UK)*

In '*Forgotten Revolution*' Liam Cahill has written a very readable account of the Limerick Soviet. He has drawn on a very wide range of sources and shed important light on a key episode of the period 1919-23. The clear, direct style of the writing makes the book accessible to the general reader while the meticulous research commends it to the academic.
— *The Meath Chronicle*

A scholarly contribution to the history of the Labour movement in Ireland and deals with a critical stage in that history. But don't be put off by the word scholarly – it is an absorbing and informative read concerning the period. Liam Cahill's account does it justice.
— *RTÉ Staff Magazine*

Liam Cahill spent ten years researching this book. It is illustrated with many period photographs and mementoes from the Limerick Soviet.
— *Public Sector Times*

'*Forgotten Revolution*' describes for the first time Labour's leading role in the developing struggle for Irish independence in the years after 1916. The book is excellently and colourfully presented.
— *The Leinster Express*

'*Forgotten Revolution*' is written in a clear, direct style, making this forgotten history available to the general reader. Liam Cahill has over twenty years' first-hand experience of trade unionism and this experience, together with the exhaustive research which he undertook, have resulted in a book of the highest academic standard, historically accurate and written from a deep and genuine interest in this dramatic episode in Irish history.
— *The Nenagh Guardian*

Written in a clear and lively style, the book is designed to appeal to the general reader with an interest in Irish history. It also puts the episode into the context of contemporary events

in Ireland, Britain and Europe.
— *The Kerryman*

Cahill has a shrewd eye for the realities of the situation.
— *The Linen Hall Review*

A welcome addition to the shelves of the Labour history enthusiast. An attractive, well produced but, above all, immensely readable recounting of a period in Irish history when everything was up for grabs and we blew it.
— *Customs Journal*

Liam Cahill tells his tale well and even-handedly and provides the serious student with a fine bibliography. Both Labour and Limerick were lucky with their chronicler.
— *An Múinteoir, INTO journal*

Liam Cahill spent ten years researching this book. It describes Labour's leading role in the developing struggle for Independence in the years after 1916.
— *Ireland's Eye*

A quick word about one of our programmes starting on radio on Monday night. If you are interested – attention Limerick! – Liam Cahill, who used to work here in our Newsroom, wrote the book called '*Forgotten Revolution*', all about the Limerick Soviet, the stirring events of the general strike in 1919, when fourteen thousand workers took over the entire running of the city.

On RTÉ Radio programme 'Book Time', starting on Monday next, ten past eleven at night, Liam Cahill will be reading his book and it goes on for a fortnight. Each week day night and you should catch it if you can, particularly if you have an interest in Limerick and its history.
— *Gay Byrne, RTÉ Radio 1*

Liam's scholarly research into the Soviet cannot be faulted and he has delved deep into the primary sources.
— *Making Sense Ireland's political and cultural review*

Cahill looks at events from a trade unionist perspective. His book is not a Marxist analysis. Having said that, he gives a detailed account of the militant struggle of the workers of Limerick against British imperialism.
— *The Leninist (UK)*

Liam Cahill is one of Ireland's most respected and authoritative journalists and commentators.
— *Centrepoint Published by Limerick Teachers' Centre*

If you can't afford to buy it, it's worth ordering from your local library.
— *Aontas*

Liam Cahill has brought this significant event back into public memory.

– Fred Powell, The Political Economy of the Irish Welfare State: Church, State and Capital

A sympathetic but scholarly study of the establishment, maintenance and demise of the general strike in Limerick of April 1919.

– Jonathan Smele, The Russian Revolution and Civil War 1917-1921: An Annotated Bibliography

Acknowledgments

For many years, the late Jim Kemmy was a lone pioneer in research and scholarship on the Limerick Soviet and he built a solid foundation on which this book rests. He was generous with access to his invaluable trove of original materials on the Soviet and his stockpile of relevant material, both published and unpublished. More importantly, perhaps, he gave freely of his advice and experience at vital stages.

Mike McNamara, President of Limerick Council of Trade Unions, has curated an impressive archive of materials about the Soviet and is an acknowledged expert on it. He has inspired me and encouraged me in writing this Centenary Edition and, at times, our work together was more like an active collaboration than passive co-operation.

Kevin O'Connor, a Limerickman and a former colleague in the newsroom of RTÉ, carried out an important interview with Charles St. George, a contemporary witness of some of the key events mentioned in the narrative and I am grateful to him.

Joe Clarke undertook important research on my behalf in London, while Michael Cannon checked newspaper archival material in Paris. At my request, Father Liam O'Sullivan (Bishop's Secretary) and Father David Bracken (Diocesan Archivist) searched the Limerick Diocesan Archives for any relevant material. I am grateful to Mike Finn for permission to use the photo of British troups outside King John's Castle.

Profound thanks are due to the administrators and staffs of several libraries and archives for their efficient and courteous assistance over several years: the National Library of Ireland, the State Paper Office, Dublin (now part of the National Archives), the Public Record Office, London, the Imperial War Museum, British Pathe, Hulton Archives/GettyImages and the British Library, Colindale. The impressively marshalled and presented online resources of the Irish Military Archives were of invaluable assistance.

In RTÉ, the former librarian Máire Ní Mhurchú and the library staff were cheerful and indefatigable in responding to a variety of queries and requests for books. Tom Holton of the Stills Department was also of great assistance.

I am grateful to John McKenna, a tutor on the Maynooth University course leading to the NUI Certificate in Creative Writing for Publication. He guided me towards unlocking insights into the writing of creative non-fiction that have helped me to present the outcome of my research in a more engaging and interesting way. Orla Kelly has been all that I could have wished for in a publisher – wise, committed, indefatigable, good humoured.

My late wife, Patricia, was always understanding about the commitment of time involved in this almost life-long project and I have felt her supportive presence at my shoulder during the writing of this book.

Liam Cahill

Contents

Foreword to the Centenary Edition

This is a completely updated, revised and enlarged edition of my original book on the Limerick Soviet, published in 1990.

In this edition, I have made extensive use of the significant official archives that were opened up in recent years, many of them available online. These include the Bureau of Military History, Witness Statements, 1913 – 21 and the Military Service Pensions Collection, 1916 – 23 – both held in the Military Archives in Dublin – as well as the British National Archives, the Imperial War Museum and a comprehensive archive of materials relating to the Soviet curated by Mike McNamara, President, Limerick Council of Trade Unions, and held in the Mechanics' Institute in Limerick. I have also benefitted from the increase in scholarship and research on the events of 1911 to 1923 in Ireland, some of it on the working-class dimension of those years, including specific work on the Limerick Soviet.

This has enabled me to make a totally refreshed analysis of information and sources about the Soviet, helping to situate it more securely in the context of the competing political forces and evolving events of its time. In particular, it has enabled a better understanding of the crucial roles of the Irish Republican Brotherhood and of socialist trade union organisers in the events before, during and after Limerick.

The number of words in this edition has increased by 25% compared with the 1990 version, from roughly 60,000 words to almost 75,000. More importantly, however, I have substantially re-organised and rewritten much of the text to make it more enjoyable and accessible to general readers, while at the same time still being of value to academic researchers and students of history. The focus now in the early chapters is much more on the stirring events and intriguing protagonists of the Soviet while the latter part analyses the theoretical and historical context locally, nationally and internationally as well as the long-term consequences.

The 1990 edition was a best seller and quickly sold out its print run of 2,000 hard back copies. Since then, I have found continuing interest in the story of the Soviet and I have often been asked when I might re-issue the book. I responded to this interest by making it available for download free on the Internet – there were more than 25,000 visits to the site – and have created popular pages on the subject on the Facebook and Twitter platforms. However, I undertook a revised edition of the book to mark the Centenary of the Soviet and as a contribution to the Decade of Commemorations.

I researched and wrote about the Soviet originally to try to answer this important question: Why were our grandmothers and grandfathers – even our great grandparents – more radical in their politics than my generation? In the late Sixties and early Seventies of the last century

I was part of a short-lived move to the Left by the Labour party. Before, during and after the General Election of 1969, that move provoked – to adapt the memorable phrase of James Connolly – a carnival of reaction from press, pulpit and people. Socialism was condemned as a foreign import that was alien to the Irish people. I hope my work has gone some way towards discrediting that charge.

So, I undertook this work originally for a political purpose, not merely from a desire to establish the facts of the Limerick Soviet. I make no apology for that approach and I take my stand on this with the distinguished British historian, EH Carr, in his seminal essay *'The Historian and His Facts:* 'Since they do not and cannot exist in pure form, they are always refracted through the mind of the recorder… History means interpretation… It is the historian who has decided for his own reasons that Caesar's crossing of that petty stream, the Rubicon, is a fact of history, whereas the crossing of the Rubicon by millions of other people before or since interests nobody at all'.

Liam Cahill

21 January 2019

Abbreviations

AOH	Ancient Order of Hibernians
BMH	Bureau of Military History
CBS	Crime Branch (Special)
CMG	Commander of the Order St. Michael and St. George
CO	Colonial Office
CSORP	Chief Secretary's Office Registered Papers
D-I	District Inspector
DSO	Distinguished Service Order
GHQ	General Headquarters
I-G	Inspector General
ILPTUC	Irish Labour Party and Trade Union Congress
IRA	Irish Republican Army
IRB	Irish Republican Brotherhood
ITGWU	Irish Transport and General Workers' Union
KC	King's Counsel
LUTLC	Limerick United Trades and Labour Council
MA	Military Archives
MSPC	Military Service Pension Collection (1913 – 21)
NLI	National Library of Ireland
PRO	Public Record Office, London
RIC	Royal Irish Constabulary
SPO	State Paper Office (now incorporated into the National Archives)
WO	War Office
WS	Witness Statement

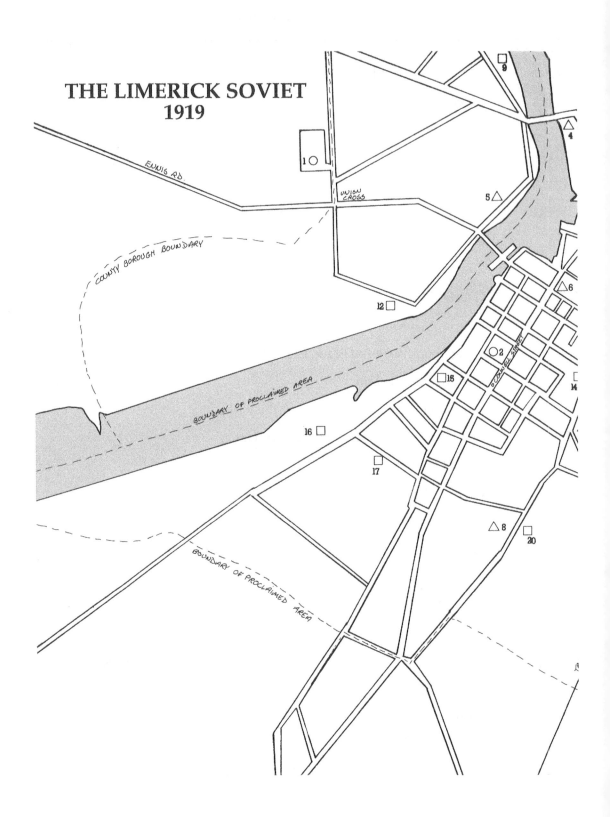

THE LIMERICK SOVIET
1919

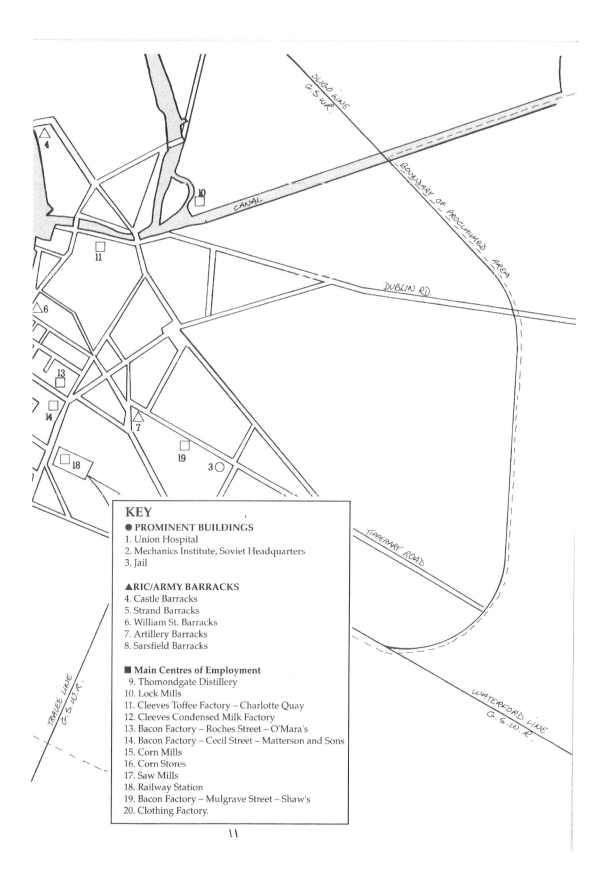

KEY

● **PROMINENT BUILDINGS**
1. Union Hospital
2. Mechanics Institute, Soviet Headquarters
3. Jail

▲**RIC/ARMY BARRACKS**
4. Castle Barracks
5. Strand Barracks
6. William St. Barracks
7. Artillery Barracks
8. Sarsfield Barracks

■ **Main Centres of Employment**
 9. Thomondgate Distillery
10. Lock Mills
11. Cleeves Toffee Factory – Charlotte Quay
12. Cleeves Condensed Milk Factory
13. Bacon Factory – Roches Street – O'Mara's
14. Bacon Factory – Cecil Street – Matterson and Sons
15. Corn Mills
16. Corn Stores
17. Saw Mills
18. Railway Station
19. Bacon Factory – Mulgrave Street – Shaw's
20. Clothing Factory.

CHAPTER ONE

<u>Robert Byrne – Republican, Trade Unionist and Hunger Striker</u>

'On Monday, April 14, there began in Limerick City a strike
protest against military tyranny, which because of its dramatic
suddenness, its completeness and the proof it offered that
workers' control signifies perfect order, excited world-
wide attention.'
– *Irish Labour Party and Trade Union Congress, Annual
Report 1919*

It began with the active life and death by gunfire of a young man named Robert Byrne, Irish Republican and trade unionist.

On Monday 14 April 1919, the '*Irish Independent*' correspondent in Limerick telegraphed the Dublin office: 'Limerick City is on strike. Shops, warehouses and factories are closed. No work is being done and no business transacted.'

The strike had been declared by Limerick United Trades and Labour Council to protest against the proclamation of the city by the British authorities as a Special Military Area, under the Defence of the Realm Act. The military control regulations required all citizens to carry special permits and thousands of workers faced the prospect of police and military scrutiny several times a day as they went to and from work. By Monday evening, fourteen thousand workers had joined the strike.

Within twenty-four hours, the Strike Committee had become the effective governing body of Ireland's fourth largest city. The Committee – or the Soviet as it soon became known – regulated the price and distribution of food, published its own newspaper and printed its own currency. It was the first workers' soviet in Britain or Ireland and it brought the Labour movement to the brink of a revolutionary confrontation with British power in Ireland.

The Limerick Soviet was organised Labour's first – and in the event, fatally flawed – intervention in the Irish War of Independence.

By a fortuitous coincidence, the soviet received worldwide newspaper coverage. The city was to be the jumping off point in an attempt by an airman to win a £10,000 prize to be won by the first person to fly the Atlantic from East to West. Scores of overseas journalists were there to cover the event, but when it – literally – failed to take off, they turned to reporting on the soviet.

The proclaiming of Limerick came hard on the dramatic events associated with the death of an IRA[1] Volunteer hunger striker, Robert Byrne, during a botched rescue attempt. He was shot in his bed in Limerick Workhouse Hospital in the afternoon of Sunday 6 April 1919 in a struggle with members of the Royal Irish Constabulary during his attempted rescue by members of the IRA. Within a few hours, he had bled to death from his wounds. A policeman was killed and another wounded. The inquest jury found that a policeman had fired the fatal shot that killed Byrne and 10,000 Irish Volunteers marched behind his coffin. The British authorities imposed the permit system in a futile move to flush out the policeman's killers and the workers retaliated with a general strike.

Robert Joseph Byrne was born on 28 November 1889 in a respectable two-storey red brick house at 5 Upper Oriel Street in Dublin. Oriel Street is in the North docklands area, behind the present-day International Financial Services Centre and the former An Post Sorting Office in Sheriff Street. He was named after his father, a fitter by trade, who was from the nearby North Strand. His father's relatively higher earnings from a trade may account for the better-quality house, particularly compared with the many single storey two-roomed cottages in the vicinity. His father was a cousin of the famous Alderman Alfie Byrne, ten times Lord Mayor of Dublin, once a Parnellite, later a Free State Senator and TD – nominally an Independent – but generally favouring Cumann na nGaedhael and, later, Fine Gael.

Robert's mother was Annie Hurley, the daughter of a shopkeeper, from Nelson Street (now called Parnell Street) in Limerick city. His parents were married in Limerick in July 1882 and lived there for a number of years before moving to Dublin. Their eldest son, John Hurley Byrne, was born at 3 Nelson Street on 27 April 1883. Robert was born in Dublin, as were his other siblings – Mary, George, Thomas and Francis – as well as some children who died in infancy. After the death of Robert Byrne senior in 1907, the family returned to Limerick and lived in Town Wall Cottage, situated in the Donovan's Row area, just off John Street. Town Wall was an old, historic part of Limerick nestling below the famous walls that had witnessed the Williamite sieges of 1690 and 1691. It was reputed to be the place where the women of Limerick had marshalled to repel the Orange besiegers. The area had a strong, nationalist tradition which influenced Byrne's outlook and for a number of years he had been active in the Sinn Féin movement.

In May 1907, when he had just turned eighteen years of age, Robert began working as a Learner in the General Post Office in Limerick. A year later, he was transferred to

---

1 – On 20 August 1919, members of Dáil Éireann and the Irish Volunteers agreed to swear allegiance to the Irish Republic. From that date onwards, the Volunteers officially became the Irish Republican Army. From April 1919 onwards, this military organisation had begun to be known colloquially as 'the IRA' or 'the Irish Republican Army'. In official documents required under the Military Service Pensions Acts, service prior to 31 March 1919 is described as being in the 'Irish Volunteers'. After that date and up to 30 September 1923, service is deemed to be with 'Óglaigh na nÉireann'. This book follows the MSPC convention.

Kinsale, county Cork as a Postal Sorter. Then, he moved to Bandon, in the same county, on promotion as a Postal Clerk. In October 1911, he returned to Limerick and worked as a Telegraph operator in the GPO. This was a responsible job, because for much of the early part of the 20th century telegraph was the most important means of rapid communication. It also put him in a position to gather much information in his own section and in the postal branch, to be passed on to intelligence officers of the Irish Volunteers.

Robert Byrne was active in his union, the Irish Post Office Clerks' Association, becoming Chairman of the Limerick branch and was a delegate to Limerick United Trades and Labour Council. Like many other unions, the IPOCA held their meetings in the Mechanics' Institute building, then located in Glantworth Street.

The veteran and respected Limerick Fenian, John Daly, died on 30 June 1916 and hundreds of Irish Volunteers, Cumann na mBan members and Fianna Éireann boy scouts marched in his funeral cortege. They included Robert Byrne whose presence marching with the Volunteers was noted by the police Special Branch and reported by them to the Post Office. In his response to this allegation, Byrne claimed that he did not march with the Volunteers but had walked after the hearse with the chef mourners and friends of the deceased.

Daly was a leading member of the Irish Republican Brotherhood. His niece, Kathleen Daly, was married to Tom Clarke, another leading member of the IRB, a signatory of the 1916 Proclamation and executed by the British for his part in the Rising. His nephew, Edward Daly, was a Commandant in the Rising and was also executed. Daly had commanded the Limerick detachment of the IRB in the Fenian Rising of 1867 in their abortive attack on the Kilmallock constabulary station. He later became a member of the Supreme Council of the IRB and organiser for Connacht and Ulster. In the general election of 1895, Daly was elected unopposed as MP for Limerick city but was disqualified because of his previous conviction for treason-felony. Three times he was elected Mayor of Limerick, from 1899 to 1901.

Daly was a close friend, not only of Clarke, but of Seán MacDiarmada, another of the IRB leadership and an executed signatory of the 1916 Proclamation. The Daly and Byrne families were friends and their political views were closely aligned. Through his friendship with John Daly, Robert Byrne became acquainted with both of these influential national leaders. It is safe to assume that, at some stage, prior to the 1916 Rising, Robert Byrne had been sworn in as a member of the clandestine IRB.

The police had been closely monitoring Byrne's connection with Clarke and MacDiarmada. On 6 June 1916 Sergeant Walsh, of the Limerick Crime (Special) Division, sent a report to Dublin Castle regarding Byrne's Republican activities. He noted that he had been observed attending meetings of the Irish Volunteers in the Drill Hall and his mother's house, where he lived, had been visited by 'the late suspects Thomas J Clarke and John MacDermott'. Sometime during 1916, his name was included in a list of Post Office officials who had 'come under the notice of the Police by reason of their connection with the Irish Volunteer or Sinn Féin movements'. The list shows an entry as follows: 'Byrne, Clerk, Limerick, reported to be Sinn Féiner – No action taken'.

In January 1917, Byrne came under further scrutiny from the Police Crime (Special) Branch in an investigation of 'alleged disloyalty of Postal officials' in Limerick. Sinn Féin in Limerick often hired Saint Ita's hall for Sunday night dances. The drapers' assistants employed by Todds had arranged to hold a dance in the same hall on the previous Wednesday night and had decorated the hall. Among the decorations used were the flags of the wartime Allies, including the Union Jack. On the Saturday prior to the Sinn Féin event Limerick Postal officials had booked the same hall for a dance. On the morning of the Postal dance, according to a police report, 'Mr R. Byrne of the Limerick Post Office' when viewing the decorations, was alleged to have said the flags would have to come down as no one would dance under the Union Jack. On another occasion during that day, a police report noted that Byrne had said the postal officials were afraid to leave up the flags fearing the Sinn Féiners would interfere with them at their regular Sunday night dance. Because of the postal clerks' objections, the drapers' assistants took down all the decorations. But the episode meant that only a handful of postal officials attended their Saturday night dance, perhaps fearing that association with the event might damage their careers.

Robert Byrne's star continued to rise in the Republican firmament. On 3 September 1918, he attended a meeting in the Town Hall to protest against the action of the Unionist Mayor, Sir Stephen Quin, in inviting the Lord Lieutenant to visit Limerick. The meeting did not disclose much opposition and the protest fizzled out. Not long after that meeting, Byrne was brought before the Post Office management to face serious disciplinary charges, including that he had attended John Daly's funeral in 1916. In late November 1918, he had been elected Adjutant of the Second Battalion, Mid-Limerick Brigade of the Irish Volunteers. The authorities' tolerance had reached its limits and in January 1919 Byrne was dismissed from the Post Office. It has been claimed that his sole attendance at a meeting of Limerick United Trades and Labour Council was for the one where his dismissal was discussed. In a report headed 'The Hidden Hand in the GPO', the local radical newspaper '*The Bottom Dog*' grimly noted the 'esteemed and respected' Byrne's dismissal. It warned that he would have the support of Post Office Clerks' Association and of the trade union movement generally.

The authorities increased the pressure on Byrne. On New Year's Eve, Monday, 31 December 1918, Head Constable Healy led a party of policemen from John Street station along the short distance to the Byrne family home at Town Wall Cottage, to conduct a search. This was a senior and experienced raiding party. It included three Sergeants – Breen, Moroney and Corry – and eight constables. When they entered, they found Robert Byrne in bed and Sergeant Breen found an unloaded large pattern Webley 1917 six-chambered revolver on the bedside dresser in Byrne's room. He asked Byrne to account for it and he replied 'I'll give you no information about it'. At the same time, Sergeant Moroney discovered eight live rounds of revolver ammunition for the Webley in a drawer in Mrs. Byrne's bedroom and a revolver bullet of smaller size. Elsewhere in the house, the searchers found a useless old-style blunderbuss – Mrs Byrne said it had been in the house for a hundred years – as well as a copy of 'Manual of Field Engineering', dated 1911, and a pair of field glasses. Newspaper reports say the searchers also found Byrne's notebook as Adjutant of the 2nd Battalion. Within only two months of confidently leading the search party, Head Constable Healy died – one of the estimated 23,000 Irish people who succumbed to the virulent Spanish flu pandemic of 1918 –19.

On 13 January 1919 Sergeant Michael Corry of the RIC arrested Byrne at his home under draconian powers accorded to police and military by the wartime Defence of the Realm Consolidation Act 1914. He was charged with possession of a revolver and ammunition and brought to Limerick Prison in Mulgrave Street, to await trial by court martial, under the DORA Regulations. The following day, Byrne refused to take food. On 15 January 1919, the Governor of Limerick Prison, AF Falkiner, phoned the General Prisons Board in Dublin Castle to inform them as follows: 'Robert J Byrne committed by the Military the day before yesterday to await his trial by Court Martial has since last night refused his food which is supplied by the Military'. In his Journal, the Medical Officer, Dr. Michael McGrath, recorded 'Prisoner Robert Byrne on hunger strike. His condition is so far satisfactory and he is supplied by the Military with sufficient food'. At 4 o'clock in the afternoon of 16 January Robert Byrne began to take food again.

On 18 January, Byrne replied to a letter he had received from his mother. He asked her to send him a thick pair of socks from the several pairs in his wardrobe. He wrote: 'I am fit and well and really there is no occasion to bother about me at all. Try and put me out of your mind and just treat my absence as if I were away for a few days. You must have enough to worry about without wasting any thought on me'. The letter disclosed an impish sense of humour. He asked for a visitor to Town Wall Cottage to be put in his room to keep his bed warm and said that they would be surprised by his tidy ways when he got home. 'I will be alright if I don't dismantle my bed and fold up all my bed clothes at the beginning', he wrote. The letter ended with these words: 'Do try and cease thinking of me and above all don't worry as there is absolutely no cause for doing so. Remember me to all, Bert'.

Robert Byrne's trial began on Tuesday, 21 January 1919 in the New Barracks, Lord Edward Street, now called Sarsfield Barracks. Coincidentally, this was the same day that Dáil Éireann held its first public meeting in Dublin and that Dan Breen, Seán Hogan,

Seamus Robinson and members of the 3rd Tipperary Brigade of the Volunteers initiated the guerrilla dimension of the Anglo-Irish War in an ambush that led to the death of two policemen. According to '*The Irish Times*' report, the prosecuting officer was Lieutenant Jones and the court members were Major Wakefield and Captains Grey and Rush. Byrne refused to recognise the court's jurisdiction and declined to plead. The prosecuting officer presented the evidence against him, he was found guilty of possession of a revolver and ammunition but sentencing was postponed until the first week of February.

When the court martial reconvened on 2 February 1919, they sentenced Byrne to twelve months imprisonment with hard labour. The official courts-martial records show such a sentence passed on 'Robert T Byrnes' of Limerick on either 2 February or 4 – one date has been typed on top of the other and it is therefore difficult to say which is the intended date but the date is confirmed by press reports on 3 February. One headline read 'Drastic Sentence on Limerick Man'. He was handed over to the civilian authorities to begin his sentence in Limerick Prison.

Byrne found himself in a prison system where solitary confinement and cruelty were the order of the day. Holding the rank of Captain, and therefore being the most senior officer imprisoned, he quickly asserted himself as leader of the Republican prisoners and immediately began organising them to campaign for treatment as political prisoners, not as ordinary criminals, establishing their own military discipline and not subject to the ordinary prison routine. On 10 February, he demanded to be accorded the status of political prisoner. Classification as a political prisoner meant that they were kept apart from other prisoners and had their own special room or cell, they were given extra food and drink and allowed to exercise their trade or profession. Limerick Prison had accommodation for ninety-nine male prisoners and there were twelve to fifteen 'special' prisoners. Three days after he began his sentence, sixteen prisoners claiming political status barricaded themselves into their cells. They smashed up the furnishings and sang Republican songs that were listened to with amusement by the large crowd of supporters who thronged the street outside the Prison. Apart from Robert Byrne, prisoners involved in the disturbances included Patrick Donegan, Michael McMahon, Jeremiah Treacy, John Morrissey, Edward Horgan, Patrick McMahon, Thomas O'Toole, Henry Meany, Maurice Culhane and Laurence Keefe.

The prison authorities reacted quickly and brutally and sent for RIC reinforcements. The prisoners were beaten, their boots and clothing removed. They were handcuffed to their beds, some were kept in solitary confinement and given only limited quantities of bread and water. Prison visits were banned. The prisoners were overpowered by the sheer force of RIC reinforcements. The Official Press Censor prevented the '*Irish Independent*' from reporting the disturbance.

Following the disturbances, the Sinn Féin Mayor, Stephen O'Mara, visited the Prison to view the conditions there. The following day, the Prison Visiting Committee made an inspection. The Committee, a feature of the supervision of all prisons, were prominent, loyal citizens who inspected and reported on conditions occasionally. In Limerick, they included Sir Charles Barrington, the owner of Glenstal Castle estate and Courtenay Croker, who had a large estate at Ballynagarde in the county. The Visiting Committee sent an extensive report on Robert Byrne and other DORA prisoners to Max Green, Chairman of the General Prisons Board, in Dublin. Green was the son-in-law of the deceased John Redmond, leader of the Irish Parliamentary Party.

A week later, the Mayor, Stephen O'Mara, and the Visiting Committee made separate visits to Robert Byrne. The Committee told him that the Government would not grant him privileges and they advised him to 'keep order'. If he did not, the Prison Governor would discharge his duty and take the necessary steps to prevent damage to Government property. They reported that Byrne had no complaint other than that he was not being treated as a political prisoner.

Early in January, the '*Irish Independent*' had reported a meeting held at the O'Connell Monument in Limerick to protest at the treatment of political prisoners in the local prison. The Limerick protest meeting was reported to be 'of large dimensions, although called at an hour's notice'. Significantly, in view of later events, the speakers included John Cronin, President of Limerick United Trades and Labour Council. Following the meeting, there was an impromptu protest march to the City Prison led by a Sinn Féin band playing nationalist airs.

The Catholic Bishop of Limerick, Dr Denis Hallinan, described the prisoners' treatment as 'a gross breach of the promise made by the Government in Ireland on the death of Thomas Ashe'. Ashe died on 25 September 1917 as a result of maladroitly administered forcible feeding in Mountjoy Prison, in Dublin, during a hunger strike. Hallinan had succeeded Bishop Edward O'Dwyer, a stern opponent of British misrule, and the new Bishop supported Sinn Féin provided they did not endorse armed rebellion or collude with secret societies. The Sinn Féin Mayor, Alphonsus O'Mara, wrote to the Chief Secretary for Ireland, Ian Macpherson MP, condemning the forcible feeding of prisoners who had not been tried or convicted.

At a meeting in Limerick City Hall, presided over by the Mayor, the Irish Post Office Clerks' Association protested against the practice of secret reporting on employees with Republican views. Copies of the protest resolution were sent to the Prime Minister, Lloyd George, the Postmaster General, the Chief Secretary for Ireland and the Secretary of the Irish Post Office, Arthur Hamilton Norway (an author and father of the celebrated English novalist Nevil Shute). Hunger strikes, forcible feeding and protests were not confined to

Limerick. By April 1919, prisoners in Dublin, Belfast and Cork had spent as many as fourteen weeks in solitary confinement in disputes over their treatment as political prisoners.

The events in Limerick Prison were reported to the office of the Chief Secretary for Ireland in Dublin Castle on a daily basis. The files there recorded the commencement of Byrne's hunger strike and a discussion of the granting of what was termed amelioration to him. There was a general report on the 'disorderly conduct' of prisoners and a report on damage to prison property by Robert J Byrne and James Kennedy. One document was entitled 'Limerick: Damage to prison property and list of mutinous DORA prisoners'. The Dublin Castle records note that this file was transferred to the Irish Free State Department of Justice on 5 May 1925, when that fledgling state presumably faced similar problems in its prisons.

Although the authorities did not attempt the forcible feeding of Robert Byrne, forcible feeding of prisoners was a major issue in Limerick during February 1919. Tension in the prison was taking it's toil on the health of staff. The Chief Warder, Webb, became ill and the Chief Warder of Dundalk Prison was despatched as a temporary replacement. A few weeks later, Webb died from his illness. On 8 February, A F Falkiner, Governor of Limerick Prison, sent Max Green, the Chairman of the General Prisons Board, a copy of what he termed a 'placard' posted in Limerick that evening. The leaflet referred to 'the horrible and revolting system of forcible feeding' and accused two Limerick doctors of 'doing (their) dirty work!'. The doctors were named as McGrath and Irwin. Dr PJ Irwin was stated, in the leaflet, to be Resident Medical Officer at the Limerick District Asylum 'at a salary of close on one thousand pounds per annum.' The leaflet alleged Irwin was ready to put the life of a fellow-countryman in danger for the sake of an additional three guineas a week. Also, on the night of 8 February, a dozen similar leaflets were found in the letter box at Limerick Post Office.

Forcible feeding of prisoners was a highly emotive topic after the death of Thomas Ashe. Details of the gruesome procedure had emerged during his inquest. It involved strapping the prisoner by hands and feet to a chair, forcing the mouth open with a wooden spoon and inserting a long rubber tube through either the mouth or the nose. The tube was connected to a bowl containing a mixture of milk and eggs which was then forced into the prisoner's digestive tract for about five or ten minutes.

On 13 February, District Inspector Craig of the RIC submitted a report on the leafletting incidents to the force's Inspector General. Both doctors were stated to be popular and not in any danger. Dr Michael McGrath had one of the city dispensaries and was Medical Officer of Health as well as being Prison Medical Officer. During 1917 and 1918, the doctor had done a good deal to highlight Limerick's appalling slum housing in a series of three articles he wrote for the '*Bottom Dog*' newspaper. Inspector Craig noted that McGrath's private practice was not large and, that for the present, he was not likely to suffer professional injury.

'But', the District Inspector remarked, 'if he has to forcibly feed Sinn Féin prisoners in the future it is very probable that he will become unpopular.'

Limerick Asylum Board met to consider the actions of Dr Irwin, their Resident Medical Officer. Dr Irwin denied he had temporarily left the asylum to forcibly feed prisoners for an additional three guineas a week. He claimed he had been acting on foot of the general rules for the management of the asylum and in accordance with the practice of his predecessor over fifteen years. The Asylum Board adopted a resolution expressing considerable indignation at Irwin's action and noting that he had promised he would refuse to continue assisting in forcible feeding. Dr Irwin's withdrawal was reported to the General Prisons Board on 14 February by Dr McGrath in his capacity as Medical Officer of Limerick Prison. Dr McGrath requested that arrangements be made to get a Consultant from somewhere else, with recognised experience, to assist in any further recourse to forcible feeding. His view was that there were no members of the medical profession in Limerick on whom he could rely to consult with him if the question arose again.

Dublin Castle studied the General Rules and Regulations for the Management of the Limerick District Asylum, drawn up in 1912, to see if the Asylum's Resident Medical Superintendent could be forced to assist the Prison Doctor. Rule Five stated: 'The Resident Medical Superintendent shall superintend and regulate the whole establishment... He shall devote the whole of his time to his office... He shall, however, be permitted to undertake the following engagements – visiting any person at the request of the Lord Lieutenant, the Lord Chancellor, the General Prisons Board, the Inspectors of Lunatics, or one of them, examining into such person's mental state, reporting, and, if necessary, giving evidence thereon.' The Castle concluded, correctly, that there was nothing in this rule to authorise Dr Irwin's assistance at forcible feeding in the prison.

Since Dr Irwin's withdrawal may have coincided with the start of Robert Byrne's hunger strike, it may explain why the prison authorities did not try to forcibly feed Byrne. The strain of forcible feeding, and its attendant unpopularity obviously took its toll of Dr McGrath. In 1919, he applied for a salary increase and later in the same year he resigned as Medical Officer of Limerick Prison. The Mayor and Corporation discussed the situation in the prison and wrote to the Castle authorities protesting at the sentences and treatment of Byrne and a prisoner named Moran. Once again, the Press Censor, deleted the major portion of the 'Independent's' report. This told how the prisoners were handcuffed and lashed with ropes in their cells, deprived of their food, papers and tobacco and how the police had assaulted the prisoners.

Understandably, since Robert Byrne was a delegate representing the Post Office clerks, Limerick Trades Council joined in the protests. At a meeting on 14 February – when pressure on the two doctors was at its height – the Council adopted a resolution and later distributed it throughout the city in leaflet form under the heading 'The Prison Infamy in Limerick'. This leaflet was duly noted in the files of Dublin Castle as a 'Sinn Féin' leaflet. The Trades Council resolution read: 'That we the members of Limerick Trades and Labour Council, assembled in conference, protest most emphatically against the treatment meted out to the political prisoners at present confined in Limerick County Prison, and view with grave alarm the inactivity of the Visiting Justices and Medical Officer. Furthermore, we call on the public representatives to do their duty to their fellow-countrymen and take the necessary steps to have the prisoners receive what they are justly entitled to, namely political treatment; that copies of this resolution be submitted to the local Press, Visiting Justices and Medical Officer.

The Trades Council leaflet contrasted the treatment of the Republican prisoners with that of a man convicted of the manslaughter of a girl 'in circumstances of the most revolting brutality'. He had been sentenced by a judge 'lenient to his ilk' to serve twelve months in the first division of the prison. The killer was not required to work, according to the leaflet, and he was supplied with every comfort – a cot, books, newspapers, slippers, glass, writing materials. 'In fact', the leaflet claimed, he had 'everything he could procure in a first-class hotel.' In an emotional appeal, the Council suggested that men 'who have never committed a crime' believed they were entitled at least to the treatment the criminal was getting. It said that one of the prisoners – Henry Meany who was on hunger strike since 6 February – was in a bad state of health yet was manacled as well as handcuffed. Meany was subsequently removed to Mountjoy Prison in Dublin in a very critical condition but resumed eating shortly after he arrived there.

Towards the end of February, a learned article on prison hunger strikes was circulated to all Governors. Previously, a copy of the authoritative but theologically conservative '*Irish Ecclesiastical Record*' had been placed in the Officers' Library in Limerick because it included an article entitled 'The Morality of the Hunger Strike' by the Chaplain to Mountjoy, the Very Reverend Canon John Waters, President of Clonliffe College in Dublin. From July to December of 1918 a debate on the morality or otherwise of hunger strikes had raged in the austere pages of the 'Record'. Canon Waters – who had little, if any sympathy with Republicans – was locked in argument with Reverend Father Patrick Cleary, the eminent Emeritus Professor of Theology in Maynooth College. Neither the Irish Hierarchy nor the Vatican, however, made any definitive pronouncement on the issue, one way or the other, and so it remained a matter purely for arcane theological disputation.

On 27 February, the Governor of Limerick Prison sent a Memorandum to the General Prisons Board in Dublin Castle on the topic 'Wrecking of Cells by Prisoners'. He reported that restraints had been removed from Prisoner McGrath because of the seriousness of his illness. The Governor stated that 'those who break cells are left in the cell with suitable covering to place over broken windows at night which can be removed during the day when the weather is mild.' The previous night, Robert Byrne and John Moran had broken their cell windows and wooden shutters had been hung on the frames of the windows. He confirmed that Byrne had been denied political concessions by order of the Government. On 1 March, the Visiting Committee, reported that when they inspected the Prison, they 'found things in good order' and heard 'no complaints'. They said that Robert Byrne and John Moran did not wish to see them but that Maurice Culhane had asked for the restoration of privileges for himself and the other political prisoners.

On 4 March, District Inspector Craig, of the RIC, commenced a prosecution under the Malicious Damage Act 1861 against Robert Byrne at Limerick Petty Sessions Court for alleged damage to furnishings – 'the property of His Majesty's Government' – in his prison cell. The witness for the prosecution was Constable Moffatt. The charges were that Byrne 'did unlawfully, wilfully and maliciously commit certain damage, injury and spoil' to items in his cell – a window, glass, shelving, a stool, a chamber pot, a water can, a table, mugs, plate and basin. The damage was alleged to have occurred on 5, 12 and 26 February and the total monetary value was stated to be more than £3, or approximately €180 in today's values. The Resident Magistrate, PJ Kelly, adjourned the charges for four weeks.

On 7 March, Robert Byrne began a hunger strike for the second time. Three days later his condition was described as 'weaker'; and he was confined to bed in the Prison hospital. Five days later – on 12 March – he was transferred to the Men's Number One Ward on the second floor of Limerick Workhouse, or the Union Infirmary as it was also called, on Shelbourne Road on the Clare side of the Shannon. He could not be transferred to Mountjoy Prison, in Dublin, because many prisoners there were suffering from severe influenza and the prison hospital was full. The Prisons Board Medical Officer, Dr McCormack, had advised that it would be highly dangerous to move a prisoner, on hunger strike for five days, to an influenza affected area. The Workhouse Board of Guardians were furious because the authorities proposed to keep him in custody while in the hospital. The Guardians declared that Byrne would be regarded as a free man while he was there. Despite this opposition, the prison authorities stationed a prison warden and armed policemen in the ward.

A couple of days after he arrived in the Infirmary, Robert Byrne resumed eating. After a fortnight, when the Workhouse doctors showed no inclination to certify him as medically fit to return to prison, the Prison Governor, AF Falkiner, became suspicious as to why Byrne had resumed eating and why the doctors were slow to certify that he was fit to return. He had already reported to the General Prisons Board on his suspicions about Warder Lilly who was guarding Robert Byrne at the Workhouse Infirmary and had been 'seen in conversation with a known Sinn Féiner'. The RIC had begun keeping tabs and reporting regularly to Dublin Castle on warders suspected of Sinn Féin sympathies. Nurses and attendants in hospitals and infirmaries were also suspected of being 'persons with SF tendencies' and the Governor of Cork Prison had warned 'no assistance could be expected from them' in keeping sick prisoners secure in their institutions. On 4 April, Falkiner warned the General Prisons Board that none of the doctors were likely to certify Byrne as fit. The Governor may have suspected that he was building up his strength again for a particular reason.

In any event, the Limerick Irish Volunteers sensed an opportunity to boost morale and embarrass the authorities by rescuing Byrne from the less secure confines of the Workhouse hospital. The intention was to secrete him in a 'safe' house somewhere in the hills of Clare where it would be extremely difficult for motorised British forces to track him down. Commandant Peadar Dunne called a council meeting of the 2nd Battalion in Hogan's Hotel, next door to Matt Boland's shop in Lower Gerald Griffin Street. Dunne was a veteran of the fighting in the Marrowbone Lane distillery during Easter Week 1916. After his participation in the Rising, and following his release from Prison, he lost his job in Guinness's brewery despite his twelve years of service there and he was unable to get other work in Dublin. Madge Daly, whose brother, Edward, was a Commandant in the Rising and had been executed, offered Dunne a job delivering bread from Dalys' bakery, located at 26 William Street, Limerick.

In 1917, the Volunteers GHQ ordered Peadar Dunne to organise a second Battalion in Limerick. There was intense dissatisfaction locally and nationally at the inept performance of the original 1st Battalion, commanded by Michael Colivet, during Easter Week 1916. In fairness to them, it should be said that Professor Eoin MacNeill's Countermanding Order, as the figure head Chief of Staff of the Irish Volunteers, cancelling the 'manoeuvres' planned for Easter Monday, caused utter confusion not just in Limerick but in many places outside of Dublin.

The Limerick men had also been in contact with the Volunteers in Kerry and were acutely aware, earlier than Dublin, that the Rising was doomed to failure because, on the Friday preceding the Rising, Roger Casement had not succeeded in his mission to land arms from Germany in Kerry. This was a major factor in Colivet's thinking in eventually standing down the Limerick 1st Battalion during Easter Week. Limerick was to be the distribution point Northwards and Eastwards along the railway network for the arms to be landed by Casement. Outside of Dublin, it was to be the fulcrum of the planned Rising. However, Limerick's failure to act decisively in 1916 was compounded by the inexplicable, naïve decision to hand over their arms 'temporarily' to the British military, with the city's unionist Mayor, Sir Stephen Quin, acting as intermediary.

Prior to the Rising, the police had observed Thomas Clarke and Seán MacDiarmada (the military 'brains' of the Irish Republican Brotherhood) visiting Robert Byrne at his home, underlining his role and the importance of Limerick in the preparations. The Report of the Royal Commission on the Rising described Clarke and MacDiarmada as part of the 'inner circle by which the plans for insurrection were no doubt nurtured.' Clarke and

MacDiamada spent Christmas 1915 in the home of the prominent Republican family, the Dalys, and it may have been during this visit that they made contact with Byrne.

In forming a battalion in Limerick openly led and directed by their own men, the Irish Republican Brotherhood – the Fenians, described in the Easter Proclamation as Ireland's 'secret military organisation' – were applying a lesson learned from the confusion caused by MacNeill's Countermanding Order. They were also correcting a fault line that had lain at the core of the Volunteer organisation since their foundation in November 1913. At the outset, the Brotherhood's strategy had been that the Volunteers would be 'fronted' in leadership and prominent positions by respectable figures from non-revolutionary organisations like the Irish Parliamentary Party, the Gaelic League, the GAA and the Ancient Order of Hibernians. This was intended to maximise recruitment numbers and popular support. However, the real power would lie with IRB men making the decisions and pulling the strings in the background. However, that strategy had come badly unstuck in the forty-eight hours preceding the Easter Rising when MacNeill, the titular head of the Volunteers, realised what was really planned and attempted to stymie it.

The main movers in the new 2nd Battalion – including Peadar Dunne, Peadar McMahon and Robert Byrne – were members of the Irish Republican Brotherhood (IRB). The 2nd Battalion could be described as the 'IRB' Battalion in Limerick and its formation underlined a determination by the IRB that, in the renewed struggle for independence post–1916, they would never again put non-IRB members in a position to thwart the organisation's strategy or tactics. Later in 1917, Dunne formed 3rd, 4th and 5th Battalions in Mid Limerick and eventually was elected Brigade Officer Commanding.

It has been suggested by authoritative sources that the 2nd Battalion was more working class in membership compared with the more 'respectable' 1st Battalion. James Gubbins was a Lieutenant in the Limerick City Regiment of the Volunteers and later Adjutant of the Mid-Limerick Brigade of the IRA. In his Witness Statement to the Bureau of Military History, he describes the relatively middle-class composition of the City Regiment (later the 1st Battalion) in October 1916: 'Tradesmen, clerks, shopkeepers, teachers, shop assistants and labourers were all represented. The Gaelic League, as might be expected, supplied many of its members as did the Sinn Féin organisation (weak at this period), past members of Fianna Éireann and the AOH. The city Rugby clubs provided a large contingent. Players and former players of the game contributed to the ranks of each of the four companies, in particular to A Company, where they provided more than half the personnel. At the start, three of the four companies had Rugby men as captain. Three of the crew of the Athlunkard Boat Club were members of the Battalion, while a fourth was closely associated with it. The GAA representation was relatively weak'.

By contrast, when the IRB set about forming the rival 2nd Battalion, its five Companies were based on GAA clubs in mainly working-class parishes. These junior hurling clubs, formed following the 1916 Rising, were linked to Sinn Féin clubs named after heroes of the 1916 Rising. Treaty Sarsfields, from Thomondgate, linked with the Ned Daly SF Club and formed A Company; St. Patrick's and Claughaun of Pennywell linked with the Thomas Ashe Club and formed B Company; the Star team, from Irishtown, associated with the Roger Casement Club and formed C Company; in the Boherbuoy district, Shamrocks affiliated with the Con Colbert SF Club and made up D Company; from the Ballysimon-Blackboy-Pike area, Faughs were linked to the Tom Clarke Club and formed E Company.

So many new companies were being formed, and so quickly, that it was difficult to agree on a suitable night for drilling and meetings. As IRB Organiser and a member of the Volunteer Executive, Ernest Blythe was deeply involved in the reorganisation of Limerick but he wryly recalled: 'I remember that in each case it proved very difficult to fix on a suitable drill night, especially was it so in the third Company, which I formed in the quarry. Between Sodalities and Confraternities there was not so much as one night in the week in which everyone was free. I do not suppose there is any city in Ireland which has so many religious societies as Limerick has.'

One of the founders of the 2nd Battalion, Peadar McMahon, made this distinction: 'The 2nd Battalion were a different type of people – decent fellows but they were all working people. The 1st Battalion were all white-collar workers. I think that was one of the reasons the 1st Battalion didn't like the fact that they were working men.' Ernie O'Malley, a senior trainer and organiser attached to the Volunteers GHQ, also noted that 'there was a good deal of working men in the 2nd Battalion and I think this was a kind of distinction between these battalions'.

As Robert Byrne lay in the Workhouse Infirmary, the Council of the 2nd Battalion agreed a rescue plan, to be executed on Sunday, 6 April. Twenty-four IRA men were to enter the ward under the guise of visitors and a covering party of fifteen would be on duty in the corridors and grounds. Five men from each IRA company would be formed into two Sections. Jack Gallagher, of D Company, would be in charge of one, Lieutenant Michael 'Batty' Stack, of E Company, the other. Only Stack and Gallagher were to be armed.

Earlier on the sunny Sunday afternoon, Eamon Dore – a veteran of the 1916 Rising in Dublin – and Batty Stack had visited Robert Byrne separately to alert him to the planned rescue. Dore left the hospital a short time before the rescue was to begin and met some of the rescue party on the stairs as they were assembling prior to entering the ward. In his Witness Statement to the Bureau of Military History he says 'When I had finished my visit, I would leave the room and go out of that particular ward, travelling round the hospital and by a roundabout way come to the same ward again. While this was happening, the remainder of my party were to visit patients in the ward and pose as friends and so work their way near to the armed guard over Byrne. The whole rescue was timed and, on the blast of a whistle from me, they were to rush the RIC guard and pin them down. At the moment when this was happening Byrne was to jump from the bed.'

The RIC had general orders to shoot prisoners in circumstances where a rescue was being attempted. That Sunday afternoon, Robert Byrne was being closely guarded by Sergeant JF Goulden of Ballyneety, county Limerick, Constable J Tierney of Kilteely, Constable J Fitzpatrick of Clarina, Constable Martin O'Brien who was attached to Caherconlish Station, Constable T Spillane of Askeaton Station and Warder John Mahoney or Mahony, Rocksborough Road, who was on the staff of Limerick Prison. O'Brien and Spillane were seated on either side of the prisoner's bed.

As the hands of the clock moved nearer to three o'clock, the pitch of conversation rose as visitors tried to cram into the remaining minutes the things that had been left unsaid during the earlier part of the visiting time. Batty Stack blew a shrill whistle in the prearranged signal. Twelve members of the rescue party moved to disarm and tie up the policemen. They were Tim Buckley, Jim Downey, 'Soaker' Ryan, Dinny Maher, 'Lefty' Egan, 'Corky' Ryan, Michael Clancy, Tarry Enright, Michael Danford (who held the rank of Captain), Billy Wallace, Mick Walters and Joe Saunders. Other participants in the rescue included Liam Forde and Cornelius McNamara as well as Brian Crowe who had cut the telephone wires to the hospital prior to the rescue so as to give the rescuers more time before the alarm could be raised.

All the accounts of what happened next agree that it was a short, decisive affray. According to the warder's later account, two men presented revolvers and ordered 'Hands Up!'. Several revolver shots rang out and patients jumped beneath their beds in terror as panic-stricken visitors scattered. People out for a Sunday afternoon stroll turned back in fright at the sound of gunfire.

As soon as the whistle was blown, Warder Mahony, Constable Spillane and another policeman ran to the bed and grabbed Byrne as he tried to rise. Constable Spillane had his revolver out, and as Robert Byrne tried to heave himself out of bed, the burly policeman hurled himself bodily on top of him. Sometime during this confused struggle, a bullet entered the body of Robert Byrne, on the left-hand side, between the 6th and 7th ribs. Batty Stack claimed that Spillane fired at Robert Byrne as he threw himself on top of him in the bed. From a range of a metre and a half, Batty Stack shattered Spillane's spine with a bullet from a .38 revolver. The other guards had been tied up but Constable O'Brien freed himself and, as he approached the fleeing rescuers, gun in hand, Stack fired a second shot and the 120-kilos policeman collapsed to the floor in an ungainly heap – dead. Stack coolly bent down to get his weapon and take it away. Constables Tierney and Fitzpatrick were wounded.

Stack pulled Constable Spillane off Byrne to get him out of the bed. One of the unarmed members of the rescue party, Thady Kelly, was to take Byrne away to a horse drawn carriage at the front of the hospital. However, there was a hitch in the transport arrangements. The Battalion driver had to leave Limerick City urgently to help Dan Breen and Sean Hogan escape through a British military cordon. They were still wanted for their part in the January 1919 killing of two RIC members in an ambush at Soloheadbeg, county Tipperary. Instead, a mourning coach was got from a local undertaker, with Nurse Mary Giltinane, a Cumann na mBan member, inside it ready with clothes and a disguise for Byrne.

Dressed only in a night-shirt and overcoat, Robert Byrne staggered down the stairs, supported by two or three comrades. The hospital's main gate was on Shelbourne Road but, by mistake, the coach driver had gone around to the mortuary at the back of the hospital. With no transport visible to them. Byrne and his rescuers were forced to go out on to the public road and set off on foot. They had gone only three hundred metres, towards Hassett's Cross, when they noticed blood oozing from Byrne's chest. At the cross roads they stopped a pony and trap driven by John Ryan of Knockalisheen, county Clare, and his young daughter Nancy. They brought the wounded IRA man to their labourer's cottage, near Meelick, in county Clare where his condition deteriorated badly.

Robert Byrne's body lay on a bed in an upper storey of Ryan's house and on his breast, close to the heart, was a hole the size of a halfpenny coin. The bullet had passed through his lungs, causing a fatal haemorrhage. Near the bed was a bloodstained Volunteer's overcoat. Mrs Ryan said that the men who had brought Byrne to the house were complete strangers to her, but they had asked her, in the name of God, to take him in. A Franciscan priest, Fr. Philip Murphy OFM, was called to give Byrne the Last Rites of the Catholic Church. The same priest had attended Byrne in Limerick Prison prior to his transfer to the Workhouse Infirmary. To Father Philip fell what he later termed 'the hideous task' of telling Mrs. Byrne of her son's fate. Sometime afterwards, Mrs. Byrne presented him with a gold cross inscribed with the words: 'To the priest who ministered to the hunted felon. From Bert Byrne's mother to Father Philip, April 6th, 1919'. He hung the gold cross on the mantelpiece in his room.

At around seven o'clock in the evening, Robert Byrne was attended to by Dr. John Holmes, the District medical practitioner, and Dr. C McDonnell. By that time, Dr. Holmes later said, his condition was 'hopeless'. When Holmes asked him who had shot him, Byrne – vomiting blood – replied: 'The man that got shot'. His last words were 'This is what is going to do for me Doctor, isn't it? I am not afraid to die in any case'. At half past eight on Sunday, 6 April Robert Byrne died.

As he had lain dying on the floor of the hospital ward, Constable O'Brien asked that a clergyman be sent for and the Chaplain, Canon O'Driscoll, administered the Last Rites of the Catholic Church to the dying man. Constable Spillane's wound, close to his spine, was also serious but the other policemen and the warder sustained only minor injuries, probably caused by being hit by a truncheon which was later found in the ward. There were bullet marks on the walls and the statue of the Infant of Prague on a little altar had been damaged by a ricochet.

Constable O'Brien was a married man, with one child. One report gives his age as fifty, but another account states that he was thirty-five, with twelve years' service in the Constabulary. O' Brien was stationed in Caherconlish, in county Limerick and he had been on temporary duty in the city for only three weeks. He was buried in his native Birr, county Offaly. There was a large attendance at the funeral, including senior Catholic clergy, and there were fifty cars in the cortege. In a sign that bitterness had not yet run too deep, some members of Sinn Féin attended the funeral. The Lord Lieutenant, Lord French, sent his condolences to Mrs O'Brien, as did the Inspector-General of the RIC, Lieutenant-General Joseph Byrne. Mrs O'Brien demanded two thousand pounds (€120,000) in compensation for the death of her husband. Dublin Castle records later show a grant made to the Constable's mother, an application by his widow to be made Post Mistress of Caherconlish, in county Limerick and the grant to her of a pension of two pounds (€120) a week. Constable Spillane, the son of an RIC Sergeant from Loughrea in county Galway, was also awarded a pension. He was lucky to have survived. He was removed to Dublin for treatment where surgeons located the bullet lodged in his spine and removed it. Constable Spillane was awarded the King's Police Medal for Gallantry but was never able to return to work because of his injury.

The area around the cottage in Meelick, where Robert Byrne died, was placed under military control and there was much police and military activity in counties Clare and Limerick. It was surrounded by detachments of police and the Scottish Horse regiment. One of the few police documents of the time still extant in the National Archives is a telegram from County Inspector Yates, of the RIC, reporting the finding of Byrne's body. The telegram was dispatched at 1.53 pm. and received in the Chief Secretary's office at 3.17 pm., on Monday 7 April. It said the body had just been discovered at the house of John Ryan of Knockalisheen, Ardnacrusha sub-District, county Clare. Death had apparently been caused by a bullet wound in the stomach. Robert Byrne was the first member of the IRA to die in the Anglo-Irish War. The Workhouse rescue was not, however, the first time police had come under fire in county Limerick. In September 1918, near Abbeyfeale, Volunteer Tommy Leahy of Tournafulla fired on a group of policemen, wounding one of them.

The vehicle in which Mrs Byrne travelled to Knockalisheen had been preceded and followed by military lorries. According to the telegram sent to Dublin Castle, the owner of the house, John Ryan, his wife, his servant girl and servant boy, Michael Dogherty, were arrested, along with others found there: Arthur Johnson, Parnell Street, Limerick, John Hurley of Town Wall Cottage (a cousin of the deceased), the prisoner's mother, Mrs

Anne Byrne, his aunt, Emily Crowe, 25 Sarsfield Street, the deceased's cousin, Thomas Crowe also of Sarsfield Street, and Patrick Brady, of Lower Gerald Griffin Street who was the undertaker's driver. Hurley, Crowe, Dogherty, Johnson and Brady were remanded in custody for eight days to Limerick Prison on a charge of being accessories after the fact in connection with the killing of Constable O'Brien. Emily Crowe, less than a year after the events at Meelick, on 15 January 1920, became the first woman ever elected to Limerick Corporation, representing Sinn Féin.

Patrick Brady, it later emerged, had been sent by an undertaker to measure the deceased for his coffin. Arthur Johnson had been Byrne's predecessor as Adjutant of the 2nd Battalion and was now Battalion Engineer in the IRA. Hurley later became Quarter Master of the mid-Limerick Brigade of the IRA. The arrested group were brought to William Street police station for questioning and the station was surrounded by a large crowd of people. In the succeeding weeks, those who had been arrested were released.

A general meeting of Limerick Trades Council held on the Friday after Byrne's death dealt only with some matters of special importance. As a mark of respect to their late fellow-member, the President, John Cronin, suggested that they adjourn after the minutes had been read. He said it was his sad duty to propose this resolution: 'That a vote of condolence be sent to Mrs Byrne on the death of her son, who for the cause of self-determination as all Irishmen are entitled to, was murdered by the minions of English Tyranny here in our midst.' But while condoling with Mrs Byrne, Cronin said he must also congratulate her in having reared a son of such heroic disposition, whose name would be handed down in generations to come as an example of what an Irishman should be.

Mrs Byrne's letter in reply is preserved in the Minute Book of the Council: '... Thank God that our dear son and brother died a free man fighting for his country's cause. I pray the Almighty that his blood has not been shed in vain and that our dear Motherland will soon shake off the shackles of the Foreigner and take her righteous place among the Nations of the Earth...'. The letter's style is reminiscent of similar letters written, for example, by the executed leaders of the 1916 Rising and their families. The death of her son seems to have badly affected his mother's health and in later years local people believed Mrs Byrne missed him deeply and regretted his death to the point of bitterness. Nevertheless, in a file in the Military Service Pensions Collection, she is recorded on lists of names and addresses of members of Limerick City Cumann na mBan on the date of the Anglo-Irish Truce, 11 July 1921 and on 1 July 1922.

In 1924, under the terms of the Army Pensions Act 1923, Mrs Byrne applied to the Government for compensation for the death of her son, because he had been her sole financial support. She rejected the initial award of a gratuity of £100 (€6,000) and it was later increased to £150. She still rejected the increased award on the grounds that it was too small and compared it to a much bigger award made to the widow of George Clancy, the Sinn Féin Mayor of Limerick who was murdered by Crown forces. Her husband's cousin, Alfie Byrne TD, was one of a number of politicians who made representations on the family's behalf. The gratuity remained unpaid to Mrs Byrne at the time of her death in 1929, after several years of ill-health. Four years later, her son Thomas, a pharmacist – with the agreement of his older brother, Lawrence, then living in America – sought payment of the gratuity. The Minister for Defence, Frank Aiken TD, favoured paying the money to her estate but he was overruled, on legal grounds, by the Minister for Finance, Seán McEntee TD.

The issue of payment of the gratuity to the Byrne family was re-opened in 1936. Ruling on a broadly similar claim from the family of a deceased named John Lacey, the Attorney-General, Conor Maguire, advised that once a gratuity had been granted during the deceased's lifetime, the legal personal representative of the deceased could properly claim payment of it. In the light of the A-G's ruling, civil servants in the Department of Defence noted that it was intended to introduce amending legislation that would confirm that awards could be paid to legal personal representatives and it was suggested that the matter of a payment to the Byrnes could await the enactment of the legislation, when a further application for payment might be received. On 4 December 1936, the final word in the Department's file – on a story that had begun more than nineteen years previously in a cottage in Knockalisheen county Clare – lay with the civil servant who wrote: 'Better let sleeping dogs lie. There is an additional reason – that a claim must now be awaited from the person concerned.'

Mrs Byrne's treatment at the cottage in Meelick and the arrest of some of the prisoner's relatives led to protests at a meeting of the Limerick Infirmary Guardians. There were incidents around William Street police station and reports of a baton charge in the city. Thus, the first week of April 1919 ended in Limerick with stirring events and passions aroused. However, there was more to come, as people learned the details of Byrne's shooting and death and Limerick prepared to mourn a dead hero. The fuse had been lit and the flame had begun its inexorable approach to the powder keg.

CHAPTER TWO

<u>An Inquest and a Funeral</u>

'The Government have no wish to interfere with the solemnity and dignity of any funeral ceremonial, but they cannot tolerate any defiance of the law.'
– *Official communiqué issued on Wednesday, 9 April 1919, in advance of Robert Byrne's funeral.*

The Coroner for East Clare, Mr Michael Brady, opened an inquest into the death of Robert Byrne on Tuesday, 8 April, in John Ryan's cottage at Meelick, where Byrne had died. Sergeant James Walshe, a plain clothes member of the RIC from Limerick, and the deceased's brother Thomas identified the remains.

Dr Aloysius Humphreys, Resident Medical Officer to the Workhouse and Dr James Brennan, visiting physician there, carried out the post mortem examination. Dr Humphreys said there was a small circular external wound just below the heart but he could not find a corresponding exit wound. Nor could he find the bullet which had taken a backward and downward course. It penetrated the left lung and the walls of the stomach and apparently lodged in the intestines. In a portent of allegations yet to come, District Inspector McClelland of the RIC objected to a line of questioning and to the admission of evidence that suggested the fatal shot had been fired at close range. The doctors cited haemorrhage, peritonitis (inflammation of the intestines) and shock as the causes of death.

The Coroner agreed to hand over Byrne's remains to his relatives for burial and adjourned the inquest for a week. Michael Brennan, of Meelick, a leading member of the IRA, complained that the Volunteer uniform had been removed from Byrne and a file was indeed opened in Dublin Castle under the title 'Robert Byrne – Forfeiture of Volunteer uniform.' This suggests that the removal complained of was a deliberate act of policy.

An estimated ten thousand citizens attended the removal of Robert Byrne's body from John Ryan's house in Meelick to Saint John's Cathedral in Limerick. The coffin, covered in the Republican tricolour, was borne the distance of three miles or so on the shoulders of IRA Volunteers. Close on ten thousand mourners from Limerick and Clare marched in a military style escort with the hearse.

There was no police interference during the parade, police and military having been withdrawn from the streets but the authorities were not prepared to accept further open defiance. On the night of the removal, an Assistant Inspector General of the RIC visited Limerick, while Major Maunsell, Chief Intelligence Officer, Southern District, arrived with other military officers. Their visit was reported to be in connection with the mapping out of a portion of Limerick to be shortly placed under martial law. The following day, Wednesday 9 April, the authorities' determination was underlined in an official communiqué issued as a public notice: 'The Government have no wish to interfere with the solemnity and dignity of any funeral ceremonial, but they cannot tolerate any defiance of law. Anything in the shape of a military parade or assembly in military formation will at once be stopped. The Government will accept no responsibility for any consequences which may arise from disobedience of this order'. All that day, thousands of people passed by Robert Byrne's coffin, lying in state before the high altar in Limerick Cathedral and the flag of the Town Hall flew at half-mast.

On Thursday, 10 April, Robert Byrne was buried in Mount Saint Lawrence's Cemetery in Limerick. Commandant Michael Brennan, Officer Commanding the East Clare Brigade of the IRA, commanded the funeral cortege because the two rival Limerick battalions could not agree on one of their own to command it. The funeral was as much a city's display of defiance as an expression of sorrow. There was a strong military presence throughout the day. Armoured cars flashed through the streets, and coming up to two o'clock, sections of soldiers with fixed bayonets and police took up positions along the funeral route. Each section was supported by an armoured car and an ambulance. Two military aeroplanes circled above the Cathedral and followed the procession for part of the way.

At ten minutes past three, the funeral left the Cathedral. The hearse was covered in wreaths, and many more were carried by IRA Volunteers following behind. The '*Irish Independent*' termed it 'a most remarkable funeral demonstration. First came the Catholic clergy of the city churches, the wreath-bedecked hearse, the flag-draped coffin borne by Volunteers, the chief mourners and a seemingly endless number of Volunteers from Limerick, Clare and Tipperary with Cumann na mBan. A further five thousand must have marched – including the Mayor and members of the Corporation in state.'

The funeral made its way through the old town, the Mall, Patrick Street, William Street, to the cemetery. The mourning throngs wore armlets of black crepe and the Sinn Féin colours of green, white and orange. As the coffin passed points where the military and police were posted, the troops presented arms. At the corner of O'Connell Street and William Street, the clatter of rifle butts on the cobbled setts and the glint of bayonets in the sunlight caused a moment of panic among the crowd. A few onlookers were slightly injured in a wild stampede. Outside the 'Household Bazaar' in William Street some British officers stood on a plinth observing the funeral and saluted the tricolour draped coffin as it passed by.

Robert Byrne was buried in a grave that already contained the remains of his father, who died in 1907, aged forty-seven, and his sister Mary Agnes (Cissie) who died in 1912, in her early twenties. As his coffin was lowered into the grave, a firing party discharged a volley of shots. The firing party was drawn from the 2nd Battalion's A Company, who operated in the district near the cemetery. They would frequently provide firing parties for IRA Volunteer funerals since their proximity to the cemetery made it easier for them to safely carry and hide arms. Cornelius McNamara, who took part in Robert Byrne's rescue, was a member of the firing party, under the command of Captain M McCann.

Among the mourners at the graveside was the deceased's cousin Alfie Byrne, a former Irish National Party MP, Alderman of Dublin Corporation, and famous Lord Mayor of that city. The mourners also included railway workers and employees of some local stores who had taken the day off when refused a half holiday to attend the funeral. Already, the emotions aroused by Byrne's death were having their effects among some workers. Byrne's Post Office clerical colleagues in Limerick, Thurles and Limerick Junction and the Limerick Postmen laid wreaths at the grave. His brother, Thomas, worked as a chemists' assistant and the assistants' Association passed a vote of condolence. More significant perhaps was the vote of sympathy passed by the ITGWU on the night of the burial.

With the funeral of Robert Byrne ended, public attention could focus again on the precise and increasingly controversial circumstances of his death. The issues arose with devastating clarity, not in the resumed inquest on Byrne himself, but in the more unlikely forum of the inquest on Constable O'Brien. The Byrne family retained Mr Patrick Lynch KC to represent their interests at the O'Brien inquest and at Byrne's own inquest. Lynch was a member of a prominent Nationalist family who had unsuccessfully challenged Eamon de Valera in the crucial East Clare by election of July 1917. In the subsequent years of the War of Independence, he represented Republican interests in a number of celebrated trials and inquests.

During the adjourned inquest on Byrne, Mr Lynch first questioned the legality of his detention at the Workhouse Hospital. The following day, at the inquest on Constable O'Brien, he developed this idea further and made a sustained legal attack on the validity of the detention. By undermining the legality of Byrne's detention, Lynch's aim was to dissuade the jury from bringing in a 'verdict at large' – in simple terms, implicating a person or persons 'unknown' in the killing of the policeman.

Lynch began his final speech to the jury by emphasising the wide powers of a Coroner's court. It could issue a warrant for the arrest of anybody, who could be tried without any intermediate intervention by a magistrate. If the jury returned a verdict beyond the actual cause of death, they would be opening up a very large field of investigation, he said. They had evidence that Byrne was a patient in the hospital, but none to show that he was sentenced to imprisonment or that he was a prisoner on the day of the rescue, any more than any other patient in the hospital. If friends and relatives came to take away a prisoner, what right had anyone to stop them? Byrne was not a prisoner, he argued, and how did his case differ from that of any other patient?

Mr Lynch said the jury could not bring in a verdict against people or attribute crimes to them without evidence, and the jury were not to assume that because a warder took up position beside him that Byrne was in legal custody. The police were bound to prevent a prisoner being taken from them and they would be justified in using a great deal of force in doing so, but there was no pretence in this case that Byrne was their prisoner. 'If the matter was probed and investigated,' said Lynch, 'it would be found that men who were ill and transferred from other prisons to hospitals for treatment did not leave in the custody or company of a warder because there was no legal sanction to send one.' If that were so, the warder John Mahony had no more right in the ward than anyone who might be a trespasser, except he was there with the courtesy of the Infirmary Guardians. He had no right to hold Byrne once he left the walls of Limerick Prison, and neither the warder nor the police had any right to detain him in the hospital.

In legal terms, the inescapable conclusion from Lynch's argument was that Byrne was not held in legal custody at the time of the shooting. Therefore, any violence used by the police or warders to restrain him had no legal backing. His death from a bullet wound sustained in the Infirmary struggle could, therefore, be characterised as contrary to law. It would amount to either murder or manslaughter.

In Dublin Castle, the authorities had requested a legal opinion on the very issue of the legality of police remaining in an Infirmary to prevent the escape of a prisoner. This was in relation to a Republican prisoner, Thomas Keane, who had been transferred in late March from Cork Prison to a Workhouse hospital. With remarkable prescience, four days prior to Robert Byrne's rescue, the Governor in Cork, J King, had warned that the police had information about the likelihood of an 'organised mob' overcoming a warder and the police guards to rescue the prisoner.

The Castle records indicate this request referred to a case in Cork Infirmary. It may, indeed, have referred to Cork, though the relevant file number is contemporaneous with the events in Limerick. The file is no longer held in Dublin Castle but the records note it was handed over to the Irish Free State Department of Justice on 5 May 1925 – an interesting example of the similarity, and continuity perhaps, of the problems faced by the new state.

In any event, Lynch's eloquent plea had the desired effect locally. In Constable O'Brien's case, the jury perfunctorily returned a verdict that his death was due to haemorrhage, the result of a bullet wound. They did not, therefore, seem to take any account of a plea from the Crown Solicitor for Limerick, Mr JS Gaffney, that the .38 calibre bullet found in the Constable's body indicated he had been shot by a non-Constabulary weapon.

The decisive evidence at Byrne's resumed inquest was that of Doctor John Holmes, of Barrington's Hospital, who spent the last hour or so with Byrne before he died. Holmes asked the dying man: 'How did this happen to you?'

He replied: 'I was jumping out of bed.'

Holmes: 'Do you know who did it to you?'

Byrne said: 'The man that was shot.' 'That was all he said', continued the witness, 'that was relevant as to how he sustained the wounds.'

This evidence pointed towards either Constable O'Brien or Spillane (since both were 'shot') as the man who had pulled the trigger on Robert Byrne. But, first, there was legal argument as to whether or not Byrne's words could be admitted in evidence.

Dr Holmes said he saw Byrne at about seven o'clock on the evening he died, and he was vomiting blood about every quarter of an hour. Byrne said to him: 'This is going to do for me doctor. Is it not?' Then he said: 'I am not afraid to die, in any case.' The State Solicitor, Gaffney, pointed out that there were only two cases where a dying declaration was admissible in evidence. One was where there was a charge of murder against a person then on trial, and the other was in the case of manslaughter and in the presence of the person being indicted for that manslaughter.

Lynch's reply was clever. He said that murder and manslaughter were both charges arising from the death of someone, but in an inquest too, it was a death they were dealing with. In such a case, he argued, what more powerful evidence could there be than the 'voice from the grave'? If the deceased man knew he was dying – if he knew he was in a dying condition – and if counsel could produce evidence for the Coroner and the jury incriminating any person, then the jury could bring in a verdict against the person incriminated, and on their finding, the Coroner could issue his warrant for the arrest of such person. If the jury had power to issue a warrant and bring in a verdict, they had the same power to receive evidence to justify a warrant. If the evidence led to a conviction afterwards, surely the hearing of such evidence in the first place was admissible?

P J Kelly, one of the Resident Magistrates for Limerick City, witnessed much of the inquest and sent a graphic account of the proceedings that day to James McMahon in Dublin Castle, the Under Secretary to the Lord Lieutenant, who was the permanent head of the British administration in Ireland. Kelly expressed concern about the inflammatory nature of comments made about him by Hugh O'Brien Moran, a solicitor representing Arthur Johnson, one of those arrested when Byrne's body was found. O'Brien-Moran was President of the Tom Clarke Sinn Féin club and was frequently called on to represent Republicans in various prosecutions and court cases. In 1917, he successfully defended the Secretary of the Limerick GAA County Board, James Ryan, against a charge of refusing police admission to a hurling match without payment. Nevertheless, Ryan and O'Brien-Moran were imprisoned for refusing to identify the origin of documents presented in evidence. On O'Brien-Moran's release from prison a few months later, a 'Sinn Féin mob' attacked two police patrols in the city and fired a number of revolver shots at that them. The Solicitor General advised the Under Secretary that the Coroner had discretion about how he conducted proceedings, unless they were irregular and could be quashed by the High Court. As regards O'Brien-Moran's speech, nothing could be done, unless proceedings were justified against him.

Kelly's report said that more than five hundred people were present in Limerick City courthouse for Byrne's inquest. There were frequent bursts of loud applause, cheering and unrestrained clapping of hands, according to Kelly. From the extended report on the inquest in the '*Irish Independent*' we get a flavour of Lynch's final speech to the jury. From the evidence, said Lynch, they could gather that Mr Byrne belonged to the Irish Volunteers, 'a body recognised by everybody as remarkable for the purity of their lives, nobility of motives and their unselfish love of the land that bore them.' That statement was received with prolonged cheering. At the conclusion of the inquest, the jury barely hesitated before reaching their verdict. After only twenty minutes of deliberation, they found that 'Robert J Byrne met his death by a revolver bullet discharged by either Constable O'Brien or Constable Spillane.'

Nearly sixty years later, in a series of conversations with the late Jim Kemmy, the Limerick historian and distinguished public representative, Batty Stack admitted that it might have been a bullet from his gun that killed Robert Byrne as he slowly tried to ease himself out of the line of fire.[2] The sixteen years old Stack himself did most of the shooting in the Workhouse Hospital ward. He fatally wounded Constable O'Brien, but may have unwittingly wounded the prisoner too, as a weakened Robert Byrne tried desperately to ease himself out of the line of fire. With the benefit of hindsight, then, the Crown Solicitor's claim that the calibre of the bullet found in Constable O'Brien's body showed that he was killed by a non-Constabulary weapon, takes on a new significance.

Within the IRA, Batty Stack had a reputation as a cool and efficient killer, a squat gunman who shot first and did not talk afterwards. Although IRA members often recounted their exploits in bolt holes like a favoured public house in Nelson Street, Stack was noted for his silence. In the aftermath of the Workhouse rescue, his coolness stood to him and he allowed the British authorities to suffer the blame for the killing of Byrne, while he kept the truth to himself.

In the early months of 1919, Stack had taken part in numerous IRA operations. Although he lived in a largely Republican community, at Carey's Road near Limerick railway station, Stack took little part in any overt anti-British demonstrations. Like others with military expertise, he was kept in the background for the 'real' fight – the armed attacks on police and army.

---

2 – Information given to author: Michael 'Batty' Stack, interview with Jim Kemmy; Charles St. George, interview with Kevin O'Connor

Commandant Michael Brennan described Stack as 'one of the best and most active Volunteers in Limerick.' Eventually, Stack's exploits came to the notice of Michael Collins, who was then intensifying the military campaign against British occupation. He was seconded to IRA Headquarters, in Dublin, and became one of Collins' select and hand-picked assassins, whose activities had such a disproportionately devastating effect on the morale of the Crown forces. Stack often disappeared from Limerick for days on end and the few people 'in the know' would scan the newspapers for details of the latest IRA shooting escapade.

The startling outcome of the inquests on O'Brien and Byrne was an unpleasant shock for the British authorities and the people of Limerick. But, while all of this was emerging behind the walls of the Courthouse, other events had been taking place in Limerick and the shock of the inquests was as nothing compared to the tremors that were being prepared.

CHAPTER THREE

<u>Soldiers, Strikers and Citizens</u>

'We, as organised workers refuse to ask them for permits to earn our daily bread and this strike is a protest against their action.'
– *John Cronin, Chairman, Limerick Strike Committee*

On the Monday morning after the shooting at the Infirmary, the following official announcement was issued: 'In consequence of the attack by armed men on police constables and the brutal murder of one of them at Limerick yesterday, the Government has decided to proclaim the district as a Special Military Area.'

As General Officer in Command of Forces in Ireland, Lieutenant-General the Right Honourable Sir Frederick Shaw KCB, Commander-in-Chief Ireland, had attended a top-level meeting that Monday morning with the Lord Lieutenant, Viscount French, at the Vice Regal Lodge in Dublin, together with the Inspector-General of the Royal Irish Constabulary, Lieutenant-General Joseph Byrne, and the head of the Dublin Metropolitan Police. Later the same day, the Lord Chancellor, James Campbell, had a meeting with the Lord Lieutenant.

On Wednesday, 8 April 1919, General Shaw appointed Brigadier-General Christopher Joseph Griffin CMG, DSO as the Competent Military Authority throughout Ireland. In a separate notice, most of Limerick City and a part of the county were placed under General Griffin's authority, as a Special Military Area. Griffin was a member of a well-to-do Cork Catholic family, the son of Patrick Griffin of Woodhill Terrace, Tivoli, in Cork city. He was commissioned into the Lancashire Fusiliers in September 1895 and was severely wounded at the battle of Spion Kop while serving in South Africa in the war against the Boers, where he took part in many battles and engagements.

He served with distinction in the Great War, on the Western Front. The Lancashire Fusiliers were among the first units sent to Belgium at the outbreak of the war, as part of the British Expeditionary Force – the army the Germans nicknamed 'The Old Contemptibles'. Until April 1917, Griffin commanded the 2nd Battalion of the Lancashire Fusiliers with great ability and determination and was then appointed to command the 103rd Infantry Brigade, followed by command of the 7th Infantry Brigade. His decorations for exemplary courage and service included the Order of St. Michael and St. George and the Distinguished Service Order, with Bar. The DSO was awarded for meritorious or distinguished service by officers during wartime, typically while under fire or in combat. He was wounded five times during the Great War and, on the final occasion in May 1918, he was fortunate not to have been killed outright when a German shell exploded, wounding Griffin and killing one of his Staff Officers.

Four months after the stirring events in Limerick had ended, at the age of forty-four, General Griffin married Ruby Ward, the widow of one of his fellow officers in the 2nd Battalion who had been killed in action in August 1914 after only three weeks in the field. Four years after Limerick, he retired from the British army and died in 1957.

The Orders declaring Limerick a Special Military Area and appointing Griffin as Military Commandant were made under the provisions of the Defence of the Realm Acts and the Regulations made under the Acts. This Act – DORA as it was usually known – was introduced by the British authorities on 8 August 1914, soon after the outbreak of World War One and it gave them sweeping powers, literally, to defend the Realm. One of its key provisions was the power to proclaim entire districts as Special Military Areas, under what was termed a Competent Military Authority. This enabled the military to issue entrance and exit permits and to weed out spies by frequent and close checking of passes. Later on, as the Anglo-Irish War increased in ferocity, Special Military Areas were used to pressurise the local citizenry into disowning the gunmen in their midst. General Shaw's signature gave legal effect to the authorities' swift response, announced on the previous Monday, to the events in Limerick.

Also on that Wednesday, Viscount French and the Chief Secretary for Ireland, Ian Macpherson MP, jointly sent an urgent, almost panic-stricken, demand for troop reinforcements to the Adjutant-General in London: 'The situation here grows worse and worse. It cannot be dealt with efficiently unless the eight battalions which were promised to the Chief Secretary by you are immediately sent. Five are understood to be ordered. These are not enough for the purpose. It is absolutely imperative that great expedition should be used in the dispatch of these troops'. In January, the War Office had promised Dublin they would not be 'let down' below the minimum requirements of troops and mechanical transport. Now the reply was that necessary steps were being taken to expedite the dispatch of troops.

Although the formal proclamation of the military area was made on Wednesday, 9 April, it was not to come into practical effect until the beginning of the following week. The military and police spent the intervening period mapping out the area to be covered, securing positions and selecting sites for military outposts leading to the city. They commandeered the extensive premises of the Shannon Rowing Club, strategically located beside Wellesley (later called Sarsfield) Bridge, something they had previously done after the disturbances of Easter Week, 1916.

On 14 April 1919, the *'Irish Independent'* carried an official Public Notice setting out the details of the Limerick Special Military Area. It provided that, on or after 9 April 1919, no person could enter the SMA without permission of the Military Commandant. For permanent residents, application for permission had to be made to the Commandant and in the case of people resident outside, applications were to be made to their local police. Contravention of the Regulations was a criminal offence and non-residents could be removed from Limerick by direction of the Commandant unless they had been residing in the city on 9 April. The Regulations did not apply to anyone under sixteen years of age nor to anyone passing through the SMA in the course of a continuous journey by railway or water from and to places outside the Area.

The SMA was defined as 'That portion of the County Borough of Limerick which lies on the Left or South Bank of the River Shannon and the area included in the following townlands and portions of townland situated in the Limerick No. 1 Rural District, that is to say, within the townlands of Spitalland, Killallee, Monamuck and Park, and within those portions of the townlands of Singland and Reboge which lie to the West of the Railway Line from Limerick to Ennis'. The order was dated 10 April 1919 and signed by CJ Griffin, Brigadier-General, Commandant Limerick Special Military Area, Competent Military Authority.

Already, the '*Irish Times*' noted that respectable citizens 'who took natural pride in the city's industries' were beginning to wonder how far they would be affected by the proclamation. Most people, the newspaper said, realised the restrictions would seriously affect the commercial interests of the city. That was indeed a classic understatement. It was as if the regulations had been drafted deliberately to punish, if not provoke, the citizens of Limerick.

The designation of the River Shannon as Northern boundary of the Special Military Area meant that the large working-class area of Thomondgate, to the West of the river, was cut off from the rest of the city. Workers from there would have to show permits and undergo military checks four times a day, on either of two bridges, as they went to and from their work. Similarly, workers who lived on the Southern side of the river would face police and military scrutiny going to Thomondgate. Between five and six thousand workers were directly affected by the restrictions. Two of the city's largest factories were North of the river and were therefore cut off – Cleeve's Condensed Milk and Butter Company, employing six hundred workers (mostly women), and Walker's Distillery. Entire suburbs had been divided under the regulations and the supply of milk to the city, mostly from Cleeve's, would be seriously disrupted. Tenants who held vegetable allotments in the rural area North of the Shannon would be unable to tend them.

People who needed permits were required to report to the offices of the Military Commandant, General Griffin, at 78, O'Connell Street – the former recruiting office. They were required to produce a letter of identification from the RIC sergeant in their district. If the police thought the applicant was a fit person to get a permit, one whose loyalty was beyond doubt, they would recommend him to the military authorities. In this way, known Republican sympathisers faced economic punishment for their views, if they could not exercise their trade or vocation. In addition, people suspected of crimes could be isolated and taken into custody. After the police recommendation, the military recorded the applicants' height, weight, colour of hair and eyes and other details. These were kept on a card, duly stamped and dated. In some cases, applicants faced the trouble of having to apply every day. Only children under the age of sixteen were permitted to cross the bridges without a permit.

At this time, people in seven districts in Ireland faced such restrictions. To add insult to injury, the ratepayers could be levied with half the cost of sending extra police to the area. In Westport, County Mayo, for example, no potatoes or other farm produce or turf were allowed in and poor people were suffering particularly badly because of the lack of fuel. Even most of the mourners at a funeral were turned back a mile outside the town. However, Limerick's strong trade union organisation and the city's history, the frequent overlapping of membership between the Labour and Republican movements and the heightened passions after the death and funeral of Robert Byrne all ensured that Limerick's response would be more robust and more effective, than that of other areas.

The IRA Volunteer who pulled the trigger at the Workhouse rescue, Batty Stack, was employed in Cleeve's factory as an apprentice mechanical engineer and many Cleeve's workers were members or sympathisers of either the IRA or Sinn Féin. For Stack and for other Republicans, the prospect of being checked and questioned by the military four times a day was dangerous. In addition, there was probably a genuine sense of grievance among Cleeve's employees over the way the military boundaries had been planned. On the Saturday before the general strike started, the Cleeve's workers – members of the ITGWU and the Irish Clerical and Allied Workers' Union – rejected an offer by the authorities to supply them with permits for the coming week and decided, instead, to go on strike from Monday the 14th.

Some authorities have suggested that the Cleeve's workers' decision forced the hand of the Trades Council but it is just as likely that the Council, caught up in the emotional atmosphere of the city, would have moved towards a stoppage anyway. A confidential police report said the strike had its origins among a number of Sinn Féin members employed at Cleeve's factory but it is also likely that their militant ITGWU Organiser, John Dowling, played a key role in encouraging the strike. A union colleague later described Dowling as 'the philosophical begetter of the Limerick Soviet'. The police report went further and said Sinn Féin had 'instigated' the general strike. Many years later, in his Witness Statement to the Bureau of Military History, Batty Stack claimed that 'The whole strike was engineered by the Battalion staff at the time, and Councillor James Casey, who was Chairman of the Trade Union Council at the time gave us his wholehearted support...'

On Sunday, 13 April 1919 – Palm Sunday in the Christian liturgy – delegates from the thirty-five unions affiliated to Limerick United Trades and Labour Council met to consider the situation. Their discussions lasted for almost twelve hours, ending at half past eleven that night. In the end, the decision was unanimous. The Council decided to call a general strike of all Limerick workers as a protest against the proclamation of the city as a Special Military Area. At a sympathetic printing works in Cornmarket Row, printers worked through the night on a strike proclamation. Within two hours, the city's walls were covered with this notice:

'Limerick United Trades and Labour Council Proclamation
The workers of Limerick, assembled in Council, hereby declare cessation of all work from 5 am on Monday April 14, 1919, as a protest against the decision of the British Government in compelling them to procure permits in order to earn their bread.
By order of the Strike Committee Mechanics' Institute.
Any information with reference to the above can be had from the Strike Committee.'

The Council elected a Strike Committee, chaired by the Council President, John Cronin, who was a delegate from the Amalgamated Society of Carpenters. Cronin was an unassuming person, but a highly skilled craftsman, having won a gold medal and certificate from the Worshipful Company of Carpenters for proficiency in his trade. Cronin's father had been also been President of the Trades Council and the son had followed diligently in his footsteps. In 1880, as Secretary of the Congregated Trades of Limerick, Cronin signed an Address of Welcome to Parnell on a visit to Limerick. Later in the Anglo-Irish War, he would be a diligent member of a Sinn Féin court when it was established in Limerick.

The Trades Council Treasurer, the printer James Casey, was elected Treasurer of the strike committee. He was an Alderman of Limerick Corporation. In March 1921 after RIC Auxiliaries had murdered the Mayor of Limerick, George Clancy, and the ex-Mayor, Michael O'Callaghan in their homes, Casey bravely filled the office of Mayor temporarily for a couple of weeks until a longer-term holder of the office could be elected. He gave the graveside oration at their funerals. He was an enthusiastic amateur boxer and referee and later became President of the Irish Amateur Boxing Union, as well playing for Garryowen for many years.

The third officer of the strike committee was an engineering worker, James Carr. Later in 1919, Carr was part of a move by Countess Markiewicz and the Dáil Cabinet, as well as the IRB, to break away from British-headquartered trade unions and form Irish ones. This was not just a nationalistic plan, but was intended to give the IRB a strong foothold and 'cover' in employments vital to maintaining British rule – such as dockyards and the rail companies. Seven hundred people attended the inaugural meeting of the Irish Engineering Industrial Union in Dublin. With support from Sinn Féin clubs and IRA units – and the ITGWU – the union grew rapidly and formed branches in Dundalk, Drogheda, Cork, Cobh, Passage West, Limerick, Galway and Sligo. The new union's head office at 6 Gardiner Row, in Dublin, was used by the Volunteer Headquarters and the Dáil Cabinet. In the folklore of Limerick trade unionists, the strike leaders were remembered as 'The Three Cs'. The strikers also elected subcommittees to take charge of propaganda, finance, food and vigilance – an early indication, perhaps, that they expected a long, rather than a short, strike.

The speedy and efficient way in which the Trades' Council meeting was organised and its decision publicised seems to confirm an element of Republican influence and support. Certainly, the normal, cumbersome methods of consultation with the members of individual affiliated unions were not followed. Indeed, from the outset, the Soviet was underpinned by remarkably effective organisation. Very early on, the '*Irish Times*' speculated that many observers detected in this 'The hand of Sinn Féin'. Years later, in their Witness Statements to the Bureau of Military History, Michael Stack and Michael Brennan (Officer Commanding, East Clare Brigade of the IRA) stated that the local IRA battalions were involved in the on-the-ground organisation of affairs and they kept Volunteer Headquarters in Dublin appraised of events in Limerick. Although he was not a member of a trade union, Michael Brennan was co-opted to the Strike Committee for the duration of the strike. Thus, there was a clear link established between the trade union leadership and the local IRA leadership. However, since Brennan and other key local IRA leaders were members of the clandestine Irish Republican Brotherhood, it might be more accurate to state that 'the hand of the IRB' was involved. This would also explain the willingness of the farmers surrounding the city – who would not normally have an affinity or sympathy with a purely Labour agitation – to supply abundant foodstuffs to the inhabitants.

On Monday April 14, 1919, the '*Irish Independent*' correspondent in Limerick cabled the Dublin office:

'Limerick City is on strike. Shops warehouses and factories are closed. No work is being done and no business transacted.'

The strike committee sanctioned the continuation of public utilities like water, gas and electricity with a skeleton crew though street lighting was turned off. The strike took the city and its workers by surprise. Nevertheless, almost all workers stayed out and, apart from the Post Office and the banks, practically every branch of industry stopped and all places of business were closed. The banks did little or no business, but the Post Office was kept busy by journalists filing reports on Robert Byrne's inquest and the start of the strike. Even the public houses followed the lead.

On the first day of the strike, to avoid the loss of perishable commodities, the Strike Committee allowed people to work at the bacon and condensed milk factories and the tanneries. The employees of Cleeve's creamery did not turn up for work, but instead, joined in a parade by thousands of workers through streets filled with a holiday style atmosphere. Bakers' and butchers' assistants joined the strike. Bread was not obtainable, but it was announced that the bakers would return to work that night, easing initial fears of a food shortage.

In all, more than fourteen thousand workers were on strike. The '*Irish Times*' noted: '... nothing doing anywhere, except a Coroner's inquest on the Sinn Féin prisoner, Byrne, who was shot during an attempt to rescue him.'

At Kingsbridge Railway Station, in Dublin, and at other stations, passengers were refused tickets to Limerick unless they had a permit from the military authorities. Some passengers persisted in making the journey. But the few who arrived in Limerick that Monday morning had considerable difficulty in getting hotel accommodation. Pickets visited all the hotels and ordered them to close their doors. Where visitors were admitted, they were told there could be no guarantee they would be supplied with food and that supplies could not last beyond the evening. Restaurants, too, were closed.

The three thousand or so members of the Irish Transport and General Workers' Union were crucial in the strike. Goods for Limerick were not dispatched from the North Wall, in Dublin, nor accepted at Kingsbridge when it became known they would not be handled by the transport workers in Limerick. The '*Irish Independent*' reported: 'Every thoroughfare in the city is full of people moving about and discussing the situation. There is considerable suppressed excitement, but the people show no disposition to be otherwise than quiet and orderly...' In a perceptive comment, the newspaper's correspondent wrote: 'The strike is in every way complete, and it looks as if there is a possibility of a fierce struggle between organised labour and the Government.'

The '*Irish Times*' report blamed the Transport Union as the 'dominating factor' in encouraging the strike decision. 'Associated to some degree with labour in its action', the newspaper claimed, 'is the irresponsible element of Sinn Féin, which, of course, regards the situation as a challenge to British law. The ordinary citizen, however, who has at heart the welfare of the city, and realises how costly will be the strike and the other incidents, is gravely concerned, and anticipates a permanent setback to its trade and commerce. The bill that he will have to meet for the maintenance of the extra police will be a heavy one...

The Chairman of the Strike Committee, John Cronin telegraphed a message to William O'Brien, General Secretary of the Irish Labour Party and Trade Union Congress: 'General strike here as protest against permit restrictions.' Cronin outlined his assessment of the causes of the strike to newspaper reporters. He said the present industrial situation had arisen out of the tragedy at the Workhouse. 'The military authorities have seen fit to place Limerick under martial law. In doing that, they have fixed their boundaries inside the city, which makes it necessary for workers to pass in and out to their work. We, as organised workers, refuse to ask them for permits to earn our daily bread, and this strike is a protest against their action. What we want is to have this ban removed so that the workers may have free access to their work in and out of their native city. It is our intention to carry on the strike until this ban is removed. This strike is likely to become more serious.'

The strike call threw the Castle authorities, particularly the RIC, into immediate difficulties. Within a half hour of the strike meeting ending, Dublin Castle was being told of the decision. At five minutes to midnight, on the Sunday, District Inspector Craig of the RIC telephoned Dublin. The succinct official record of the telephone message shows that Craig asked for at least three hundred extra constables, if possible, to be sent on the first morning train. Alternatively, he would settle for a hundred men sent in advance from the Dublin Depot. Craig's initial assessment was wise: 'The situation looks very serious.'

The message from Craig prompted a handwritten message to Brigadier-General Joseph Byrne, the Inspector-General of the RIC, from the Deputy Inspector-General WM Davies, at twenty to two in the morning. The request for three hundred police reinforcements was impossible to meet, even with more time available. Davies pointed out that he was reluctant to take men from any of the Southern companies, because 'there are so many strikes going on elsewhere' – an interesting insight into the level of trade union militancy at the time. Although he knew the military did not intervene in strikes, they would have to do so if disorder arose. This comment suggests that this very senior RIC officer did not quite appreciate the extraordinary challenge to authority posed by this particular strike. Indeed, the whole tone of his message to the Inspector General is querulous and indecisive.

Forty minutes later, at twenty minutes past two in the morning, a decisive reply came back. Fifty men were to be sent from the Depot on the first train. GHQ were to be informed of the policing difficulties. The Inspector General's assessment was blunt: 'Say to GHQ that as this is no ordinary strike it is presumed instruction will be tonight sent for military to help police.'

On the same file in Dublin Castle on the headed notepaper of the Vice Regal Lodge, is a note of two matters decided upon there, that Monday. The first was the text of a communiqué to be telegraphed to Limerick and issued to the Dublin press by the Press Censor's Office. This read: 'The public of Limerick are informed that although Limerick has been proclaimed a military area, this in no way prevents the inhabitants from getting their supplies in the ordinary way. If, owing to the wanton action of ill-disposed persons, the inhabitants suffer through lack of the necessities of life, the Government are in no way responsible, and cannot do anything to ameliorate the consequences of such action.' The second decision noted was an instruction to inform the C in C that 'the Government instructs him to give every possible assistance in the maintenance of Law and Order, especially in view of the fact that Limerick is a military area.' After a slight initial hesitancy, Dublin Castle had recognised the challenge for what it was and made its dispositions to deal with it.

If the lives of Limerick's workers were disrupted by the military regulations, so too were the arrangements of more 'respectable' citizens elsewhere. The Company Secretary of Switzer's department store in Dublin, Mr WF Hanna, applied for a permit, saying it was 'of extreme importance' that he travel on the Thursday. He wished to be in his native Limerick for the Easter holidays. In the initial period prior to the exact details of the control regulations being published, the Limerick RIC had referred Mr Hanna to the Dublin Metropolitan Police. Indignantly, he pointed out that they professed 'complete ignorance – or rather absence of information!' Mr Hanna said that he was a 'most law-abiding citizen anxious to mind my own business and no politician.' In exasperation, he asked the Chief Secretary for Ireland: 'Tell me what I am to do please.'

From 56 Monson Street, in Lincoln, came a request from Patrick Noonan for a permit to return to Rathkeale, in county Limerick, also for the Easter Holidays. Noonan explained that he had gone to Lincoln to replace a man who had gone to fight at the Front, being too old himself for military service. He enclosed a newspaper clipping showing he was the author of a telegram to the Lord Lieutenant of Ireland, from the 'loyal Irishmen of Lincoln', expressing deepest sympathy at the sinking of the passenger ferry 'Leinster' in October 1918, with a loss of more than five hundred lives. The telegram had expressed the hope that the 'fiendish outrage which called aloud to Heaven for vengeance would fire the youth of Ireland with the fighting spirit of their race to give, even at the eleventh hour, the final knockout blow to the murderers of our countrymen!

Noonan also enclosed a copy of a reference written for him in 1916 by Major General TF Lloyd, Colonel the Prince of Wales North Stafford Regiment, at Rathkeale, county Limerick. Apart from describing Noonan as a strong Loyalist, the reference said his life had been erratic, taking up various pursuits, among others, correspondent to newspapers, writing especially articles on hunting. 'And I never saw anything written by him that was not loyal in every sense of the word', the General commented. Not surprisingly, Noonan got his permit. Other applicants were referred to their local police. One came from WF Enright, a wholesale spirits, cork, butter and general produce merchant in Belfast and another from a person named Walsh in Liverpool.

A week into the strike, the Chief Secretary for Ireland, the Scot Ian Macpherson, received an anonymous letter from Limerick, signed 'An Anxious One'. The letter began by endorsing a recent Speech by Macpherson in the House of Commons. Of this speech, the Parliamentary Correspondent of the '*British Weekly*' – himself an experienced Scottish member of the Press Gallery – had laconically commented: 'This was not the type of speech which Mr. Macpherson, a Home Ruler, would have liked to deliver, but the man who becomes Chief Secretary for Ireland cannot always do what he likes.'

In general, the Chief Secretary's anonymous Limerick correspondent berated him about the dangers facing the country and the need to maintain morale in the police force. Unless the force was supported, the writer warned, the younger men especially would go over to the Rebels, 'leaving the country in a bad way and all loyal citizens at the mercy of Rebels who will turn the place into another Russia.' This letter was written after the strike had lasted for a week and the writer's reference to Russia is of interest.

The tribulations of the Loyal citizens of Limerick even found their way into the hallowed chambers of Buckingham Palace. On the fourth day of the strike, Mrs Anna Worrall of Catherine Place, in Limerick, wrote to his Majesty King George V to ask a favour of the King, knowing she said, that since the War he was 'only too ready to hear all about his subjects.' She hoped the letter would not be thrown in the wastepaper basket but would be given to the King himself. Mrs Worrall's request was to have the military tanks removed from the Wellesley Bridge (now called Sarsfield Bridge) to the Borough Boundary at the Workhouse Cross in County Clare. This, she pointed out, would allow the men and women workers to go freely to Cleeve's factory.

The General Strike, she complained, 'makes it hard for everyone'. The grocers and bakers were the only shops allowed to open, from 2 pm. to 5 pm. 'They are all 'Sinn Féiners',' she declared, 'but the Government ought to think a little of us few loyal subjects and it is no use making them more bitter than they are, nor do we want bloodshed here over it. No one knows I am writing to your Majesty. Will you send orders to Head Quarters in Dublin by return and grant the request I ask?'

King George's Private Secretary passed the letter to Dublin Castle. District Inspector Rodwell reported from Limerick that Mrs Worrall was a most respectable and loyal old lady, but was considered 'slightly eccentric'. She frequently visited her brother, the well-known auctioneer Mr Fitt, who lived on the Ennis Road and had to show her pass when crossing the Wellesley Bridge. Laconically, Rodwell noted: 'She probably does not like doing this.'

Other concerned citizens were expressing their views too on the effects of the proclamation. Limerick Corporation adopted a resolution criticising the allocation of extra police and the ever-active P J Kelly, Resident Magistrate, convened a meeting of his colleagues to consider the state of the city.

Now the powder keg had exploded, and the pieces could never be put back again.

CHAPTER FOUR

<u>Food, Money and Newspapers</u>

'Limerick, famous all over the world for the quality of its
bacon, will at the present rate soon be without the morning
rasher.'
– *The Irish Independent, 19 April, 1919*

The first and most fundamental task facing the strikers was that of literally feeding Limerick's thirty-eight thousand inhabitants.

The suddenness with which the strike was called and became effective meant that rich and poor alike were taken unawares. On the first Monday of the strike there was panic over the continuity of food supply and an '*Irish Independent*' headline warned of 'The Peril of Famine'. That evening, in its first major assertion of power, the Strike Committee ordered the bakers to resume work. In its report on this development, the '*Irish Times*' for the first time referred to the Committee as the local 'Soviet', though it is not quite clear from the context whether the reference was sarcastic or not. In any event, however, the report indicates that even on the first day of the strike it was being referred to in some quarters as a 'Soviet'. After the Soviet's order, at an early hour on Tuesday morning, crowds of women and children lined up outside the bakeries in the hope of getting bread and it was handed out to them fresh from the ovens.

Describing the shortage of food on the first day of the Soviet, the '*Irish Times*' waxed lyrical: 'In this land of plenty, in the heart of the Golden Vale, it is not easy for the stranger to procure food. The bakeries are closed and the butchers' shops are shut, with the result that the hotel larders are scantily stocked. Biscuits and cheese were never so appetising as today, when they sustained many a weary traveller through a trying time. Milk, however, could hardly be had, though there are creameries everywhere. The visitor from Dublin, of course, did not mind the shortage of butter, but he did miss his margarine...'

On that first day, other foodstuffs – potatoes for example – were running alarmingly low, and fresh meat was impossible to obtain. All the public houses rigidly enforced the order to close. Even the most favoured customers could not buy a drink anywhere and the '*Irish Independent*' wryly noted in heavy black type: 'Limerick is an absolutely dry city.'

If there were no public houses, at least the citizens still had the cinemas for entertainment. Some of these were glad to open with notices outside the door saying 'Open by authority of the Strike Committee' and they donated their profits to the strikers' fund. On its masthead the *'Limerick Leader'* announced that it was being published 'by permission of the Strike Committee'. But there was a plaintive letter of protest to the *'Irish Independent'* about the closure of the Limerick Free Library. The writer, 'Munchin', admitted that the general strike was in defence of the public but he warned the new 'powers-that-be that in striving for the public rights they should not trample on public privileges'. The Public Park, where the Library was situated, had not been closed. So, 'Munchin' enquired, if it was possible to look after the recreation of the body, why not recreation of the mind? This, he argued, was especially true when 'time hangs heavily on many men's hands, and newspapers, even for money, are hard to get.'

From early on, the Soviet claimed to have the food situation well in hand. They sat in session in the Mechanics' Institute, in Lower Glentworth Street, from early morning until late at night, carrying out their arrangements with thoroughness and completeness of detail. They issued hundreds – another report says 'sheaves' – of permits to shops to open and supply foodstuffs, between two and five o'clock in the afternoon. The Soviet strictly controlled the price of food. They issued posters throughout the city showing a list of retail prices for essential foodstuffs. The posters warned that drastic measures would be taken to prevent profiteering. If there was evidence of this, the shops involved would be closed down. Pickets wearing distinctive badges patrolled the streets. They ensured no shops opened without permission and that they were not overcrowded during the hours of opening. Shops received special permits to display and opened only during the hours permitted by the Soviet.

In general, the provision merchants acted in harmony with the Soviet and they kept prices at normal levels. After a week, the *'Irish Independent'* commented: 'It is certainly a remarkable tribute to the skill and organisation of the Strike Committee that while there has been a general suspension of all branches of industry in the city now for seven days, there has been no scarcity of food.' Large purchases were discouraged, so hoarding was prevented.

Given that the *'Irish Times'* was always critical of the strike, its grudgingly favourable comments on the food situation on the same date are an interesting indication of the Soviet's effectiveness. In a comment on the food supply, the newspaper said: '.... though it is daily diminishing, it should not be thought there is immediate danger of serious distress... the people there are, therefore, well supplied with milk, and they also have fair supplies of other necessaries.'

The general strike was expected to have wide repercussions and the IRB/Volunteers made plans to respond to them but these were never fully implemented. On the first Friday of the strike, 18 April, the Sinn Féin Comhairle Cheantair – in response to an approach by the Strike Committee – issued a circular seeking gifts of foodstuffs – particularly butter, milk, eggs, potatoes and vegetables. It said that the foodstuffs would be paid for at prices agreed on by the Strike Committee. The circular said the hardships 'inflicted on the citizens were particularly severe, especially for the poorer classes who now find it difficult to procure ordinary food.'

It would be wrong to give the impression, though, that the Soviet's relations with the city's business people were entirely harmonious. For many of them, believers in the rights of property, it must have been galling having to take orders from a group of mere workers and to hear John Cronin declare: 'The necessary steps have been taken to ensure a sufficient supply of food for the people...' After the first week of the strike, the '*Irish Times*' found some business people who were 'suffering considerable inconvenience and loss as a result of closing their establishments, and they would be glad to see the strike ended and the old order of things restored.' They may have been among the traders who, at that time, threatened to open their premises in spite of Soviet opposition. On the second Monday of the Soviet, some shopkeepers did, indeed, do that but they were punished the following day by having their opening delayed.

Throughout the life of the Soviet, the problem of bread supplies remained crucial. It was closely linked to supplies of flour, obviously, but also to supplies of coal, since the bakery ovens were coal-fired. To ensure supplies of flour, the Soviet gave permission for the unloading of seven thousand tons of Canadian grain at the docks. No deliveries of bread were allowed to shops or private homes – everyone had to buy their supplies directly from the bakeries. Farmers from outside the city, normally dependent on bread carts for deliveries, had to come in to collect their supplies. As the '*Irish Independent*' noted: '...it was no uncommon spectacle to see an aged peasant driving an ass and cart laden with bread through the streets.'

It appears that in some instances the Soviet tried to requisition food supplies. Dublin Castle records refer to a file about a demand to Cleeve's factory for 'butter etc. required by the Transport Union.'

Limerick's food problems offered the first opportunity for those who sympathised with the strike outside the city to give practical help. A Catholic priest, Father Charles Kennedy of Ennis, County Clare, helped to organise the farmers in the South East of the county, near the city, to supply food to Limerick. His efforts in this direction earned him the title of 'A Fighting Soggarth' in an edition of the Soviet's own newspaper '*The Workers' Bulletin*'. The Soviet Food Committee was divided into two sections – one to receive food and the other to distribute it. Food depots were set up in Thomondgate, on the Clare side of the Shannon, because it was outside the controlled area. Four city councillors controlled the collection and distribution of food through four depots established by the Soviet.

The Clare farmers sent potatoes, milk, eggs, butter, tea, sugar and home-made bread into the depots and these were sold at prices considerably below the market value. Through a combination of circumstances, the people of Limerick suffered no shortage of milk and it was available at a very cheap price. Because of the closure of Cleeve's condensed milk factory, the farmers found themselves with supplies on hand. This was sold to the city's poor at three pence or four pence a litre, compared with the usual price of seven pence. The maximum price set by the Soviet was four pence.

Towards the end of the Soviet's existence, the supply of food from county Clare received ecclesiastical approval at a high level. At Sunday Masses in the Diocese of Killaloe, the priests appealed to the congregations to help Limerick with food supplies, saying they did so with the sanction and approval of the Bishop, Doctor Fogarty. There was a generous response, including one gift of twenty tons of potatoes. Unorthodox methods were used to bring in food. In a memoir of the Soviet, the Trades Council Treasurer, James Casey, recalls that relays of boats with muffled oars were successfully used to run food and other supplies through the blockade. On other occasions, Casey recalled, the funeral hearses from the Union Hospital, outside the military cordon, did not always contain corpses!

Cork and other centres offered to send food, as did a number of British trade unions. Farmers and shopkeepers outside Limerick who wished to send gifts of food were asked to send them by rail to the city, consigned to the 'Food Commission, Mechanics' Hall, Limerick.' Any food received in this way was to be stocked in wholesale stores under the Commission's control and then distributed to shopkeepers who were willing to recognise the authority of the Strike Committee. If necessary, the Commission would open supplementary retail shops.

The quantity of food sent by farmers, especially from County Clare, in support of what was clearly a Labour agitation raises intriguing questions in view of the many strikes involving farm labourers at that time. Not all farmers were willing donors to the strikers' stockpile of food. A veteran of the Soviet, Dan Clancy, recalled an incident that occurred in the 'Little Market', off Robert Street, when the strikers compelled the farmers to give away food for 'half nothing'. As the police stood by helplessly, the strikers ordered the farmers from the market. Clancy recalled sardonically: 'They all flocked to the Republic'. Since the normal methods and outlets for disposing of their produce were closed, many farmers decided to make a patriotic virtue out of necessity. But the involvement of Father Kennedy, in Ennis, suggests a degree of organisation by Sinn Fein and its sympathisers, and of course, one cannot rule out feelings of genuine nationalism on the part of some farmers.

Pig and cattle fairs were seriously disrupted by the Strike. The April Munster Fair, held in the second week of the strike, had no more than one tenth of the usual supply of cattle. Buyers were few and little business was done. The pig-buyers were seriously affected by a prohibition on the killing of about two hundred pigs which had been bought during the first two days of the Soviet. Bacon supplies were exhausted in some of the shops. 'Limerick', the '*Irish Independent*' noted, 'famous all over the world for the quality of its bacon will, at the present rate, soon be without the morning rasher.' The military themselves were forced to make special arrangements to bring supplies by train to Limerick from Dublin and Cork.

Soviet control of the city's business ran deep. Drapery and boot shops were not opened, so that anyone needing a collar and tie had to get it surreptitiously from a friendly proprietor or get a Soviet permit. An American journalist staying in the city had to make an eloquent appeal to a Soviet subcommittee for permission to buy a shirt. Even chemists' shops were confined to limited Sunday opening hours.

After food, fuel was next in importance. The Soviet allowed coal and coke merchants to open between ten and five o'clock, but supplies were running alarmingly low, and very limited quantities were given out. In general, the coal merchants were hostile and refused to open their yards. Rather than force a violent confrontation, however, the Soviet reluctantly accepted this. But they warned the coal merchants that they were not to co-operate with the military by supplying them with fuel, nor should they supply customers who had obtained military permits.

After a week, the cautious '*Irish Times*' commented that 'while the food question seems to have been solved for the present, the question of money is causing anxiety to many families...' The majority of trade unions seemed to have been prepared to pay their members strike pay for the duration of the Soviet but a key trade union, the National Union of Railwaymen, made it clear that it would not. In addition, at the end of the first week, outside food supplies were readily forthcoming but little money had been received. It would have cost €400,000 weekly (in today's values) to maintain the strike but after two weeks only €85,000 had been received. Faced with this prospect, the Soviet took one of its most historic and, indeed, self-confident decisions. This was to print its own currency, in denominations of one, five and ten shillings – equivalent in today's values to roughly €30, €15 and €3, respectively. The decision does not seem to have been based on any ideological considerations but was a straightforward pragmatic response to a shortage of money.

The notes were printed at the Record Printing Works owned by Michael Gleeson in Cornmarket Row and were about the size of an ordinary Treasury note. On the outside border were the words: 'General Strike against British Militarism 1919' and on the face was printed: 'The workers of Limerick promise to pay the bearer the sum of _____ shillings.' A subcommittee of the propaganda committee was responsible for the printing and issuing of the currency and, not unexpectedly, it mainly consisted of accounts staff from large firms like Cleeve's, the bacon factories, the flour mills and the Corporation. James Casey, as Treasurer, and John Cronin, as Chairman, signed the notes for the Trades Council and they varied in colour according to their face value.

Cronin announced that a fund was being set up to supply the Soviet with money that was needed to make purchases outside the city and to retain circulation within the city as well. Legally, the currency was in the format of promissory notes. Strikers could purchase necessities on credit, tender a promissory note and the Soviet promised to redeem the note from the trader when the strike was over, out of the funds donated in support of Limerick. Tom Johnson, Treasurer of the Trade Union Congress, who had been sent by the Executive to liaise with the Limerick strikers, said the security for the notes, in the first place, would be the stocks of food being presented free by outside sympathisers, then the financial support and integrity of the workers of Limerick, backed by the national feeling. Later, the currency was backed by the Trades Council and the Trade Union Congress itself and accepted by approved shops. A list was compiled of merchants and shopkeepers who were willing to give credit to the Trades Council. Johnson said the notes issue was 'sound finance' and was a sign the strike could be prolonged. The '*Irish Times*' saw the currency more as a type of promissory note or food voucher and therefore as 'a sign of growing financial weakness... The impression, therefore, is gaining ground that the crisis has passed and the that the close of the week will synchronise with the close of the strike.' According to James Casey, when the notes were ultimately redeemed, a small surplus remained in a fund that had been subscribed to by sympathisers in all parts of Ireland. Many of the notes were redeemed in this way but some people retained them as souvenirs.

Whatever the original motivation for the issuing of currency, that decision alone places Limerick in a unique position in Labour history. At the time, the significance of issuing the currency was not lost on socialists. At the annual conference of the Independent Labour Party, in Britain, 'Councillor Cradford of Edinburgh said that they ought to do something to encourage the 'Limerick Soviet' which had got over its financial difficulties by the issue of a paper currency of its own. He would like to see the working-class of this country do the same. In spite of what Mr (Ramsay) McDonald had said, the 'Limerick Soviet' was the first working-class Soviet on practical lines established in these islands...'

An article by the late Jim Kemmy in the '*Irish Times*', in May 1969, was accompanied by illustrations of two notes. The illustrations were originally published in '*Fifty Years of Liberty Hall*', edited by Cathal O'Shannon. In a letter to the newspaper, John Cronin's son, Jeremiah, challenged the authenticity of his father's signature on the notes reproduced but he offered no explanation or theory as to how the difference arose. The signature in the illustration accompanying his letter was certainly different from the illustration accompanying the earlier article. The contested notes might well have been forged or signed by someone else with authority from John Cronin or run off after the strike as souvenirs.

Transport and communications were important enough to merit the setting up of a permits committee under the charge of four city councillors. The carters who worked at conveying perishable goods displayed printed cards, sometimes on the horse's bridle:

'Working under the authority of the Strike Committee.' The committee issued permits to merchants to obtain and carry commodities like coal, butter and flour from the railway station to shops. Doctors, chauffeurs and car drivers got permits when necessary. The only vehicles allowed on the streets were those owned by people who had appeared before the permits committee. Any other cars were immediately ordered off the streets by the workers' patrols. In all, the Soviet issued thousands of transport permits.

An American army officer arrived by train and got the necessary military permit to enter the city. He intended to visit relatives outside Limerick but he could not induce any of the hackney carriers to drive him to his destination. After a time, he appeared before the permits committee and got permission to travel. He delivered a spirited speech, in which he promised to expose British rule in Ireland when he returned to the United States. 'I guess', he concluded, 'it is some puzzle to know who rules in these parts. You have to get a military permit to get in, and be brought before a committee to get a permit to leave.'

All in all, the Soviet and its subcommittees carried off the job of feeding and regulating the lives of the thirty-eight thousand Limerick citizens with remarkable effectiveness. Not a single case of looting was reported, nor did a single court case come up for hearing at the petty sessions. After eight days in the city, an American journalist commented that he had not seen one person under the influence of drink nor a single disorderly incident. Given human nature, however, that generalised assertion seems unlikely to be true. But in several reports, various newspapers commented favourably on the peace and good order prevailing in the city and the absolute control exercised by the Soviet and its 'Ministers'.

But the name of Limerick, and its remarkable achievements, were soon to receive world-wide news coverage due to the fortuitously planned arrival there of a celebrated traveller and adventurer.

CHAPTER FIVE

<u>The World Watches</u>

'We are spectators today of a very bold and candid experiment in Irish Syndicalism.'
– 'Irish Times' editorial on 'The Strike at Limerick', 23 April, 1919

In April 1919, an intrepid flier named Major JCP Wood intended to fly the Atlantic from East to West, using Limerick as his departure point, to win a ten thousand pounds prize (equivalent to €520,000 today) offered by the London 'Daily Mail'. The Major never quite made it to Limerick in his attempt but his plan ensured the presence in the city, from the very start of the Soviet, of a large international press corps. Expecting to cover one major news story, these journalists found another one under their noses and cabled their reports diligently around the world.

The strides made by aircraft and flying during World War One meant there was considerable post-War interest in the commercial and other possibilities offered by air travel. In early 1919, the Air Ministry still controlled the air and prohibited civilian flying, though it was announced that civilian flying would resume on the first of May. The newspapers speculated eagerly on the changes the establishment of civilian air links would bring. Schemes had been put forward for a service between London and Cape Town and London to Egypt had already been flown. Hull Chamber of Commerce was supporting a scheme for a service to Scandinavia across the North Sea. There was talk of linking Ireland to the North of England and Wales by a service to Liverpool.

But, overshadowing all of these proposals was the challenge of the unconquered Atlantic. The 'Daily Mail' offered its lucrative prize to the first aviator to cross the Atlantic, and the manufacturers of 'State Express' cigarettes were prepared to add two thousand guineas (approximately, €120,000 in today's values) to it. The 'Daily Mail' rules stipulated that an Eastward flight had to land in either Ireland or Britain. Six contestants came forward to try for the prize.

The big problem facing the flyers was the weather. 'Like Cleopatra', the 'Irish Times' commented in an editorial, 'the Atlantic weather has an infinite variety. Anticyclones drift hither and thither above the Ocean's broad expanse, and the airman may encounter seventeen different brands of weather in his flight in as many hundreds of miles. The pioneer of the crossing will owe his success partly to daring, partly to skill, but most of all, perhaps, to luck.'

By flying Westward from Ireland, Major Wood was facing into the prevailing winds, increasing the estimated flight time from twenty to thirty hours but he would have the advantage of spending most of his flying time in daylight. By following the line of the River Shannon to Loop Head, in county Clare, the Major was positioning himself for a direct flight line across the Atlantic to St. John's in Newfoundland, a distance of around 2,800 kilometres. Another not inconsiderable advantage was the much greater likelihood in a Westward flight of making landfall in North America, compared with an Eastward flight which might miss the British Isles altogether, if the plane was blown off course.

The Major's planned departure caused great excitement in Limerick. A twenty-eight hectare field at Bawnmore, some kilometres the city, was prepared for the flight, with a huge whitewashed cross marked in the centre of the flying ground. Bawnmore had no hangars, but it had been temporarily used before the War by the Royal Flying Corps and it was close to the Shannon, an admirable navigational guide. It had the advantage too of being an elevated site, and the flight would not be delayed by a boggy runway if the weather was bad.

Two thousand three hundred litres of fuel were stored in Limerick in preparation for the flight and it was speculated that the military might move it to Bawnmore, if the carters refused to carry it because of the strike. But this proved not to be necessary. Sir Stephen Quin, one of the local notables involved in assisting the Major's preparations, went to see the Strike Committee. John Cronin said that they had no objection to the Major starting his flight from Limerick, provided he admitted he was starting there by permission of the strikers. Sir Stephen said he would convey the message to Wood, and subsequently the fuel was moved to Bawnmore. The Soviet also granted permits to drivers to bring press reporters and photographers to the take off point.

Wood planned to make his flight, with his navigator Captain Wyllie, in a two thousand three hundred kilos weight Short-Rolls Royce machine called 'The Shamrock'. The idea was that as the fuel was consumed the plane would become lighter, and it could stay in the air for up to forty-two hours at speeds of between 135 and 150 kilometres an hour. Both airmen wore a complicated type of heated clothing. Wires ran through their combination suits from a small dynamo operated by a propeller, and with the flick of a switch, they were able to heat themselves electrically. On the left side of the cockpit was a row of thermos flasks filled with hot coffee and a couple of flasks of brandy. Wood and Wyllie proposed to take plenty of sandwiches and tablet preparations of chocolate, fruit cake and meat. These, '*The Times*' of London noted, were in case they were blown a long way off course and had 'to land in some out-of-the-way part of the American continent.'

After several postponements because of bad weather, excitement in Limerick reached fever pitch as people awaited the Major's arrival from England. On the second day of the strike, crowds of people went to Bawnmore in anticipation of his arrival. Two days later, there was another exodus from the city by car and bicycle. A score of cinema newsreel photographers prepared stands to get the best vantage point and stills photographers took up positions on walls or on the adjoining hills. There were journalists there from all parts of the world, including a big American contingent with waiting cars on standby to carry special telegraph messengers with express dispatches. At one stage, a military scouting plane hovered over the crowds.

All eyes strained Eastwards, towards the Silvermines and Galtee Mountains, for the first glimpse of 'The Shamrock'. But it was not to be seen. After four hours flying, Major Wood's plane cut out over the Irish Sea and he was forced to ditch a short distance from the Anglesey coast. A group of picnickers who saw the plane in difficulties put a small boat out to sea and picked up the plane's two occupants. Wood made this laconic comment to one of the rescuers: 'Atlantic flight biffed!' Wood had left the Royal Flying Corps aerodrome at Eastchurch, Isle of Sheppey, in beautiful weather and in good spirits. Over the eleven previous days, three engines had been tested before one was fitted permanently. To find eight reliable sparking plugs, four hundred were tested. A Church of England chaplain prayed 'God Speed!' for the flyers and all the aerodrome hands gave hearty cheers as the Major took off.

Major Wood's adventure was only one of several transatlantic flights planned that week. But his was the only one to go Westward and he was actually the first competitor into the air in the '*Daily Mail*' race. In Newfoundland, flight pioneers like Hawker, Morgan and the Australian Raynham grappled with snowstorms, preventing take-off. A journalist asked Raynham why, unlike other contestants, his plane did not carry a life raft. He replied that this was due to the fact that he intended to cross the Atlantic, not to fall into it!

All along the West coast of Ireland preparations were made to keep a look-out for the first plane to make land, and to convey the news to London. The '*Irish Times*' said the first 'watcher of the skies' who got a glimpse of the first arrival would be a humble actor in one of the most notable events in the history of the world, whether fisherman, coastguard or village curate going his daily round. On 15 June 1919, the intrepid aviators Captain John William Alcock and Lieutenant Arthur Whitten Brown landed their plane in a boggy field near Clifden, in county Galway, and claimed the place in history that Wood and the others had so desperately sought.

Apart from bringing news of the Soviet to a world-wide readership, the presence of the international press corps had an added advantage for John Cronin and his colleagues. The foreign journalists were able to file their copy through the American cable station at Valentia Island, in county Kerry, and so could avoid censorship or interference with their material by the British authorities. On the other hand, all reports sent, and published, in Irish and British newspapers were still subject to official censorship – another one of the powers exercised under the Defence of the Realm Act. Indeed, many contemporary newspapers reports on Limerick carry the legend 'Passed by the Official Censor'.

Among the foreign journalists based in Limerick at the time were Mr Morris of the Associated Press of America, whose reports were syndicated to seven hundred and fifty United States newspapers, Ruth Russell of the '*Chicago Tribune*', who wrote a book called '*What's the Matter with Ireland?*', and Mr Philmore of the Paris '*Le Matin*'. In its edition of 15 April 1919, '*Le Matin*' carried a short report on what it called 'A Political Strike at Limerick'. Each evening, the Soviet propaganda committee held briefings for the foreign journalists, indicating the sophistication with which they undertook their task.

Another visiting journalist was the British writer, VS Pritchett. In the second volume of his memoirs, '*Midnight Oil*', he recalls an encounter with the strike leaders: 'There was a strike on at the bacon factories; and there was an attempt to start a Soviet. I went to see the committee and politely took my hat off and made a small French bow when I went into their room. The leader told me to put my hat on; they had finished, they said, with bourgeois manners. We had a wrangle about this and a rapid duel of sarcasms. He was one of those 'black' Irishmen one occasionally comes across; there was another, a waiter at the hotel in Limerick who threw a plate of bacon and eggs at a customer'.

Relations between the Soviet and the press did not always run smoothly. One British pictorial daily carried a paragraph describing 'Limerick's Comic Opera Strike'. When the newspaper reached Limerick, a picket was immediately sent to the hotel where the offending correspondent was staying. In less than half an hour, he was standing before the Strike Committee. Pale and trembling, he pleaded the classical reporter's response to such criticism – the heading had been written by a sub-editor and he could not be held responsible. The Committee warned him that if anything further detrimental to the strike appeared in his newspaper, they would cut off light, food and water from his hotel. The warning had the desired effect.

The London Correspondent of the '*Cork Constitution*' claimed the strikers were trying to intimidate correspondents. He alleged threats were being made to reporters if the reports which appeared did not suit the views of the strike leaders. An English news agency alleged that Post Office staff in Limerick were scrutinising reporters' cables and that 'any journalist who told the truth was a marked man.' However, some days later, British and American journalists repudiated allegations that they were being intimidated in their work by sympathisers of the Soviet. A letter refuting the allegation was sent to the Limerick Postmaster by the special correspondents of the '*Daily News*', '*Daily Express*', '*Daily Chronicle*', '*Manchester Guardian*' and '*Daily Mail*'. As representatives of the British press, they said, they desired to dissociate themselves from this reflection on the integrity of the Limerick Post Office staff. At the same time, they wanted to thank the Postmaster and his staff for the great courtesy they had shown them during the strike.

The '*Manchester Guardian*' was severely critical of the Government's use of what it termed one of the most drastic provisions of the DORA regulations against Limerick. It called for the attention of Parliament. The scheduling of special military areas under DORA was intended purely as a safeguard against German espionage during the War in great naval and military centres such as the North of Scotland and Dover. The permit system was used only to detain suspects. The '*Guardian*' concluded: 'It was certainly never contemplated as an instrument for the punishment of Irish districts in which casual outrages had been committed.' In another comment, the '*Guardian*', obviously enjoying the Government's discomfiture, pointed out that the workers of Limerick in setting up a 'provisional government' were merely following the example of Sir Edward Carson and his supporters who had blocked Home Rule for Ireland by threatening to establish the same in Ulster.

Understandably, other British newspapers were more critical of the Soviet itself, of the motives behind it and of what it might lead to. '*The Times*' said Ireland had never been more prosperous and the bulk of the community objected very strongly to the wanton creation of industrial strife. The newspaper said any general strike could not last long without funds, and the Limerick workers were looking to England for help. 'But we fancy that English working men have other uses for their money, now none too plentiful, and will hardly be willing to put it into a country which has grown affluent during the War', '*The Times*' speculated. The newspaper consoled itself with the belief that there was in reality no country where the doctrines of syndicalism were less likely to obtain a firm hold than Ireland.

The '*Morning Post*' took a serious view of the events in Limerick. The '*Post*' claimed that Sinn Féin was secretly conducting affairs according to a definite plan. 'When the local Soviets have obtained possession and control of the local resources Sinn Féin will thus control the greater part of Ireland... Unless the Government intervene, local control by Sinn Féin will include what is most important of all – control of the roads and railways.' The '*Morning Post*', therefore, called for tougher Government measures. The '*Daily Chronicle*' too was convinced the strike was part of a Sinn Féin campaign.

From Limerick, the special correspondent of the '*Daily Express*' sent these graphic words: 'The city is as much in military occupation as Cologne...There is nothing comparable with the situation today, outside certain Continental European countries. The leadership mean to win, and it certainly seems as if the workers of Ireland were with them... I have witnessed many strikes in England but never one bearing any resemblance to this. It is the grand slam, and it suggests possibilities on which it is not pleasant to ponder.'

The '*Westminster Gazette*' was measured in its comments. It said the transport workers were credited with the plan of attempting a general strike in Ireland, but it was admitted that this idea required financial support from Britain. The newspaper ruled that out as a possibility, and it said the Government had taken measures and was 'very wisely allowing the strike to blow off steam.' The '*Pall Mall Gazette*' said it was not sure that the military measures from which the strike arose were free from a provocative element, but the strike was for political and not for industrial purposes and therefore 'without justification from the standpoint of constitutional Labour.'

In Belfast, the Unionist '*News Letter*' saw the direction of Government policy as being in capable hands and it commended General Griffin's 'tactful' behaviour. The '*Irish News*', a long-time supporter of the now declining Irish National Party was scathing in its criticism of the strike. It denounced it as a 'picturesque form of protest, but it will not worry Dublin Castle in the slightest degree...', while Limerick itself would suffer severely if the strike continued for many days. 'What could be gained', the '*Irish News*' asked, 'even if the people remained idle for a week, a fortnight or a month? Many traders and a few manufacturers might be beggared, thousands of wage-earners would sacrifice their incomes, thousands would go hungry, but no soldiers' rations would be curtailed to the extent of an ounce (about 28 grams).' The voice of old-fashioned Belfast Nationalism concluded: 'The wisdom of those who invented and promoted this costly kind of protest against an unjust Castle 'proclamation' must be regarded as more than questionable.'

While the news reporting of the '*Irish Independent*' on the Soviet was often colourful, and seemed fair, the paper's only editorial on the matter was a curious mixture of criticism of the authorities balanced by criticism of the strikers and, above all, a fear that matters might escalate into a general strike. Given the conservative nature of its proprietors' politics –William Martin Murphy had led the employers during the Dublin Lockout in 1913 – the '*Independent*' was happy to see the Government challenged, but not by a movement led by organised Labour. Down that road lay dangers for the Nationalist middle-classes themselves.

The '*Independent*' began on a stirring note: 'Militarism has been crushed in Prussia only to be set up in Ireland in a way that is a negation of civil liberty.' The authorities were going too far; the ordinary criminal law was enough to deal with outrages or raids. Putting an entire city under practically the same rule as if it were in a war zone did not capture and punish the evildoers. A whole community was punished and subjected to needless and wanton inconvenience. The resulting resentment lessened the chances of catching the perpetrators of crimes. 'Limerick, a singularly crimeless city before the unfortunate occurrence of a few weeks ago, is besieged and treated as if all its inhabitants were diabolical criminals', the editorial complained. In a neat twist of argument, the paper reminded the authorities that brutal and savage murders were not uncommon in Britain and there had been serious riots there, but no city or district 'on the other side of the Channel' had been put under military rule.

Turning to the workers, the '*Independent*' thought their action 'hasty' but felt sure that, while Irish Nationalists differed as to the wisdom of the action, the majority of them would sympathise with its objects. But the paper would not countenance an escalation of Limerick into a national, general strike, saying it would be 'productive of very serious results for the country as a whole.' The paper asserted that the Limerick strikers had, unthinkingly, played into the Government's hands by their action and instead of embarrassing the authorities were simply increasing the loss, inconvenience and suffering of the people at large. In any event, the *'Independent'* pointed out, Ulster, or a large part of it, would not respond to any call for a national strike, 'so that the loss and inconvenience would fall exclusively on Nationalist Ireland.'

The *'Irish Times'* devoted three editorials to the Soviet. On the morning after the rescue of Robert Byrne the newspaper had three targets in its editorial sights. Seizing on the phrase 'no arrests have been made', the *'Irish Times'* said that sentence had been the burden of all the recent stories of outrage. In its view, a state of terrorism prevailed throughout the country. The Government owed an urgent duty to the people to strengthen the arm of the law to assure decent men of such protection as would embolden them to help it to save their country's peace and honour. If the Crown forces were insufficient, they must be increased; if the law was inadequate, the Government must seek new powers from Parliament, the editorial declared.

The *'Irish Times'* then turned to two other sources for support. They appealed to 'the acknowledged leaders of the Sinn Féin movement' to express their horror for the crime of murder and they called on the Roman Catholic Church to 'enlist all its tremendous sanctions on the side of morality and law.' Individual churchmen had denounced individual crimes with fitting fervour, but the hour demanded nothing less than a solemn protest and warning from the whole body of the Hierarchy.

A week later, after the first day of the Soviet had ended, the *'Irish Times'* returned to the theme of 'Lawlessness in Ireland'. The teachings of Sinn Féin, the *'Irish Times'* said, had created a far-reaching atmosphere of sedition. It had got into the heads of thousands of young Irishmen who thought it was a fine thing to give the maximum of trouble to authority – and the Irishman was the most ingenious maker of trouble in the world.

Referring specifically to Limerick, the newspaper conceded that the measures taken were pure coercion and furnished no remedy for the root-causes of Nationalist discontent. But they were not intended to be, the editorial pointed out. The Government's first duty was 'the maintenance of the King's authority and the protection of life and property... So long as crime and violence can be committed with impunity throughout large areas of Ireland, the Government must suppress them forcibly.'

The *'Irish Times'* turned again to 'moderate' Nationalists and the Catholic Church. The Government's actions, it argued, were an unsatisfactory substitute for a public opinion that would discourage, denounce and expose violence. 'We have no such public opinion today because the leaders of one half of Nationalist Ireland are preachers of sedition, and the leaders of the other half are unwilling, or afraid, to open their mouths.' The Roman Catholic Bishop of Ross, Doctor Kelly, had told his people 'the plain truth in his sermon on Palm Sunday.' The Bishop's fear of 'the influence of Irish Bolshevism on the religious authority of the Church' seemed to the '*Irish Times*' to be so well-founded that the silence of the Church as a whole filled the editorial writer with surprise.

Just over a week later, the '*Irish Times*' devoted its final editorial to 'The Strike at Limerick', once again using the term 'Soviet' to describe the way the city was being run. The paper saw the attempts to extend the strike to all of Ireland as a 'very bold and candid experiment in Irish Syndicalism.' But, taking the same view as the '*Irish Independent*', the '*Irish Times*' said there could not be a national strike because 'the sturdy and well-organised Labour of North East Ulster will have nothing to say to it. The truth is that Syndicalism and Bolshevism, with their common motto 'What is yours is mine, and what is mine is my own' never will make any headway in this country. In our farming classes the sense of property is as sacred and strong as in the French. Our middle-classes are hard-working individualists. The bulk of Irish Labour, both urban and rural, is restless today, but it is shrewd and intelligent.'

More specifically on Limerick, the '*Irish Times*' hoped the Irish people would be sobered and instructed by the story. 'We are not sorry General Griffin decided to give the local Soviet a free hand.' The Soviet, the paper argued, had inflicted 'more arbitrary restrictions on individual liberties than were ever attempted by Prussian bureaucracy in its mightiest hour.'

This time, there was no reference to the Catholic Church's influence, but there was another appeal to moderate Nationalists: 'The agitation is a challenge to British government in Ireland, against which some Irishmen have worked themselves up to a pitch so mad that they would prefer a bloodstained and bankrupt Bolshevism to an Ireland safe and progressive under British rule. Today, however, these men are acting with the tacit consent – though not, we are convinced with the genuine approval – of a majority of Irish Nationalists. The Nationalist Press does not criticise them. No Nationalist organisation has warned the country against their schemes.'

Despite that type of critical comment, the people of Limerick were eager for news during the Soviet. When the morning mail train arrived, there was a wild rush for the Dublin morning papers and in twenty minutes they were all bought up. Demand for newspapers was so great that, in the evening, the newsboys were selling the '*Herald*' at three pence to six pence a copy.

The Soviet allowed the local Limerick papers to publish one issue a week carrying an imprint in bold type: 'Published by Permission of the Strike Committee.' But the Soviet itself also went into the newspaper business, publishing a regular news sheet called '*The Worker's Bulletin*'. The '*Bulletin*' started simply enough, as a single sheet, more like a propaganda leaflet. But it ran for at least seven issues, and in its final editions was very much like a local newspaper of the time in content and format. Each edition of the *'Bulletin'* carried in bold type the legend: 'Issued by the Limerick Proletariat'. It was a clever mixture of news reports and propaganda leavened by some humour and it represented a fine achievement by the Propaganda Committee.

Another initiative of that Committee was their reply to the Government's statement disclaiming any responsibility for hardship caused to the citizens. The military posted typewritten copies of the statement in the streets but because they could not commandeer a printing works, they were severely handicapped in the propaganda war. The Soviet's reply was that they would rely on the old and proud traditions of Limerick to suffer any difficulties patiently.

At the end of its first week, the Soviet had succeeded better than either its friends or enemies could have imagined. Food, travel, finances and propaganda all appeared to be under control. The scene was set for the first major physical confrontation with the British military and for General Griffin's first divisive concession.

CHAPTER SIX

<u>Compromise and Confrontation</u>

'The whole scene made a remarkable picture. The crowds on the
bridge, the military fully accoutred, and the cordons of police
furnished a centre-piece to a setting as peaceful as any artist
could conceive. The brackish waters of the Shannon, sparkling
in the evening sunlight, moved lazily by as if nothing was
happening, and the church bells intensified the calmness of the
scene.'
— The 'Irish Times' 22 April 1919

The success and strength of the Soviet may be gauged from the fact that only four days after
it began the authorities offered a tempting compromise.

On the first Thursday of the strike, Brigadier-General Griffin attended a special meeting
of the Chamber of Commerce, accompanied by his secretary, Captain Wallace, County
Inspector Crane from the RIC and District Inspector Craig. The proceedings were private
but a formal report was given to the press. In order to facilitate the business of the city,
General Griffin said, the authorities had decided to allow the employers to issue permits to
their employees. The military would give the employers duplicate blocks of permits for this
purpose. Furthermore, at the request of the Chairman and other members of the Chamber,
he would put before Headquarters the idea of granting a further concession so that traders
would be empowered to issue permits to their rural customers to come in to shop in the city.

The General's meeting with the Chamber may have been preceded by behind the scenes
contacts with major business people who were concerned about the losses they would sustain
in a continued strike. His concession represented a considerable climbdown on his part.
At the start of the strike, Cleeve's had asked for a permit to cover all six hundred of their
workers, but this was refused because the military had insisted on individual applications.

The General's offer was an ingenious stratagem, firstly, to divide what had hitherto been
a united community on the issue of permits, and secondly, to turn the employers – who had
at least acquiesced in the Soviet's controls up to then – into a pressure point on the workers
to settle. It appears also that the General was to some extent trying to use the employers
as intermediaries to effect an overall solution to the problem. According to the *'Workers'*
Bulletin', General Griffin said that if the Chamber saw fit, they might consider conveying
his decision to the Strike Committee. After General Griffin had left the Chamber a strikers'

delegation, led by John Cronin, was invited in and told of the offer. The employers made it clear that they hoped the offer would be accepted, emphasising that they viewed it as a substantial concession. Cronin and his colleagues said they would report the matter to the full strike committee, but nothing further was heard on the matter and it was, in effect, rejected out of hand.

It is not surprising that the General's offer was unacceptable. Rank and file strikers interpreted his compromise as giving the employers the right to decide who was fit to enter the city and who was not, something they could no more countenance than military checking. The danger was that some employers might abuse the power to discriminate against certain workers. Disappointed perhaps with this outcome, the Chamber vented their irritation on the Government and sent a resolution to Andrew Bonar Law, the Acting Prime Minister, demanding that martial law be ended. Law held the 'Acting' position while Lloyd George was absorbed in labyrinthine deliberations of the Paris Peace Conference, in Versailles.

Easter Sunday, 20 April 1919, a week exactly after the strike began was both a high point and a watershed of the Limerick Soviet. Apart from its celebratory connotations in the Christian world, Easter in Nationalist Ireland has an added significance. It is the time people commemorate the Rising and executions of Easter 1916, seen as the modern spring from which the waters of freedom ran. Easter Sunday in Limerick became the occasion of a mass confrontation with the troops and police, that had many humorous aspects but was also a serious test by both sides of their will-power and resolution. One newspaper described the confrontation as 'a situation of considerable menace' and another as 'an ominous development'.

That Sunday afternoon – a fine and sunny day – a crowd of about a thousand people, mostly young men and women dressed in their Sunday best, moved out of the city to the nearby Caherdavin Heights, about three to four kilometres out along the Ennis Road, under the guise of attending a hurling or Gaelic football match. Some survivors have asserted that a match was never, in fact, planned and that the exodus was nothing more than a ruse to cover a mass movement of people out of the city as a prelude to challenging the permits regulation and testing the military's resolve. What is certain, however, is that an *aeríocht*, an outdoor festival of traditional Irish dancing, music and singing, took place because some of the newspapers carried photographs of what the *'Daily Sketch'* captioned as 'Irish colleens dancing at the Caherdavin gathering, the object of which was to protest against the necessity of permits to enter the city'.

By this juncture in the evolution of the Soviet, military permits were not needed to leave the city though they had been at the beginning of the strike. In any event, the checkpoints were on only the main thoroughfares and it was always possible to leave the city along the railway bridges and embankments or by crossing the Shannon in a boat. Among the crowd were many of the strike leaders, including Tom Johnson, Treasurer of the Irish Labour Party and Trade Union Congress.

After several hours, the crowd moved back from the county Clare side of the Shannon, towards the sentries on Sarsfield Bridge. A soldier fired a blank shot and immediately military reinforcements rushed out of the Shannon Rowing Club and a dozen troops with loaded rifles and fixed bayonets went to strengthen the sentries facing the crowd. In the upper windows of the clubhouse, troops placed guns in position. Officers rushed to and fro with their hands ominously on their revolvers and a nearby whippet tank on standby got up steam, tested its machine guns and moved into position.

For a time, it looked as if a serious crisis had been reached. The leaders of the crowd demanded entry to the city, without permits. This was refused. In an impressive display of passive resistance, the crowd then formed itself into a giant circle and, one by one, approached the sentries and demanded entry into Limerick, all the time just brushing off the bayonets. As each person was refused entry, they wheeled away and their place was taken by another. Fifty policemen marched down Sarsfield Street from William Street Station to reinforce the men on the bridge but they carried only side arms and batons. A staff officer from military headquarters arrived on a motor-cycle and, a few minutes later, an armoured car – with machine guns ready for action – drove at a furious pace to the scene. News of the incident spread like wildfire through the city and thousands of people lined the city side of the river to watch the confrontation. A large number of journalists, including some American reporters, observed the scene.

Again, and again, continuing until nightfall, the demonstrators marched up to the military and police lines. The soldiers surveyed the parade in silence, but stood ready all the while with rifles and bayonets. Shortly after nine o'clock, the spectators scattered in panic as a rumour swept the crowd that the military were about to open fire. At one stage, a Franciscan priest crossed the bridge and appealed to the demonstrators, over the heads of the cordon, to disperse. General Griffin himself arrived to evaluate the problem at first hand. The Mayor, Alphonsus O'Mara, and a number of prominent citizens demanded that Griffin allow the demonstrators return to their homes. He offered to send an officer to give them permits, but this was refused and the Mayor repeated his demand for unhindered passage, without success.

The '*Irish Times*', no friend of the strikers, carried this lyrical description of the demonstration: 'The whole scene made a remarkable picture. The crowds on the bridge, the military fully accoutred, and the cordons of police furnished a centre-piece to a setting as peaceful as any artist could conceive. The brackish waters of the Shannon, sparkling in the evening sunlight, flowed lazily by as if nothing was happening, and the church bells intensified the calmness of the scene.'

From the city side of the river, there were shouts of encouragement and the demonstrators sang Irish songs to keep their spirits up. Shortly after midnight, a number of demonstrators managed to cross the river in boats. Despite the cold, others, including a large number of determined young women, maintained their vigil on the bridge. In the morning, some of the women passed unhindered through the military pickets. According to a local newspaper, the sentry's heart was softened by 'their charming looks and the magic of their brogue'. Most of the demonstrators, however, spent the night in some comfort on the Clare side of the river.

The women were accommodated in people's homes in the working-class Thomondgate district, famed in a local poem for 'its social joys and the birthplace of the devil's boys.' The young men held an all-night concert and dance in Saint Munchin's Temperance Hall. Next morning, the Clare farmers brought hundreds of boxes of eggs, butter, gallons of new milk and loaves of home-made bread into Thomondgate. The residents cooked the food and the demonstrators ate a hearty breakfast.

Fortified by their meal, after midday, around two hundred men and women lined up outside the Temperance Hall and marched about two kilometres to the Long Pavement railway station. They were cheered by crowds along the route. Long Pavement was the first station out of Limerick on the line to Ennis, county Clare. Some of the organisers of the exodus, through their contacts among the rail workers, knew that a goods train with sixty to seventy empty carriages was due to pass through there from Ennis. They contacted the signal man further up the line, at Ballycar, and it was arranged for him to stop the train at Long Pavement. When the demonstrators got to the station, they boarded the train. The station master and his staff were so astounded at this influx of passengers at a remote wayside station that they apparently overlooked to ask for tickets. The train crossed the Shannon over the railway bridge a few kilometres below the city centre and looped round to the city terminus.

At the check platform outside the Limerick terminus, checkers got on board and were amazed to find so many passengers without tickets. All of them paid their fare, however, without demurring. A number of military officers then arrived and demanded permits. When these were not forthcoming, they ordered the carriage doors to be locked and sentries placed outside. An attempt to segregate passengers who had permits, from the others, was abandoned as too laborious and time-consuming. After a delay of half an hour, the train pulled in to the left-hand platform where double lines of sentries barred the way to the exits. A number of priests and nuns, who had permits, appealed in vain to be released from the carriages. All the while, the young passengers sang rebel songs.

Suddenly, all the carriage doors on the offside of the train from the military were opened, some of the young men having got keys, possibly from a friendly railway official. Between two and three hundred men and women rushed out on to the centre platform and towards the main gate. Here armed sentries blocked the exit, but without pausing, the crowd rushed towards a side platform where only a solitary military policeman stood on guard. In vain, he held out his arms to block the rush. He was quickly brushed aside, and to the cheers of hundreds of onlookers gathered outside the station, the Caherdavin demonstrators broke the military blockade and were free. The demonstration may have made the troops a bit 'jittery' because, the following day, troops fired shots at the Munster Fair Green in the Garryowen district of the city.

The *'Workers' Bulletin'* revelled in the success of the demonstration. They described it as a highly successful entertainment put on by the Soviet's 'Amusement Committee' and watched by one of the largest audiences ever seen in Limerick. 'The helmets shone, the rifles pealed, the police force performed acrobatic feats, the armoured cars ran wild, and even the auld tank – which apparently got more Scotch than soda – struck up 'Rule Britannia' and sprawled out to greet the citizens of Limerick, and it was so delighted to meet them that it couldn't leave the way clear for them to get home.' 'HMT Scotch & Soda' was the nickname stencilled on the side of one of the tanks, possibly belonging to a Scottish regiment, 'HMT' being the initials of the words 'His Majesty's Tank'.

The British officers who boarded the train to check for permits had been in remarkably good spirits and exchanged banter with the strikers. There were few unpleasant incidents between the military and the civilian population. In some instances, the strike leaders wearing their distinctive badges were even saluted by the military. In general, the soldiers were considered to be carrying out their duties with tact and without unnecessarily interfering with people. Some of them became quite at home on the banks of the Shannon and 'when freed from duty spend their time luring rebellious fish from its russet waters.' The biggest contingent of British military serving in Limerick during the Soviet was the 3rd Battalion, Royal Welch Fusiliers. They had been posted to the city in November 1917 for internal security duties and by July 1918 they numbered about four thousand troops. A few months after the Soviet ended, and as the Anglo-Irish War was intensifying, the 2nd Battalion was despatched to Limerick.

As the strike continued, the soldiers began to tire of doing police work and a major was court-martialled for refusing to do duties he considered proper to the constabulary. The *'Workers' Bulletin'* claimed an entire Scottish regiment was sent home for allowing people to go back and forth without passes. Obviously, so soon after the end of the Great War, the British Army still contained many conscripts who held strong trade union or socialist views. As the *'Bulletin'* observed: 'Men like to fight men on equal terms, but when it comes to dragooning one's own class, especially women and tender babes, in the interests of autocracy, it may become a different story.'

In the Easter Monday issue of the *'Workers' Bulletin'*, after the Caherdavin episode, a writer expressed 'the greatest feelings of joy that our fellow Trade Unionists in khaki are refusing to do the dirty work, which is only fit for such invertebrates as the RIC.' Occasionally, the *'Bulletin'* referred to the RIC as 'swine', sometimes as the 'Royal Irish Swine' or 'Royal Irish Cowards'. On the other hand, the British soldiers were referred to as 'Tommy', who was not the real enemy, merely 'a tool of his Imperialistic, Capitalistic Government'. The RIC were particularly resented as being 'the eyes and ears' of British administration in Ireland. They were a semi-military force, armed with carbines and revolvers, and maintained at a strength of nearly eleven thousand – well above the establishment of a normal police force. The force had a peculiar legal status. It was not governed by the Army Act but was an armed force governed by its own regulations. In this sense, it was unique in the British Empire.

After the 1916 Rising, the Commander in Chief in Ireland, General Maxwell, had argued that the crisis had shown that he should have power to bring the Constabulary under his direct orders in the event of another rebellion or an invasion and that, when so employed, they should be subject to military law. The RIC were native Irishmen, but in order to minimise intimidation of their relatives they were not stationed in their home counties. There was hardly a village without an RIC barracks, in districts where ordinary crime was unknown. One of their principal tasks was to observe, and report on, anyone involved in any activity that threatened the state. That definition was wide enough to include Irish language and dancing classes and the Gaelic Athletic Association, the trade unions – especially the burgeoning Irish Transport and General Workers' Union – moderate Nationalist groups like the Irish National Foresters, as well as Sinn Féin. Their reports were so comprehensive that a Chief Secretary for Ireland, Augustine Birrell, was able to boast to Parliament: 'We have the reports of the RIC who send us in, almost daily, reports from almost every district in Ireland, which enable us to form a correct general estimate of the feeling of the countryside in different localities.' An official report in 1919 said that it was largely due to the efficiency of the RIC's excellent organisation that the 1916 rebellion had been kept within bounds and speedily suppressed throughout the country.

On 10 April, as the events were unfolding in Limerick, the Dáil had formally passed a decree of what it termed 'social ostracisation' of the police. On behalf of Sinn Féin, Harry Boland pledged the organisation's full support for the decision but 'respectfully' submitted that the term 'social ostracisation' admitted of many interpretations and he requested a more explicit definition. Having consulted with the Minister for Home Affairs, Arthur Griffith, the Secretary to the Dáil Cabinet and Clerk of the Dáil, Diarmuid O'Hegarty – a close friend of Boland and a member of the IRB – replied that with a broad catch-all definition: 'Social Ostracisation of the police implies that the police force must receive no social recognition from the people; that no intercourse except such as is absolutely necessary on business is permitted with them; that they should not be saluted or spoken to in the streets or elsewhere or their salutes returned; that they should not be invited to nor received in private houses as friends or as guests; that they should be debarred from participation in games, sports, dances and all social functions conducted by the people; that intermarriage with them be discouraged; that, in a word, the police should be treated as persons who, having been found guilty of treason to their country, are regarded unworthy to enjoy any of the privileges or comforts which arise from cordial relations with the public'.

The Dáil decree was enforced very effectively, forcing many policemen – particularly older members nearing pension age – to resign and making it difficult to recruit replacements. Together with a large decrease in numbers to below its establishment requirement, the decree ensured morale among the RIC was chronically poor during the Anglo-Irish War. It was partly for this reason that the authorities later turned to recruiting thousands of demobbed ex-servicemen and officers as members of the RIC. Because of the incongruous mix of khaki and bottle green in their early, makeshift uniforms they were called the 'Black and Tans' and the temporary Auxiliary Cadets were dubbed 'The Auxies'. They became notorious for their reprisals against the civilian population. In Limerick, the circumstances of Robert Byrne's death – the jury's verdict blaming a policeman for the fatal wound – added to the bitterness with which the police were regarded. At the annual conference of the Drapers' Assistants' Association, held in Dublin during the period of the Soviet, a Limerick delegate said: 'the military seemed to be friendly and the police were the only body who were not friendly.'

In his speech to Robert Byrne's inquest, Patrick Lynch KC set the tone of Limerick's differing attitude to the military and police in the days that followed. He asked how the semi-military police force had not turned their revolvers upon the attacking party of healthy men, but had killed the patient in the bed. The Army, he said, were discharging what to them was a disagreeable and unpleasant task. He would say nothing that would make anyone think that those for whom he appeared entertained any feelings but one towards the military, because, by the instructions of the relatives of Mr. Byrne, he would state publicly that they wished to express their appreciation of the courtesy and kindness extended to them in their trouble and sorrow by the military officers and men with whom they were brought into contact. When they left the city, they would leave it with the good wishes of every friend of Mr. Byrne.

Mr Lynch regretted to say he could not join in a similar expression of the manner in which the RIC force acted since the unfortunate tragedy. He could only attribute that to want of judgement. They lost their heads. Some of them acted in a manner which, he was sure, they, on cool reflection, would regret. Lynch's words were harsh, though in mitigation of the RIC's behaviour, it might be argued that they had seen one of their own members shot dead in the Workhouse incident and another seriously wounded. The military, who had not suffered casualties, could perhaps therefore take a more benign view of events and they were possibly under orders from General Griffin to exercise restraint as part of his strategy of not provoking unnecessary confrontation.

After its first week of triumphant success, the Limerick Soviet was about to move into its most testing period. Now, the attitudes of the local employers, the Catholic Bishop and clergy and the national trade union leadership became crucial to what would happen next.

CHAPTER SEVEN

<u>Bosses and Clergy</u>

'I wish to state that neither his Lordship nor the clergy were consulted before the strike
was declared and they were teetotally opposed to its continuance.'
– *Rev. Fr. W Dwane, Administrator, Saint Michael's Parish, reported in several newspapers.*

If the first week of the Limerick Soviet had its moments of drama and comedy, the second week turned into tragedy and, at times, farce. The main players in determining the nature of this Second Act of the Soviet were the Catholic Bishop, Dr Denis Hallinan, the Mayor, Alphonsus O'Mara, the military commander, General Griffin, the leadership of the Irish Labour Party and Trade Union Congress and an assorted cast of strikers, employers and clergy.

The small shopkeepers and small businesses generally had co-operated with the Soviet from the beginning. But the major employers, represented by the Chamber of Commerce, never did more than reluctantly acquiesce in the workers' control of business life. Given the natural antagonism of interests between the two classes this is not surprising. Almost from the start, the major employers were champing at the bit. They met daily, testing ideas, probing weaknesses, drafting formulae to allow the strike to be called off, liaising with the British authorities, and in general, trying to restore what they saw as the natural order of things in Limerick as quickly as possible.

On the first day of the strike, the Chamber of Commerce protested against the proclamation of the city as a military area, particularly the irritating system of permits, and they called for the immediate withdrawal of the restrictions. They sent copies of their resolution to the Lord Lieutenant, Lord French, to General Griffin and to the Acting Prime Minister, Bonar Law. This may have prompted the first concession by General Griffin, which we have already noted, that of allowing the employers to issue their own officially-provided permits.

Only twenty-four hours after the strike started, prominent business people were actively discussing the situation and complaining that their interests were seriously affected. They suggested to the authorities that a slight alteration in the mapping of the boundaries would overcome the difficulties that had provoked the strike – clearly underestimating the desire of the Government to punish Limerick and the workers' revulsion at the prospect of having to obtain permits from any authority in order to go to work.

The Coal Merchants' Association publicly lost their patience with the strikers' controls more quickly than the other employers. On the first Wednesday of the strike, the Strike Committee ordered the coal merchants to open their yards. This was complied with, and coal was sold to the citizens for a number of hours but this type of workers' control was obviously too much for some of the coal merchants to swallow. The following day, six of the principal merchants refused to open, and the police stood on duty outside their gates.

A deputation from the Strike Committee met the secretary of the Coal Merchants' Association and requested that the yards be re-opened. The merchants refused, saying they had no employees with which to do the necessary work. The deputation then offered to supply the necessary labour but the secretary repeated that the yards would not be opened. There was little the strikers could do then – if a potentially violent confrontation was to be avoided – except to express considerable indignation at the merchants' attitude and point out that they had done everything possible to facilitate them since the strike was called. In contrast, the provision merchants generally were reported to have acted in harmony with the Strike Committee and had kept prices normal.

By the end of the first week, some employers were advocating a reopening of business premises on the Tuesday following the Easter weekend. They were prepared to carry on business as best they could in defiance of the Strike Committee. John Cronin, Chairman of the Strike Committee, warned they would oppose any such reopening, but without abusing the power in their hands. The proposal was discussed at a private meeting of the Chamber of Commerce but the vast majority of opinion was against such a line of action. The Chamber adjourned its meeting inconclusively.

A number of trade unions paid their members strike pay for the first week, and some employers decided to pay wages as well. T Geary and Sons, the Shannon Confectionery Works, paid their staff full wages and Miss Madge Daly paid the van drivers employed in the family's bakery. She was a member of a prominent Limerick Republican family. Her brother Edward, the only son, and the youngest among a family of ten, was one of the Commandants of the Easter Week Rebellion, in 1916, and had been executed by firing squad in the aftermath. Madge Daly and two of her sisters were leaders of Cumann na mBan, the Republican women's auxiliary group, and later during the Anglo-Irish War their home was ransacked by the Black and Tans as part of official reprisals for an attack on British forces in Limerick.

Midway through the second week of the strike, the employers were still holding meetings and complaining about the strike's effect on their businesses. They saw themselves as the chief sufferers in a dispute to which they were not parties. They claimed many of their employees were anxious to return to work but that the sinister spectre of the Soviet stood in the way. Clerks in some offices returned to their desks but they were immediately picketed. Some of the clerks stayed at work but others re-joined the strikers.

A prominent employer made his representations directly to the Acting Prime Minister, Bonar Law, at Number Ten, Downing Street and to the Lord Lieutenant, Lord French. He was George Clancy, a wholesale and retail draper. Clancy's suggestion was that the military restrictions be withdrawn or suspended, ostensibly temporarily, but that in reality the agitation that had caused the strike would then fizzle out. His clever argument was that since the citizens had behaved so peaceably during the strike, the authorities could claim they were lifting the restrictions as a reward for good behaviour. Now was the time to solve the problem, while it was easy to do so and no harm had been done. In his letter to Bonar Law he helpfully enclosed a copy of the '*Irish Independent*' to brief him on events in Limerick!

Clancy said that for many years prior to the strike, Limerick was perhaps 'the quietest, most peaceful and most orderly place in the Empire.' Describing the rescuers of Robert Byrne as 'a party of foolish young fellows', he said the strike had been immediate and 'down to the last man. The whole city was shut down. Factories, shops, business places of all kinds, large and small, solicitors' offices, Medical Halls. Everything shut down more rigorously than even on Sunday... Everything is exceptionally quiet, and most orderly so far.' But Clancy was worried the strike might lead to something more serious, and extend 'over the whole of Ireland, North, South, East and West and it may be to England, Scotland and Wales, and I need not say what the result will be.'

Clancy claimed he had made it his business to consult 'a great many on both sides' – strike leaders and the heads of major firms like Cleeve's. They were all quite unanimous his idea was a splendid one. In his view, the 'temporary' lifting of the restrictions would be 'a great day's work for the Empire.' Clancy then cleverly couched his plea as one of concern for the Prime Minister, Lloyd George, who was in Paris 'so terribly busy and his hands so very full finishing up in a highly satisfactory manner the mighty work of the Peace Conference.' It would be cruel and inconsiderate on their part, Clancy wrote, to do anything that would cause the Prime Minister annoyance and worry and put more weight on his shoulders. On the contrary, they should try to make things as 'Easy and Pleasant' for him. Mr Clancy received no more than a routine acknowledgement of his letter from the Acting Prime Minister at Number Ten.

Other prominent citizens were preoccupied too with the military controls on the city. On the first Saturday night of the strike, Holy Saturday, the Mayor, Alphonsus O'Mara presided at a large meeting of citizens in the City Hall. The Mayor had cleverly evaded the military restrictions by staying in a hotel on the Southern side of the Shannon rather than in his home on the Northern side (where the Limerick Strand hotel is now located). They passed a resolution protesting against the imposition of the military area system in Limerick. The resolution was proposed by Michael Colivet, the local Sinn Féin TD. Father O'Connor, Parish Priest of Saint Mary's, proposed an addendum demanding the instant withdrawal of the military cordon around the city since it prevented the workers from having free access to their work.

John Cronin complained that coal and foodstuffs were being held up and another resolution was passed calling on people who had foodstuffs to place them at the disposal of the people once they had got full market value for them. Cronin's appeal is a significant measure of the weakness of the strikers' control over fuel and food. The meeting also decided that the various bodies represented should appoint delegates to a committee to help raise funds to alleviate distress. Significantly, even at this relatively early stage, the Chamber of Commerce stood aloof. Mr Goodbody, Vice-President of the Chamber, said he and some other members were present, not to express any views, but to hold a sort of watching brief and report to the Chamber.

The Mayor said that if the Government was capable of governing, they should do so without punishing innocent people. If constitutional law existed in the country, the city should not have been proclaimed. Michael Colivet TD called for support for the Strike Committee, saying they had arrived at an acute stage of the struggle. Colivet said that if a policeman had been killed or murdered in England, under the existing laws a military area such as had been enforced in Limerick could not be maintained. If the people were beaten on that question it would result in police law.

In his speech, John Cronin, announced one of the most crucial developments of the Soviet – the impending arrival in the city of the entire Executive Council of the Irish Labour Party and Trade Union Congress. On Monday and Tuesday, Cronin predicted, 'the seat of their Labour Parliament would be transferred from Dublin to Limerick.' Indicating that he was thinking along the lines of a general, national strike as a result, Cronin said: 'In the next day or two all Ireland will be doing what Limerick is doing today.' Cronin declared that in calling the strike they had done so with full responsibility and were prepared to take the consequences.

Cronin's expectation of a national escalation in support of Limerick seems reasonable in the light of comments made by the Congress Treasurer, Tom Johnson, on his arrival in Limerick, on 17 April, when he said that he had gone there 'with authority for announcing that the full strength of the Labour movement in Ireland, backed by the general public, would be exerted on behalf of the men and women of Limerick.' In a statement to the Strike Committee, Johnson claimed that the National Executive were 'all determined to give you and your fellow-workers of this city all possible support in your fight against aggressive militarism' and he suggested that 'your fellow-workers throughout the country are ready to join in the protest'. The National Executive's adjournment to Limerick would be 'to meet you in consultation and to perfect arrangements for carrying on the fight. It is no longer a local struggle, it is a National one, and our reports from other centres prove that all Ireland is ready to give active assistance'. Later, Johnson seemed to promise wider support too when he said that Labour movements all over the world would respond to the call of Limerick. 'It was no longer a Limerick fight, but a fight of workers against military domination and Imperialist forces.'

On Easter Saturday morning, the Mayor had presided at a meeting of the City magistrates. Mr RJ Daly proposed a resolution and it was seconded by the City Coroner, Mr James F Barry. It appealed in the present grave crisis which had arisen, to all lovers of peace and liberty to do all in their power to alleviate the deplorable conditions now prevailing, and declared that the military authorities would be well advised to extend the military area to such an extent that the citizens would be at liberty to attend their daily avocations without having to produce permits. There were two dissenting voices – O'Mara himself, and the Resident Magistrate, PJ Kelly. The Mayor opposed the resolution on the formal grounds that the magistrates had not been consulted before the city was proclaimed, though probably his real objection was to the idea of extending the military boundaries further. The Resident Magistrate, on the other hand, rejected any implied criticism of the military arrangements.

The diligent Mr Kelly recounted all this in a report to the Under Secretary for Ireland in Dublin Castle. Mr Kelly apparently had the support of two others in opposing criticism of the military permits system. They were satisfied the military authorities had assessed all the facts before deciding on the boundaries of the proclaimed area. According to Kelly's report, 'The majority of the Magistrates, with the Mayor, expressed themselves very strongly and pointedly showing that they are not at all in sympathy with the efforts of the authorities in the steps taken to maintain order. Some of them even went so far as to ignore the fact that a serious outrage took place at the Workhouse in the raid that was made and I'm sorry to say some conveyed that they thought it was the police who committed an outrage on that occasion.' Kelly seems to have been particularly energetic in sniffing out sedition and promptly reporting it to senior officials in the Castle and his comments give an illuminating insight into how far the attitudes of respectable and loyal citizens had gone in supporting the grievances that caused the strike.

By the time the Limerick Grand Jury convened for the Summer Assizes, in July, opinion of the RIC among the city's loyal and propertied classes had returned to more conventional lines. Sir Charles Barrington Bart., proposed a resolution expressing most emphatically their admiration and high appreciation of the manner in which the members of the RIC had discharged their duty during the trying times through which they were now passing. The Grand Jury tendered their warm sympathy with the relatives of those who had lost their lives, and they had much pleasure in sending a donation to the Central Benevolent Fund, RIC. The resolution was seconded by the Grand Jury Foreman, Mr J O'G Delmege. The Presiding Judge, Mr Samuels, directed that it be forwarded to the Chief Secretary for

Ireland. On 17 July, he replied fully endorsing the tribute paid by the Grand Jury to the members of the Royal Irish Constabulary and sharing their expression of sympathy with the relatives of those who had lost their lives.

However, in any part of Nationalist Ireland at this time the attitude of the Catholic Bishop and clergy was crucial. Initially, the Bishop, Dr Hallinan, and the senior clergy came out strongly against the military proclamation and part of their statement was considered so strong in tone by the authorities that it was deleted by the Censor. The Bishop met with clergy from the city parishes and the religious orders at the diocesan seminary in Saint Munchin's College, Corbally, on the third day of the strike. Afterwards, the newspapers published this statement:

'[1] That we consider the proclaiming of the city of Limerick under existing circumstances as quite unwarrantable. Without explanation of any kind, the citizens of Limerick are being penalised for the lamentable events at the Limerick Workhouse.

[3] That in fixing the boundaries of the military area, the responsible authorities have shown a lamentable want of consideration for the citizens at large, and especially of the working classes.' The censored portion included strong criticism of the military surveillance of Robert Byrne's funeral:

'[2] That the military arrangements of the funeral of the late Mr Robert Byrne were unnecessarily aggressive and provocative. The presence of armoured cars on the route and the hovering of aeroplanes over the city during the funeral procession were quite an uncalled-for display, in the circumstances, of military power, and calculated to fill every right-minded person with feelings of disgust and abhorrence.'

This statement was signed by Denis Hallinan, Bishop of Limerick, Canon David O' Driscoll, Vicar General and Parish Priest of Saint Munchin's, Canon David Keane, President Saint Munchin's College, Father Michael Murphy, Parish Priest of Saint Patrick's, Father O'Connor, Parish Priest of Saint Mary's, Father Connolly, Administrator of Saint John's Cathedral, Father Bonaventure, Guardian of the Franciscans, Father Hennessy, Prior of the Augustinians, Father Fahy, Prior of the Dominicans, the Jesuit Rector, Father Potter, Father Dwane, Administrator of Saint Michael's and the Redemptorist Father Kelly, Director of the city's powerful Men's' Archconfraternity.

Not unexpectedly, there was no explicit approval for the strike, but the statement still indicated a degree of very significant and influential clerical support for a redressing of the grievances that had provoked the workers' action. With the Bishop and the Catholic clergy apparently so firmly on their side, many strikers believed their success was assured. The *Irish Times*' reported that the statement was generally regarded as a justification for the strike, and it had 'infused fresh vigour into the members of the local 'Soviet'.'

The apparent clerical approval continued during the Masses of the following Sunday, Easter Day. In some Catholic churches, the priests congratulated the people on their good conduct, but appealed to juveniles not to congregate at street corners or jeer at the military sentries. This, apparently, was a practice that was increasingly irritating young soldiers. On Holy Saturday night, a sentry had fired a warning shot at some youths.

The Catholic Bishops of Limerick and of the county Clare diocese of Killaloe were broadly supporters of the strike against the military restrictions, certainly in the first week. Indeed, Dr. Fogarty, of Killaloe, was an enthusiastic advocate of food supplies for Limerick. However, the attitude of the Limerick and Clare Bishops contrasts with the remarks of the Catholic Bishop of Ross, Dr. Kelly, preaching in the pro-Cathedral at Skibbereen, county Cork, a week after the Workhouse shooting. Dr. Kelly said they knew there were deeds done in Ireland at present that were greatly against the doctrine of the Lord. They affected everyone, and were a blot on their country. He knew they were shocked at them and he wanted them to do penance for them during Holy Week.

But the Bishop was particularly concerned about expressions of approval for the Soviet-led governments in Russia and Hungary that had been made that week during the sessions of Dáil Éireann. It was his duty as Bishop to ask his flock to protest at those remarks, since the Russian and Austro-Hungarian revolutions were striking at the foundations of religion. The Bishop said he had not been too concerned when Madame Markiewicz – one of the Citizen Army leaders in the 1916 Rebellion and a member of the Dáil – had proclaimed support for the Russian Revolution, because he thought she stood alone. But now he was worried to read in his newspaper that these views were held by responsible members of Parliament and some officials of the new 'Government'. As their Bishop, he warned his congregation that if these ideas were spread among them, if they were picked up, 'the faith of Saint Patrick would not stand.'

In its first edition of May, looking back at Limerick, the *'Irish Catholic'* carried an even more forthright condemnation under the heading 'Irish Bolshevism'. The newspaper first rejected the 'crazy theories' that had 'brought Russia to the verge of abyss.' Then it turned to Limerick: 'There is only one element of danger in the situation. That is the peril that arises from the possibility of the workers allowing themselves to be unconsciously misled. What has occurred in the city of Limerick is fresh in the public memory. As the result of certain manoeuvres, the import and true significance of which were certainly not manifest to the workmen when they struck, a crisis fraught with potentialities of grave trouble, not merely on a local, but on a national scale, was suddenly precipitated.'

The *'Catholic'* continued: 'The British sympathisers with Sovietism were naturally delighted at this development, but it is in accordance with the traditional tactics of these agitators that their social and industrial experiments should first be tried on the Irish dog.

However, regarding the Limerick episode, it is one of those developments regarding which it can be said that all is well that ends well.' The editorial writer then trained his sights on Irish 'agitators' who did not hesitate to invoke the example of Russian anarchism in furtherance of their political as well as their industrial propaganda. One of them had recently said Ireland had two chances: the first was President Wilson, the other was the Bolshevik rising in Russia. Rejecting what it called the 'abominable evangel of Bolshevism', the newspaper said Lenin and his associates stood for relentless class warfare – the negation of democracy. Between those principles and the principles of the faithful Catholic people of Ireland there could be no compromise.

With attitudes like these so prevalent among influential Catholic leaders of the time, it was inevitable that the uneasy coalition of interests opposing the military proclamation would come under strain, and then crumble. The catalyst for this development was the arrival in Limerick, in the second week of the Soviet, of the Executive of the Irish Labour Party and Trade Union Congress.

Robert Byrne was active in his union, the Irish Post Office Clerks' Association, becoming Chairman of the Limerick branch and was a delegate to Limerick United Trades and Labour Council. He was a Captain and Adjutant of the 2nd Battalion, Mid-Limerick Brigade, Irish Volunteers.

Photo Credit: Limerick Council of Trade Unions Archive

THE JAIL INFAMY.

Since Wednesday evening, when a considerable number of people were attracted to the neighbourhood of the Jail by shouting and other noises, many are asking what happened. The following are the facts :—

On Saturday, 1st February, R. G. Byrne, of Town Wall Cottage, a well-known citizen, was sentenced to 12 months imprisonment with hard labour, because a revolver and some ammunition were found in his mother's house. Naturally, he protested against the barbarous sentence. He was backed up by the political prisoners at present in Limerick Jail.

At first they resorted to constitutional methods, but, finding these unavailing, they resorted to the more vigorous methods of Wednesday evening. A force of police were sent for. When they reached the prisoners' cells they deprived the men of their boots, handcuffed them, and, in addition, strapped many of them. In that shocking condition, as far as their friends know, they still are, and the night brings no change from the day.

In the same jail is a man convicted of the manslaughter of a girl, in circumstances of revolting brutality, and sentenced by a judge, lenient to his ilk, to 12 months in the 2nd division. He has nothing to do, and is supplied with every comfort. Men who have never committed a crime, believe that they are entitled at least to the treatment that criminal is receiving. But those responsible for the administration of law in Ireland treat him as a gentleman, and try to degrade the others. But those men, who demonstrated on Wednesday evening hold honour dearer than life, and while ready to suffer for their national principles, will never willingly submit to be branded as criminals. In that attitude they naturally expect the vigorous support of the people of Limerick.

It is pertinent to ask, what are the visiting justices doing? Are they willing to continue in their ornamental positions, and thereby give implicit sanction to the barbarity of having political prisoners manacled during meal time and sleeping time?

And what of our popular magistrates? Are they willing to assist in the administration of "law" which perpetrates such infamies?

If the last spark of humanity, as well as the last spark of patriotism, has not deserted them, they will quickly return the "honours" conferred on them by the foreigner, in return for their oaths of allegiance.

One of the prisoners, Henry Meany, is in a bad state of health, yet is manacled as well as handcuffed. His relations have been sent for as the Governor fears he may die.

Leaflet from LUTLC protesting against the harsh treatment of Republican prisoners in Limerick Prison in February 1919.

Photo Credit: Limerick Council of Trade Unions Archive

Michael 'Batty' Stack, E Company, 2nd Battalion, Mid-Limerick Brigade, Irish Volunteers, one of the leaders of the rescue of Robert Byrne from the Workhouse Infirmary. He was later a member of Michael Collins's 'Squad' and served in the Free State Army. His right arm suffered serious injury in an ambush during the Civil War.

Photo Credit: Limerick Council of Trade Unions Archive

The British *Sunday Pictorial* of 13 April 1919. Stringent security precautions were imposed during Robert Byrne's funeral but it passed off peacefully. Troops of the Royal Welsh Fusiliers in a side street with fixed bayonets and an armoured car with policeman seated at the back. Group of police on the footpath.

Photo Credit: The BMH Photo Series Album P28 Events of National Interest 1919-1920; File 18 of 22, Military Archives, Ireland

British troops, outside King John's Castle, blocking Thomond Bridge on Easter Sunday 1919 – the day almost a thousand young men and women challenged the military restrictions by leaving the city as a group for recreational events at Caherdavin Heights.

Photo Credit: Courtesy of Mike Finn

Nicknamed 'His Majesty's Tank 'Scotch and Soda' and used as part of the military barricade on Wellesley (now Sarsfield) Bridge.

Photo Credit: Hulton Archive/Getty Images

A soldier and officer inspecting a Military Pass on Wellesley (now Sarsfield) Bridge under the watchful gaze of an RIC constable and some curious boys.

Photo Credit: British Pathé

A soldier on Wellesley (now Sarsfield) Bridge inspects a cyclist's Military Pass as a dog waits patiently to pass.

Photo Credit: British Pathé

Tank and barricade blocking Wellesley (now Sarsfield) Bridge and Brunswick (now Sarsfield) Street.

Photo Credit: British Pathé

The British '*Daily Mail*' 19 April 1919. (Left) Troops placing bar barbed wire on a bridge to prevent it being rushed. (Right) A priest inspects one of the barbed-wire entanglements.

Photo Credit: The BMH Photo Series Album P28 Events of National Interest 1919-1920; File 20 of 22, Military Archives,Ireland,

A typical Military Pass required for moving in and out of the Special Military Area.

Photo Credit: Limerick Council of Trade Unions Archive

Sample of information and authorisation required on a Military Pass.

Photo Credit: Limerick Council of Trade Unions Archive

The Military Commandant of the Special Military Area, Brigadier General Christopher Griffin, served with distinction on the Western Front during World War One. He began the war in command of 2nd Battalion, Lancashire Fusiliers, with the rank of Major. In this group of officers, photographed after a gas attack in May 1915 at Ypres, in Belgium, he is seated in the front row, second from left.

Photo Credit: Imperial War Museums Archives

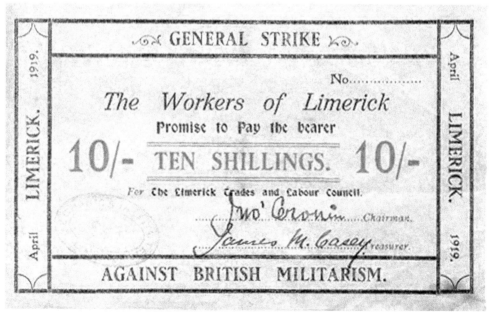

Soviet currency notes were issued in denominations of one, five and ten shillings – equivalent in today's values to roughly €30, €15 and €3, respectively. They were printed at the Record Printing Works, owned by Michael Gleeson in Cornmarket Row, and were about the size of an ordinary Treasury note.

Photo Credit: Limerick Council of Trade Unions Archive

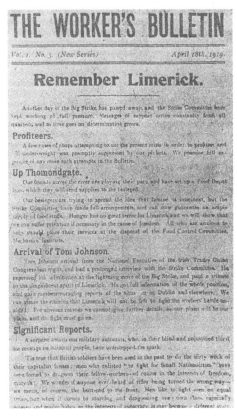

THE WORKER'S BULLETIN

Vol. 1. No. 3. (New Series)   April 18th, 1919.

Remember Limerick.

Another day of the Big Strike has passed away, and the Strike Committee have kept working at full pressure. Messages of support arrive constantly from all quarters, and as time goes on determination grows.

Profiteers.

A few cases of shops attempting to use the present crisis in order to profiteer and by under-weight was promptly suppressed by our pickets. We promise full exposure of any more such attempts in the Bulletin.

Up Thomondgate.

Our friends across the river are playing their part, and have set up a Food Depot from which they will send supplies to the besieged.

Our besiegers are trying to spread the idea that famine is imminent, but the Strike Committee have made full arrangements, and can now guarantee an ample supply of food stuffs. Hunger has no great terror for Limerick and we will show that we can suffer privation if necessary in the cause of freedom. All who are anxious to help should place their services at the disposal of the Food Control Committee, Mechanics' Institute.

Arrival of Tom Johnson.

Tom Johnson arrived from the National Executive of the Irish Trades Union Congress last night, and had a prolonged interview with the Strike Committee. He expressed his admiration at the lightning move of the Big Strike, and paid a tribute to the magnificent spirit of Limerick. He got full information of the whole position, and gave most encouraging reports of the situation in Dublin and elsewhere. We can assure the citizens that Limerick will not be left to fight the workers' battle unaided. For obvious reasons we cannot give further details, as our plans will be our plans, and the fight must go on.

Significant Reports.

A surprise awaits our military autocrats, who, in their blind and unjustified thirst for revenge on innocent people, have overstepped the mark.

'Tis true that British soldiers have been used in the past to do the dirty work of their capitalist bosses; men who enlisted "to fight for Small Nationalities" have been forced to dragoon their fellow-workers—of course in the interests of freedom, maybe!. We wonder if anyone ever heard of rifles being turned the wrong way—we mean, of course, the butt-end to the front. Men like to fight even on equal terms, but when it comes to starving and dragooning one's own class, especially women and tender babes, in the interests of autocracy, it may become a different state.

'*The Worker's Bulletin*' was a clever mixture of news reports and propaganda leavened by some humour. It began simply enough, as a single sheet, like a propaganda leaflet. It ran for at least seven issues and in its final editions was very similar to a local newspaper of the time in content and format.

Photo Credit: National Library of Ireland

Delegates to Limerick United Trades and Labour Council in 1919, the leaders of the Limerick Soviet.

Photo Credit: Limerick Council of Trade Unions Archive

"SCOTCH AND SODA" AFTER THE RIOT AT LIMERICK.

The Tank "Scotch and Soda" mounted on Wesley Bridge, at Limerick, near the spot where the riot took place.—(Daily Sketch.)

The Limerick Strike Committee considering applications for food and other permits. Mr. John Cronin, the chairman, is seen at the head of the table.

British '*Daily Sketch*' 17 April 1919. The 'Scotch and Soda' tank mounted on Wellesley (now Sarsfield) Bridge and members of the Limerick Soviet dealing with applications for permits for food and transport. John Cronin, the Chairman, sits at the head of the table.

Photo Credit: The BMH Photo Series Album P28 Events of National Interest 1919-1920; File 22 of 22, Military Archives, Ireland

'Yes, this is a soviet,' said John Cronin to an American journalist who described him as 'the carpenter who was father of the baby soviet'. A highly skilled craftsman, he won a gold medal and certificate from the Worshipful Company of Carpenters in London for proficiency in his trade.

Photo Credit: Limerick Council of Trade Unions Archive

John (Jack) Dowling - better known in Limerick as Seán – was an ITGWU Organiser. A Socialist comrade of James Connolly, he pleaded with Connolly to allow him to participate in the 1916 Rising. Instead, Connolly ordered him to 'Go down to the Galtees and organise workers into the union'. Dowling was a pivotal figure in the Limerick Soviet and he and the other radical Socialist ITGWU Organisers, Jack Hedley and Jack McGrath, were key figures in the militant events that followed the Soviet in county Limerick and the rest of Munster.

Photo Credit: Limerick Council of Trade Unions Archive

British '*Daily Sketch*' 24 April 1919. Young men and women on Easter Sunday returning from their GAA match and outdoor céilí at Caherdavin were faced with a strengthened military barricade on Wellesley (Sarsfield) Bridge. The closing of produce processors meant there was a surplus of milk and a tankard cost very little.

Photo Credit: The BMH Photo Series Album P28 Events of National Interest 1919-1920; File 06 of 22, Military Archives, Ireland

One of the notes issued by the Strikers' Committee as a protest against Limerick being placed under martial law.—(*Daily Sketch*.)

Irish colleens dancing at the Cahirdavin gathering, the object of which was to protest against the necessity of permits to enter the city.—(*Daily Sketch*.)

The British '*Daily Sketch*' on 24 April 1919 shows a Soviet currency note and what it terms 'Irish colleens' dancing at the big gathering at Caherdavin on Easter Sunday.
Photo Credit: The BMH Photo Series Album P28 Events of National Interest 1919-1920; File 16 of 22, Military Archives, Ireland

The Catholic Bishop of Limerick, Dr. Denis Hallinan with his senior clergy. The Bishop supported Sinn Féin provided they did not endorse armed rebellion or collude with secret societies. He was sympathetic to the plight of Republican prisoners and the Catholic church's tacit support was important in the early days of the Soviet. That stance changed once the workers sought a national escalation and he was centrally involved in the mediation that ended the confrontation.

Photo Credit: Limerick Council of Trade Unions Archive

When Alphonsus O'Mara was elected Mayor of Limerick in 1918, he was the first member of Sinn Féin to hold that office. He supported the prisoners' campaign for political status and was critical of the military restrictions. However, once the workers sought to escalate matters to the national level, he became involved in mediation efforts to end their protest.

Photo Credit: Mark Humphrys, http://humphrysfamilytree.com/

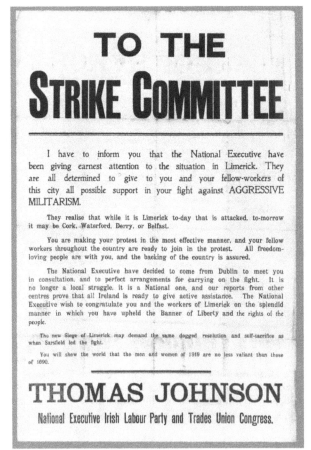

This Proclamation issued by Tom Johnson, Treasurer, Irish Labour Party and Trade Union Congress, when he arrived in Limerick on 17 April 1919 gave the misleading impression of imminent support from national trade union leaders for an escalation of the Soviet.

Photo Credit: Limerick Council of Trade Unions Archive

CHAPTER EIGHT

Defeat or Draw?

'The struggle would have dragged on for some time longer had not his Lordship, Most Rev Dr Hallinan and the Mayor, as representing the spiritual and temporal interests of the citizens, sent a joint letter to the Trades Council on Thursday requesting the immediate end of the strike...'
– 'The Munster News', Editorial entitled 'The Strike–And After'

The first notification the Executive of the Irish Labour Party and Trade Union Congress had of Limerick was a telegram sent by John Cronin, and received by William O'Brien, General Secretary of the Congress, on the first day of the strike, Monday 14 April 1919. The telegram read: 'General strike here as protest against military restrictions.' O'Brien replied by telegram wishing the strikers success and asking to be kept informed of events. The General Secretary got no reply and rang up the newspaper offices looking for information. He got what information appeared in the evening papers. Communications were obviously not easy and some union leaders in Dublin suspected the authorities were intercepting messages from Limerick, and so, information was hard to come by. On Tuesday, there was still no information from Limerick, so the following day, O'Brien called together all the available members of the Executive and they discussed the matter informally. In the absence of information, they decided the best thing to do was to send someone to Limerick and that job was given to Thomas Johnson, the Congress Treasurer.

Johnson got a permit from the authorities and arrived in Limerick on the third day of the strike. He was born in Liverpool in 1872 and served from 1914 to 1916 as President of the Irish Trade Union Congress, having attended his first Congress in 1911, as a delegate of the National Union of Shop Assistants and Clerks. From 1903 onwards, he had worked in Belfast for a cattle food firm until dismissed from his job as a commercial traveller because of his public opposition to conscription, but his attitude to Republicanism was cautious. In 1918, he was appointed full-time Treasurer of the Congress. Johnson was a little old-fashioned in his trade unionism, neither Marxist nor nationalist. Yet he showed a remarkable sensitivity to the complexity of Irish society and had the capacity to understand North and South, both Belfast and Dublin. Johnson was born in Britain as had been the great leaders of Irish trade unionism of the early decades of this century, Connolly and Larkin. But in many ways, Johnson typified British trade unionism much more than the other two who developed a brand of syndicalist trade unionism tailored to Irish conditions.

Johnson was a hardworking organiser and a thoughtful public speaker, and he seems to have established an immediate rapport with the strike leaders. He was one of the most prominent people involved in the Caherdavin Incident, and the '*Workers' Bulletin*' of 23 April paid him this tribute: 'To the splendid efforts of Tom Johnson, the defence of Limerick owes much, and his intrepid bravery has won him many friends in Limerick and elsewhere.'

Meanwhile, back in Dublin, two Limerick railway men had arrived to look for support for the strike. They met their colleagues of the National Union of Railwaymen at the Inchicore Engineering works, a pivotal part of the network of the Great Southern and Western Railways. The response was lukewarm. The Dublin NUR men said that unless there was an extension of the strike to places like Cork and Tralee, Dublin would remain uninvolved. A spokesman for one of the biggest NUR branches in Dublin told the '*Irish Independent*' that while he sympathised with the Limerick people, he thought the policy adopted was a mistaken one. It did not inconvenience the military, who had ample means of transporting their supplies but it meant starvation for their own people. They in Dublin had painful recollections of a somewhat similar state of things during their 1916 strike.

The two NUR men briefed Congress Executive members on the position in Limerick as it stood at their departure. The Executive also met a delegation from the Railway Workers' Emergency Committee, a national co-ordinating body representing the major rail unions. The Emergency Committee pointed out that if the Limerick men stopped work, the whole Great Southern Railways system would be 'put out of gear.' The railway men made it clear they were prepared to come out on strike but only with other workers as part of a national strike.

That same day, William O'Brien and other TUC leaders began a series of meetings spread over three days with the Executive, or Cabinet, elected by the separatist parliament, Dáil Éireann. The aim, presumably, was to see to what extent the two bodies could, or should, co-ordinate their action over Limerick. O'Brien had significant credibility in engaging in these discussions because he was a member of the IRB and had been interned after the 1916 Rising. He, together with the other senior union leaders Tom Johnson, Cathal O'Shannon, Thomas Farren and Thomas McPartlin were the medium through which Labour maintained contact with Sinn Féin and the Irish Volunteers.

Not unexpectedly, the Dáil Executive did not encourage escalation of the trade union action. It is very likely that there were diverging views on the issue between the President, Eamon De Valera, with the Minister for Defence, Cathal Brugha, agreeing with him, and on the other hand, the Minister for Finance, Michael Collins, and Assistant Minister of Defence and Chief of Staff, Richard Mulcahy, taking a different view. Mulcahy was being regularly updated on developments in Limerick by the trusted Commandant Michael Brennan and was favourably disposed, and he enjoyed friendly relations with senior Labour leaders. As leaders of the clandestine Irish Republican Brotherhood, the view of Mulcahy and Collins seems to have been to welcome any action – whatever its source – that increased pressure on the British and stretched their military and police resources while the IRB prepared to intensify the war in the second half of 1919.

The Dáil Cabinet minutes show that Limerick was listed for discussion on three dates after the full resumption of work had been announced. On 26 April under agenda item 6 (a), dealing with matters from the Ministry of Labour, there is a terse note: 'Limerick – Mulcahy to go to Dev with O'Mara' [Alphonsus O'Mara, Mayor of Limerick]. On 2 May, the Cabinet had before it a 'Limerick – letter' but it was 'not dealt with' and on 16 May agenda item 6 referred to 'Letters from Limerick' but no discussion or decision is recorded. The majority of the Cabinet – largely a 'shadow' government at this time – may have had practical objections to supporting trade union action, and equally likely, they may not have relished the prospect of effectively handing over leadership of the militant part of the independence struggle to the trade unions. The Dáil Executive preferred to maintain control, and the premier position, for themselves.

It began to dawn on the Congress leaders that any further escalation of support for Limerick would be entirely on their own heads and would lack the support of Republicans nationally. They had to look for an alternative that would save face all round. At some stage over the three days of meetings with the Dáil representatives, Tom Johnson and William MacPartlin suggested the idea of a peaceful evacuation of the entire city. This reflected a strategy that had been developed, but never used, to evacuate Dublin and other cities as part of the trade union campaign against the proposed introduction of conscription in 1918. By doing this, they hoped to focus world-wide attention on the plight of the workers in Limerick, without the prospect of bloodshed.

The available, resident members of the Executive met and discussed the idea and O'Brien summoned the non-resident members, by telegram, to a meeting the following day, Holy Thursday. The full Executive agreed on the evacuation plan of action and arranged to meet in Limerick after the Easter weekend. In the meantime, O'Brien and the Vice-President, Thomas Farren of the ITGWU, who was also Secretary of the influential Dublin Trades Council, were to join Tom Johnson in Limerick immediately. O'Brien, in fact, never travelled to Limerick and this later became a focus of friction between local trade unionists and the national leadership.

Outwardly, the National Executive seemed determined in its support for the Limerick strike. It unanimously condemned the action of the military authorities in proclaiming a Special Military Area, in preventing the free movement of Limerick trade unionists to and from their work, and in depriving them of their rights as workers and citizens. In a statement, it called for the immediate abrogation of the Order making permits obligatory.

The statement went on: 'In view of this wanton attack on trade unionists, the National Executive appeals to the unbiased opinion of the workers and peoples of all countries as to on whose shoulders lies responsibility for the probably grave consequences which this unwarrantable and unnecessary action by the military may precipitate.'

The following day, in Limerick, before any of his colleagues had arrived, Tom Johnson seemed to commit them to a national stoppage in support of the city. In a statement to the press, he interpreted the Executive's resolution as an endorsement of, and full support for, Limerick. Johnson said he had authority to announce that the full strength of the Labour movement in Ireland, backed by the general public, would be exerted on behalf of the men and women of Limerick. The National Executive, in collaboration with the Strike Committee, would take such action as would ensure victory. 'This', Johnson declared, 'is, in the first instance, Labour's fight against the attempt by the British military authorities to choose who shall, or shall not, proceed to or from his or her daily work, but it is also Limerick's reply to President Wilson's question, 'Shall the military power of any nation or group of nations, be suffered to determine the fortunes of peoples over whom they have no right to rule, except the right of force?' Limerick's reply is 'No', and all Ireland is at her back.'

Johnson said the National Executive were determined to give the Strike Committee all possible support. They realised that while it was Limerick today, tomorrow it might be other great cities like Cork, Waterford, Dublin, Derry or Belfast. The National Executive, he said, congratulated the Committee and workers on the splendid way they had upheld the banner of liberty. It would show that the men and women of 1919 were no less valiant than those of 1690, the year of the first Williamite siege of Limerick. The Limerick strikers could be forgiven for thinking the full weight of the Irish trade union movement was about to be thrown behind them in a national strike. But it was not to be.

There appeared to be difficulties about a speedy transfer of the full Executive to Limerick. No trains were running on Good Friday but four members of the Executive made it to the city on Easter Tuesday. They were Thomas Farren of the ITGWU, Vice-President of Congress, John T O'Farrell of the Irish Railway Clerks' Association, Rose Timmons and TC Daly, a member of the National Union of Railwaymen. Thomas Farren took part in the 1916 Rising and was one of a group of trade union leaders with nationalist sympathies who were arrested afterwards. O'Farrell, in the 1922 General Election, missed a seat in the Irish Free State Dáil by only thirteen votes but was elected to the Senate. Another visitor to Limerick that day was the General Officer Commanding-in-Chief, Ireland, Sir Frederick Shaw, who conferred with General Griffin, the Commandant, Military Area.

Matters cannot have been helped by the involvement of the Congress President, Thomas Cassidy, in organising the Easter Conference of his union. His Association's General President had come over from Britain to assist him and was, in fact, the first person to tell Cassidy about the Limerick strike. Apparently, Cassidy and his President were travelling around the country on union business. That prevented him going to Dublin for the full Executive meeting summoned by O'Brien. Instead, on Easter Monday and Tuesday his Association's Executive ordered him to Drogheda, county Louth, on union business. Cassidy considered, rightly or wrongly it is difficult to judge at this remove, that his own union's affairs should take precedence over consideration of Limerick.

William O'Brien felt it was better to wait to have the full Executive available to take decisions on what was a very serious issue. Consequently, Easter Tuesday, eight days after the strike had started, was the first day on which members of the Executive could travel to Limerick. In fact, they did not arrive in the city until the Wednesday, the ninth day of the strike, when they went into a long session of talks with the Strike Committee. The '*Irish Times*' – with hindsight, it seems correctly – interpreted the failure to meet the Tuesday appointment as 'an indication that all is not well in official labour circles.'

From the moment they arrived in Limerick that Wednesday, the full Congress leadership were in almost continuous meetings with the Strike Committee discussing strategy and tactics. At their first long meeting, chaired by John Cronin, the Congress delegation consisted of: Thomas Farren, the Vice-President TC Daly, National Union of Railwaymen, John T O'Farrell, Irish Railway Clerks' Association, Michael O'Lehane, Drapers' Assistants, Councillor Michael J Egan, a coachmaker from Cork, Tom Johnson, the Congress Treasurer, and Rose Timmons. O'Lehane was a staunch member of Sinn Féin. Egan was one of three Congress delegates, along with senior figures like O'Brien and Johnson on the nine man 'national cabinet' put forward by the Mansion House Conference to oppose conscription in 1918. The RIC duly reported to Dublin Castle on a strikers' meeting held following the Executive's arrival in Limerick.

Officially, the Congress leaders claimed they were there to assist the Strike Committee, not to take charge of the dispute. But differences of opinion emerged even on that first day. Understandably, in the light of the earlier statements by the Executive and Johnson, John Cronin and the other strike leaders wanted the Congress to declare a national strike in support of Limerick. Some of the Congress leaders claimed their Constitution did not give them the power to do that – the calling of strikes, local or national, was a matter for the individual union affiliates.

But the Congress leaders' opposition to a national strike was much more fundamental than any rule book niceties. They recognised the potential for Limerick to escalate into a bloody, revolutionary conflict with Britain if it was pushed to a national strike. The Congress had neither the physical means nor had it developed the political consciousness among its rank and file members to pursue or defend such a strategy. From their meetings in Dublin, they already knew they could not count on the wholehearted support of Sinn Féin, the IRA or the Dáil. There were doubts over whether the National Union of Railwaymen could be relied on to paralyse transport in such a strike, and without doubt, the Unionist workforces of Ulster would actively oppose it. There was uncertainty too over how trade unionists and Socialists in Britain would react to such a development in Ireland.

Leaders like Tom Johnson might accept that Limerick was justified in calling for a national strike, but the real question was whether it was the correct strategy, knowing it would have resulted in armed revolt. Johnson believed that someday an insurrection might be developed out of Labour agitation but it should not be because of Limerick. The Congress leaders advanced the alternative – but hare-brained – plan they had already hatched before leaving Dublin: the complete evacuation of the city by its inhabitants, leaving it an empty shell in the hands of the military. The Executive leaders stressed that they did not propose this in any haphazard way but had made undisclosed arrangements to house and feed the people of Limerick if they agreed to the plan. The merit they saw in their proposal was that it did not involve the prospect of any blood being shed, and it would make for very effective propaganda in Britain, Europe and the United States.

A similar proposal – but confined to women and children – was made by General Richard Mulcahy, Chief of Staff of the IRA, Assistant Minister for Defence in the Dáil Cabinet and a leading member of the Irish Republican Brotherhood. The Cabinet had instructed him to go to Limerick 'to supervise the situation on its behalf'. He bought a train ticket to Ennis but got off at Limerick, availing of a loophole in the military regulations that exempted travellers passing through the city to have to seek a special pass. Mulcahy immediately made contact with Commandant Michael Brennan, Officer Commanding the East Clare Brigade of the IRA, a member of the IRB and – according to Mulcahy – 'a fine officer'. Brennan organised the fullest co-operation of all the neighbouring IRA units in support of Limerick.

On Friday, 18 April, the Limerick Sinn Féin Comhairle Cheantair issued a circular stating that they had been approached by the Strike Committee with a request for help. Citizens were suffering severe hardships and the poorer classes, especially, found it difficult to procure food. They appealed for assistance of any kind, particularly food such as butter, milk, eggs, potatoes and vegetables which would be paid for at prices agreed on by the Strike Committee. Communications were to be sent to the Catholic Club in Barrington Street so that the supplies could be apportioned to the four depots established by the Soviet.

On 22 April, the Commandant of the IRA's Galtee Battalion, Seán Riordan, circulated important orders that had been received and asked for immediate attention to them. His circular referred to the imminent possibility of 'a large number of refugees leaving the city under press of food scarcity.' It further stated that 'a great national effort must be made to win the fight either (1) by putting the whole resources of the nation behind the workers of Limerick or (2) by extending the area of the struggle.'

Commandant Riordan ordered the Battalions to ascertain billeting accommodation for the anticipated refugees in their areas as an immediate and urgent task. Each Volunteer Company was required to notify to a Company officer the names and addresses of people willing to house and feed a certain number of refugees for a fortnight or a month: 'The Battalion officers should be instructed to see personally that their Company officers use the whole of their Company resources thoroughly to cover their whole Company area in their enquiries and that the information is made available at once.' Further weekly updates were to be provided. Riordan ordered that every single householder must be approached without fail. If he was not satisfied with the return from a District, there would be an enquiry to see if officers had performed the duties assigned to them to the best of their ability.

Four days after this order was issued, there had been little or no response. On 26 April, Riordan issued a second order, this time invoking the authority of the respected Brigade Commandant, Seán Wall, stating that the order to begin preparations for the evacuation of Limerick still stood and must be carried out. Republicans – operating through Sinn Féin, IRA and IRB networks – and their sympathisers, had responded well to the request to supply food to the beleaguered inhabitants of Limerick. But, for a variety of reasons, they appear to have baulked at the more complex task of arranging accommodation for evacuees on a mass scale.

Reasons for the lack of response are set out in an account of the evacuation plan in a Witness Statement to the Bureau of Military History by John (Jack) McCarthy, a member of the IRB, Vice-Commandant of the 5th Battalion (Kilfinane), later, Adjutant of the East Limerick Brigade of the IRA, and a combatant with the extremely active East Limerick Flying Column. In later life, he attained the rank of Lieutenant-Colonel in the Irish Defence Forces and edited '*Limerick's Fighting Story*', a classic account of the War of Independence in the city and county, first published by Anvil Books, Tralee, county Kerry in 1947.

McCarthy was a member of a wealthy landowning and merchant family. His family's extensive business interests included a wholesale, retail and distribution business as well as a well-known stud farm, Sycamore Lodge. His father was a big employer and McCarthy asserts that he treated his employees generously. The father was patron of the Kilfinane team when they won Limerick's first ever All Ireland senior hurling title in 1897. McCarthy was antipathetic towards farm labourers and other workers, especially members of the recently arrived and increasingly militant Irish Transport and General Workers' Union.

 McCarthy's account of events relating to the possible evacuation of Limerick during the Soviet is undoubtedly influenced by his class experience and attitudes. His assessment of Seán Riordan as Commandant of the IRA's 5th Battalion (Kilfinane) was that he was 'a square peg in a round hole' and 'sincere and hardworking but very impractical in the military sphere.' As a solicitor's clerk, Riordan had access to typewriting and duplicating facilities and his services were much in demand and made him well-known in both Sinn Féin and the

Volunteers. McCarthy was scathing about the Battalion's Adjutant, Patrick O'Carroll, of Kilfinane, describing him as 'an acute problem.' According to McCarthy, O'Carroll 'drank excessively, ceased to practice his religion and professed socialistic ideas.' The local Parish Priest – 'a saintly man and a good and useful friend of the Volunteers' – had commented publicly on the unreliability of 'bad Catholics' in national affairs. O'Carroll was Secretary of the local branch of the ITGWU. He often negotiated on their behalf with McCarthy as an employer, while on other occasions they met in the roles of Battalion Vice-Commandant and Battalion Adjutant. This paradox made for a difficult and uneasy relationship between the two men.

McCarthy's recollections disclose a deep antipathy among IRA/IRB officers in county Limerick towards supporting the proposed evacuation. McCarthy himself was favourably disposed towards the first request from the Sinn Féin Comhairle Cheantair for assistance by way of food supplies. However, he disobeyed the follow-up orders to source accommodation issued by Commandant Seán Riordan. Among his reasons for this stance he cites the difficulty of convincing people that the evacuation was necessary: 'I just could not visualise myself approaching such people – or commissioning others to do so in my name – knowing that, to the persons who would have to be so approached, the scheme would appear revolutionary, fantastic and unrelated to the needs of the actual situation. In brief, these two documents seemed to us to reflect more than an undertone of hysteria and to be exaggerated and impractical.' McCarthy admitted that he 'stalled from the outset in relation to these instructions, an attitude which I think – but cannot vouch for – was also that of most officers of other battalions and companies.' McCarthy claims that this assessment is supported by the fact that the Battalion Commandant, Riordan, felt obliged to repeat his order four days after he had first issued it.

McCarthy was convinced that there would be no refugees from the city and he was suspicious of the Adjutant, O'Carroll's enthusiasm for the evacuation scheme. In his BMH Witness Statement, he claimed that, as Secretary of the local union branch, O'Carroll was interested in the evacuation's potentiality for propaganda on behalf of Labour and in the promotion of 'socialistic doctrine and class war.' McCarthy's view was that because O'Carroll was in bad standing with the local Catholic clergy, they would oppose the housing of refugees and the householders' attitudes would have been conditioned by that and by O'Carroll's Labour affiliations: 'For most of them, it would have spelled Larkinism and carried echoes of Larkin's scheme during the strike in 1913 in Dublin when it was planned to send 'refugee' children to England – a scheme that was abandoned largely because of its condemnation by the clergy.'

McCarthy's account is an interesting insight into the class tensions that lay uneasily beneath the superficial unity of the movement for independence. Whatever the reasons, the bottom line was that nothing was done by Republicans in the farming areas of Mid and East Limerick to prepare for the evacuation of civilians from the city in support of the Soviet. Battalion orders were wilfully ignored or disobeyed in what might reasonably be characterised as a mutiny or quasi-mutiny.

In any event, the strike leaders themselves had flatly rejected any evacuation proposal. Whatever chance there was of feeding and housing people in their own city, with outside help, they could have little faith in the ability of the ILPTUC to feed and house about forty thousand men, women and children re-located outside of Limerick. In addition, property owners and professional people like doctors, solicitors or dentists, many of whom were sullen and reluctant inhabitants of Limerick under the Soviet, were not likely to abandon the city on the recommendation of a trade union body.

Apart from the Dáil Cabinet's attitude, the railwaymen were central to the Executive's dilemma. The railways were the pre-eminent method of mass transport of people and goods over long distances and were therefore of crucial strategic and economic importance. Johnson's assessment that the military would not stand idly by and let the railways be paralysed was almost certainly correct. The Limerick railway workers had served strike notice which was due to expire at midnight on 16 April, the first Wednesday of the general strike. But, even as Tom Johnson was setting off for Limerick, his colleague William O'Brien was telegraphing the rail workers saying: 'Railwaymen should defer stoppage pending national action. National Executive specially summoned for tomorrow.' This was sent after the TUC had consulted the rail delegates from Limerick, the Dublin rail workers at Inchicore, the Railwaymen's' Emergency Committee, a national co-ordinating body of all rail unions, as well as the national Republican leadership. That telegram had been the first real indication that whatever ways the Limerick strike might develop, they did not include a national strike.

Some rail employees in Limerick had already gone on strike on Tuesday 15 April. These were members of the Amalgamated Society of Engineers, employed in the smith, machine and fitting shops. They were followed the next day by the boilermakers, but the stoppage of those categories in no way interfered with the running of the trains. The leaders of the Limerick strike remained optimistic that their strike would spread to the other parts of the province of Munster served by the Great Southern and Western Railway. Towards the end of their first week, John Cronin said delegates who had visited various centres had returned to Limerick with reports that other workers were unanimous in their support for Limerick. He said the railway workers in other districts were ready to go out 'when the call was made'.

But despite those early indications of some trade union help elsewhere in Ireland, the attitude of the British unions with members in Ireland and especially the National Union of Railwaymen, remained crucial. As the '*Daily Herald*' put it: 'The success or failure of the strike is dependent on the railwaymens' action.' The British trade union answer was clear and sharp. The General Secretary of the National Union of Railwaymen, Jimmy Thomas

MP, sent a circular directing their Irish branches to advise their members that: 'they must not take any official part in what appears to be an industrial move against political action, without the authority from the Executive Committee.' On Thomas' instructions, a copy of his circular was sent to the Limerick Branch of the NUR and to all railway branches in Ireland. The circular followed a report on Limerick and a discussion at the National Executive of the NUR.

For the British Trade Union Congress, HR Stockman issued a statement to the press. The Executives of the British trade unions concerned held that their Irish branches could not be allowed to strike in Ireland, because they were opposed to the use of trade union machinery for political ends. Significantly, officials were advised that their members in Belfast were 'almost entirely opposed to a strike.' This was a point noted too by the '*Irish Times*' in its editorial on the morning the rest of the Executive arrived in Limerick.

Irish emigrants were not without influence in the British trade unions. There was speculation that if an unauthorised stoppage went ahead in Ireland, there would be sympathetic strikes of rail men and other workers in areas where there were large Irish communities. The same was said about the general transport workers, particularly at Liverpool and other towns with big Irish populations. Stockman himself admitted that there was a very strong agitation among the rank-and-file of the railwaymen 'on the English side of the Channel' in favour of sympathetic action in support of the Irish strikers. In August 1919, as the Anglo-Irish War intensified, Tom Johnson, as Secretary of the ILPTUC, reported that Irish workers on Tyneside and Clydeside wanted to organise and be affiliated to the Irish Congress. In April 1920, Irish workers in Liverpool and Hull struck in sympathy with Sinn Féin prisoners in Wormwood Scrubs Prison.

The leaders of the British trade unions were not without sympathy for the Limerick workers in their difficulties but they insisted that any action should be in accordance with their union rule books. It was decided to ask the Labour Party to raise the issue in Parliament without delay and to enlist the support of Liberal and other MPs for a demand that the Government deal with the Irish question on lines likely to remove the necessity for maintaining martial law in Limerick or anywhere else.

The local newspaper the '*Munster News*' took the view that Stockman's statement very probably marked the turning point of the dispute. It seemed to this newspaper that while Irish trade unions were frequently called upon to support strikes in Britain, reciprocity could not be counted on. Without the support of the British trade union Executives, the Irish Labour Party and Trade Union Congress probably had little option but to rule out a national strike. But it was their 'extreme' proposal of the peaceful evacuation of Limerick that prompted, and allowed, the Catholic Bishop to intervene in the strike and set in motion the events that led to its eventual end.

On Thursday 24 April, the Bishop, Doctor Hallinan and the Mayor, Alphonsus O'Mara, began what would be termed in modern parlance 'a round of shuttle diplomacy'. The '*Irish Independent*' described it as 'an anxious day of conferences and 'conversations'.' As a member of a celebrated Limerick family long involved in bacon processing, O'Mara was well attuned to the growing anger among the city's business class. It was the National Executive's second day in Limerick, and in the morning the Bishop and the Mayor met the strikers and the national union leaders. That meeting was adjourned, while the two public figures went to a lengthy meeting with General Griffin. He repeated his earlier offer, to allow the employers and traders to issue permits themselves to their workers and customers. And he offered further major concessions. To lighten the restrictions on workers, he would agree not to check passes when they were going to or from their meals. Furthermore, if the strike ended promptly and the cessation was followed by a trouble-free week in the city, he would revoke the Order requiring military permits. These combined concessions were enough to change the minds of the Bishop and the Mayor and convince them that the strike must end.

When the joint Strike/Congress Committee resumed their deliberations in the afternoon, they had before them a joint letter sent by the Bishop and the Mayor. They urged the leaders to end the strike The importance of the joint letter is underlined in an editorial headed 'The Strike – And After' in the local newspaper, the '*Munster News*': 'The struggle would have dragged on for some time longer had not his Lordship, Most Rev Dr Hallinan and the Mayor, as representing the spiritual and temporal interests of the citizens, sent a joint letter to the Trades Council on Thursday, requesting the immediate end of the strike...' A search of the Limerick Catholic Diocesan Archive, failed to locate a copy of the letter so its contents must be inferred from contemporary reports and comments. With the Catholic Church, the Chamber of Commerce and even some merchants with Sinn Féin sympathies now ranged against the strike, and the Irish Trade Union Congress more a hindrance than a help, the strikers had run out of options.

The '*Irish Times*' had no doubt that the change of attitude on the part of the Catholic Church was decisive. The Church's earlier position of support was not maintained. 'It is freely stated here that their views of the situation completely changed when they learnt of the drastic plans submitted by the Labour Executive to force the issue. They naturally discountenanced extreme measures and the Executive, knowing that the people would be guided by their clergy, wisely abandoned their plans.'

As night drew in and word spread that momentous matters were being discussed, several thousand people gathered outside the Mechanics' Institute in Glantworth Street. John Cronin appeared at a window and congratulated the people on their magnificent stand against tyranny. He said the fight would go on, and the flag would be kept flying. But it fell to Tom Johnson to make a dramatic announcement to the press. The Strike Committee called on all workers who could resume work without having to apply for permits to do so the following morning. Other workers who still needed permits would remain on strike but there would be a national congress of the ILPTUC to consider further action. The effect of this decision was to allow the majority of strikers to resume work but the six hundred employees of Cleeve's would still be affected, as would a considerable number of other workers in the Thomondgate district. From the subsequent debate at the 1919 annual conference of the Irish Labour Party and Trade Union Congress, in Drogheda county Louth, it is clear that the proposal to hold a special conference was never intended as a serious proposition. It was intended more to ease the psychological blow of capitulation for the strikers and to maintain a semblance of continuing pressure against the permits system.

Councillor Robert O'Connor, a member of the Strike Committee, read the proclamation which was to be posted up on the streets:

'Whereas the workers of Limerick have been on strike since Monday, April 14, as a protest against the military ban on our city; and whereas, in the meantime the question has become a national issue, we hereby call upon all workers who can resume work without permits to do so on tomorrow (Friday) morning. We further call upon all those workers whose daily occupation requires them to procure military permits to continue in their refusal to accept this sign of subjugation and slavery, pending a decision of the Irish Trade Union Congress, to be called immediately.

We also call upon all our fellow-countrymen and lovers of freedom all over the world to provide the necessary funds to enable us to continue this struggle against military tyranny.

Strike Committee, April 24, 1919'

The assembled strikers received the announcement with mixed feelings and in silence. Many were glad to be returning to work, though others regarded the result as a defeat and felt their sacrifices had gone for nothing. The *'Irish Times'* reported that Johnson was received with cheers but the *'Irish Independent'* said the speeches of their leaders did not put the strikers in better heart. In his speech, Johnson said that, taking everything into account, they had taken the best course for the moment. They believed the fight had been taken up by the workers of Limerick on behalf of the people of Ireland as a whole. It was the duty of Ireland to continue it and if Ireland was going to let the workers of Limerick down, Ireland must be ashamed of herself and need no longer call herself a fighter for freedom. He complimented the workers on the way they had governed the city so well – as good as any Government.

The crowds dispersed quietly and during the evening copies of the proclamation were posted throughout the city. Some members of the ITGWU, employed in Cleeve's, were far from happy. They tore up the posters and burned them in disgust. Some of them threatened to set up another soviet but these threats were probably not intended to be taken seriously. The feeling of resentment against the strike leaders was short-lived. The following day,

Friday, there was a hurried attempt to resume business but it was mainly confined to a small section of traders. For some factories, there was a shortage of raw materials and in others, where furnaces had to be stoked up, there was not enough time overnight to prepare them for re-opening. In the case of the bacon factories, they had no pigs to slaughter since fairs and buying had been suspended.

For General Griffin, the decision in favour of a return to work by a large number of strikers was a vindication of the careful and shrewd way he had handled the strike. His background as a member of a Catholic family from Cork may have been a help. Griffin applied the military regulations with a firm, but light, hand. He was anxious, no doubt, to avoid any provocative action or confrontation that might spark off an escalation of the strike.

The General was shrewd enough not to try to break the strike by military intervention. That might have provided further martyrs and justification for stronger action on the other side. He did not try to prevent the pickets from closing down businesses. In contrast to the days preceding Robert Byrne's burial, there was not a high level of military or police activity in the city under the military regulations. Most troops and police were confined to barracks and the emphasis was on manning checkpoints on the boundaries of the military area. Even that was done in a low-key way. Only the bridges facing North across the Shannon were fully manned. After some days, no one was prevented from leaving the city without a permit and it was easy enough to cross the river by boat. On the South side of the city – where it touched the boundary with county Limerick – access was uninhibited. No one was actually charged with illegal entry and on only two occasions did soldiers shoot to prevent entry. On neither occasion was anyone caught, though on one of them, it was claimed a donkey was shot and became the first victim of the siege! Griffin's position was strengthened by the resolute way the military had seen off the challenge of the Caherdavin demonstrators on Easter Monday. His only disadvantage was being unable to use any of the city's printing works to produce counter-propaganda. For example, on the first evening of the strike, his soldiers had to resort to posting a typewritten notice blaming the strikers for any hardship caused and that was the only feeble attempt to counteract the strikers' very active Propaganda Committee.

Griffin chose to wait for the realisation to dawn that the strike either had to escalate or be ended. In this, he proved ultimately to have a number of unlikely and unexpected allies, that included the national and local Republican leadership, the Catholic Bishop and clergy, the Mayor and the leadership of the Irish Labour Party and Trade Union Congress. Griffin's 'wait and see' strategy relied on splitting the city's solidarity by offering tempting concessions to the employers, who were at best, reluctant parties to the dispute at any time. The initial strength of the strikers, and the early support of prominent Sinn Féin people like O'Mara and Colivet had been enough to stave off an employers' revolt. But once it became clear, in the second week of the strike, that the ILPTUC was not going to support a national strike, the General had only to restate his earlier concessions for them to be accepted with alacrity. In thus achieving the ending of the strike, the General maintained the Government's status and the military's morale, by dealing only with the employers, the Mayor and the Bishop. In that way, he denied any recognition to the strike leaders, something the employers probably welcomed because of its long-term beneficial side effects for them.

On 26 April, the Saturday after the partial return to work, a statement from Johnson made it clear there had been a clash over strategy and tactics between the local leaders and the national leadership. The Executive had submitted 'certain proposals of a drastic character' which they believed would be the most effective way of countering the military tyranny using peaceful means. To their regret, the Strike Committee had told them their proposals were not likely to receive the necessary support and they accepted that decision as final. Curiously, the '*Irish Times*' report says the Executive 'endorsed' the local decision. It is not quite clear from the statement whether the Strike Committee had turned down the 'drastic' evacuation proposal on its merits, or whether they were influenced by the Bishop's opposition.

Johnson made the, by then, almost ritualistic comments congratulating the workers on their administrative and organisational abilities and he called for financial assistance to meet the losses already incurred and to continue the fight. The National Executive asked that any money be sent to James Casey, the Trades Council Treasurer, at the Mechanics' Institute in Limerick. With that final statement, all the members of the Congress Executive, except Johnson, left Limerick. The conduct of the strike was now back in the hands of the local Strike Committee. The various subcommittees remained at work and concentrated on helping people who needed money or food.

For a time, the question of employers issuing permits to their own employees flared as an issue. This was one thing on which the Strike Committee and the Congress Executive could agree on, even at the height of their disagreements – no worker could accept a permit to work from the hands of their employer. Some workers who took these permits were, on that final Saturday, stopped by pickets and ordered back, while some carters refused employers' permits given to them to make deliveries outside the city.

The Thomondgate people seemed determined to continue a protest and they held a general meeting of some of the residents on the Friday night. On Saturday morning, a number of them blocked Thomond Bridge and deterred some people from crossing. The police were called and dispersed what seems like a half-hearted attempt at a blockade. Other workers resorted to ingenious devices to return to work without having to request permits. A few procured tents to camp outside the military boundaries and others went to live temporarily in the areas where they were employed.

Late on Sunday night, 27 April, the Strike Committee issued another proclamation:

'Whereas for the past fortnight the workers of Limerick have entered an emphatic and dignified protest against military tyranny, and have loyally obeyed the orders of the Strike Committee, we, at a special meeting assembled, after carefully considering the circumstances, have decided to call upon the workers to resume work on Monday morning.

We take this opportunity of returning our thanks to every class of the community for the help tendered during the period of the strike.'

John Cronin sent a telegram to the Congress Executive in Dublin announcing the end of the strike and stating that the strikers had decided the holding of a special Trade Union Congress should be abandoned.

The Limerick Soviet had ended as suddenly as it began, exactly fourteen days previously.

CHAPTER NINE

<u>Green, Red and Orange</u>

'They were all anxious for unity and no threat of cleavage had been made if the motion brought forward by the Limerick delegates failed. Unity was very good, but if it came to a question of principle, then let them scrap unity.'
– *Tipperary Delegate, Mansfield, to the Irish National Teachers' Organisation Annual Congress, Good Friday, 25 April 1919*

The Catholic clergy and the employers were quick to recriminate against the strikers. On the final Sunday of the strike – the day the full resumption of work was decided on – Father Dwane, Administrator of Saint Michael's Parish, strongly criticised its conduct. Addressing the congregation at twelve o'clock Mass, he said neither the Bishop nor the clergy were consulted before the strike was declared, and they were totally opposed to its continuance.

Father Dwane said his sympathies were always with the working classes. He was a great believer in the dignity of labour and any help he could give in raising the dignity of labour would be rendered by him on all occasions. But he had a stern warning for his listeners: 'He hoped the honest workingmen of Limerick would in future duly consider any action they were about to take and be guided only by leaders upon whom they could rely and in whom they could have full confidence, and not allow themselves to be fooled or deceived by anybody whatsoever. He was very glad the strike had ended and it was highly creditable that during its continuance everything was so peaceable and orderly in the city.'

The employers were piqued because they were not told officially of the strike's partial end on the Thursday. The Chamber of Commerce at that stage decided on a phased reopening of business starting with shops and flour mills, leaving the factories until after the weekend. But in a later statement, they made what they termed an emphatic protest against the calling of a general strike without giving due notice to the employers. Had the positions been reversed, and the employers had closed their premises without notice, they believed the workers would have bitterly resented the action. The Chamber of Commerce argued that if the workers had consulted with them before calling the strike, they might have been able to take joint action that would have saved the city from a 'disastrous' strike. As it was, the Chamber estimated the employers had lost about a quarter of a million pounds in turnover (equivalent to approximately €15 million in today's values) and that the workers had lost forty-two thousand pounds (€2.5 million) in wages.

The disdainful attitude of the employers and other prominent citizens towards the strike was underlined some days after the permit system was withdrawn when a delegation of Irish-American politicians visited Limerick. This stop-over was part of a fact-finding tour of Ireland to observe the situation at first hand. At no time during the welcoming speeches of the Mayor or High Sheriff was the strike or the military occupation mentioned. None of the visitors referred to it either, an indication perhaps that it was regarded as an aberration and not part of the mainstream nationalist tradition. However, whatever about local begrudgery, criticism or opposition from employers or clergy, the Limerick Soviet attracted widespread interest and some support outside the city during its existence. This support came, not unexpectedly, from trade union and Labour organisations, but also from public bodies and the Gaelic Athletic Association, and it came from Britain as well as other parts of Ireland.

Waterford Trades Council was one of the first outside bodies to protest against the military restrictions. On the day the strike began, they passed a resolution demanding the immediate withdrawal of military law from all the areas affected. A copy of the resolution was forwarded to Macpherson, the Chief Secretary for Ireland. Other Trades Councils sent messages of support, money and other practical help to Limerick. Galway Trades Council planned to organise a May Day concert for Limerick. Cork Trades Council set up a fund and protested against the 'military dictatorship established by the army of occupation.' Cork Grocers' and Allied Trades' Assistants had called for the setting up of such a fund and the gas workers there promised support. Tralee Trades Council collected forty pounds (€2,400) for the strikers. Other Trades Councils, faced with local strikes of their own, found it difficult to raise money for Limerick, so there was little question of the councils banding together outside the control of the Irish TUC to produce sympathetic action. Wexford Trades Council expressed regret that, because of a local foundry dispute, they could not help. Similar problems arose in Dundalk, Drogheda, Boyle and other areas. In neighbouring county Clare, however, Ennis Trades Council assured Limerick of their unqualified support in whatever the Irish TUC deemed necessary to secure victory.

The National Executive of the Irish Transport and General Workers' Union voted the considerable sum of a thousand pounds (€60,000) towards the strike. As a first instalment, the National Executive of the Irish Clerical Workers' Union sent a hundred pounds (€6,000) to the Strike Committee. There was further Clerical Workers' support from the Dublin branches of that union. The National Executive of the Irish Automobile Drivers' Union voted a hundred pounds. A double levy of four pence (€1) was made on workers in Athlone, county Westmeath and in the same county, the Mullingar branch of the ITGWU opened a subscription list and passed a resolution condemning the action of the authorities in Limerick. From Derry came a pledge of support from the city's dockers and carters for Limerick in the 'fight against militarism.'

The annual conference of the Drapers' Assistants' Association, representing five thousand shop assistants and clerks, unanimously condemned the action of the Government or military authorities in their treatment of the workers of Limerick, in preventing them from freely earning their daily bread and they pledged them their strongest support in the struggle for freedom. The Association's General Secretary, MJ O'Lehane, who was due in Limerick later that week as a member of the Congress Executive, said they had sent two hundred pounds (€12,000) to their Limerick Branch Secretary. He anticipated that they would send a very substantial sum to the Strike Committee itself. Impressive though some of the amounts donated may sound, they came nowhere near the weekly seven to eight thousand pounds (about €500,000 today) it was calculated would be needed to keep the strike going. At the end of ten days, it was estimated that a thousand pounds (€60,000) had been received in Limerick, and some days later that figure had increased to only fifteen hundred pounds (€90,000).

At the draper's assistants' conference, two Limerick delegates gave interesting insights into conditions there. Mr Daly said the military seemed to be friendly and the police were not. He said the strike committee's control was so complete that even Major Wood had to apply for a permit before he could attempt his flight to America, and he had acknowledged that he did so with the Committee's permission. Mr Connaughton, also from Limerick, referred to the anomalies in the way the military had mapped the boundaries. In Saint Patrick's Parish, he said, the barrier came between the priest's house and the church.

Throughout nationalist Ireland there was strong support among political bodies. The second biggest financial donation, five hundred pounds (€30,000 in today's values), came from the Mansion House Conference, a body that had commanded wide support in the 1918 campaign against conscription in Ireland. At a large demonstration in Cavan, to welcome home Peadar Galligan, a Sinn Féin TD released from internment, a resolution was passed unanimously congratulating the Limerick citizens on their magnificent fight against English militarism and pledging them moral and material support. Galligan said that no attempt to create a breach between Labour and Sinn Féin would succeed.

In county Westmeath, Mullingar Rural District Council adopted a resolution congratulating the workers of Limerick on their fight against oppression. North Tipperary Sinn Féin Executive appealed to all clubs in the constituency for potatoes, oatmeal, eggs and other foodstuffs for the relief of Limerick. The Chairman of Limerick County Council wrote to the authorities protesting at the restrictions, and two members said they could not attend a Council meeting because they refused to ask for permission from anyone to discharge their duties as elected public representatives.

Cork Guardians also passed a resolution of condemnation and pledged support for Limerick. At this meeting, controversy broke out over the role of the National Union of

Railwaymen. The motion had been moved by John Good, the local Secretary of the NUR. He was criticised by Mr D Williams for pretending it was a labour matter, and trying to get Sinn Féin involved, while at the same time 'he took care to carry out the orders of his master in England, Mr Thomas.'

Traditionally, the Annual Congress of the Gaelic Athletic Association is held at Easter. As at the trade union conferences held around that time, a Limerick delegate moved to get support for the strike. Newspaper reports differ as to whether, in this case, the speaker was an ordinary delegate or someone sent to represent the Strike Committee. Again, however, he gave an insight into how well the Soviet was coping. The workers were as well fed as at any time in their lives; they were getting milk at the right price and potatoes for nearly nothing. No distress had occurred so far, but the Strike Committee wanted to have funds in hand for any unforeseen eventualities. Two prominent Republicans, Harry Boland and JJ Walsh, proposed and seconded a resolution to grant a hundred pounds (€6,000) to the strike funds from the Association. A delegate from the Munster Council of the GAA pledged ten pounds, and after other delegates had pledged money, a collection on the spot realised over thirty pounds.

As a sports organisation, the GAA offered help in the most practical way it could. Four matches were arranged to raise money for the strike fund. At the Association's headquarters in Croke Park, Louth would play Dublin in Gaelic football, and in another football game, at Roscommon, Galway were matched against Roscommon. Two hurling matches were arranged. At Cork, the home county would play Tipperary and Cork would travel to Tralee to play Kerry. However, the delegates baulked at the suggestion of playing the games on May Day. Whatever about protesting at the situation in Limerick, they clearly drew the line at anything that smacked of 'Socialism' or 'Politics'. The Gaelic football game at Croke Park drew between three and four thousand spectators. It is difficult to judge whether this was evidence of widespread support for the strike or merely reflected the attractiveness of the fixture. Dublin, in any event, defeated Louth comprehensively, by a goal and seven points to a single point.

Further afield, in Britain, the advanced Left were in support. At the Independent Labour Party Conference, in Huddersfield, Councillor Cradford, of Edinburgh, said they ought to do something to encourage 'The Limerick Soviet'. He would like to see the working classes of Great Britain following the Soviet's example in offering a paper currency of their own. Cradford said they were with their Irish friends in spirit against the military regime. The future Prime Minister of Britain, Ramsay MacDonald, opposed the strike, declaring that the nearest thing to a 'Soviet' in Britain was the House of Lords! Cradford retorted that the Limerick Soviet was the first working-class soviet on practical lines established in the British Isles but the conference was so divided on the issue that no vote was taken.

The '*Irish Times*' noted what it called the 'injurious praise' of the Independent Labour Party and the British Socialist Party. The Socialist Party's Annual Conference, in Sheffield, passed a resolution wishing success to their fellow-workers of Limerick in their struggle for civil liberty. Cathal O'Shannon, a prominent official of the ITGWU and a leading light in the Socialist Party of Ireland, made a fiery speech to the delegates. To laughter, O'Shannon said it was bad enough having to work without having to get a permit to do so. If a general strike was called, he said, it would not end with a Limerick Soviet. To cheers, he predicted it might end with something more than the British occupation of Ireland would want to stomach. O'Shannon said that, if necessary, arrangements could be made for a general strike, including JH Thomas' railway men. He said he looked to a combination of the elements of the Left in Scotland and South Wales, Ireland and England, which would bring about an alliance of revolutionary socialists and end what he termed 'the white terror' now prevailing.

The Workers' Socialist Federation dispatched a correspondent to Limerick to report at first hand for its newspaper '*The Workers' Dreadnought*', edited by the noted women's rights activist Sylvia Pankhurst. The '*Dreadnought*' later carried a series of articles entitled 'The Truth about the Limerick Soviet' and their reporter filed graphic, harrowing accounts of the conditions under which women workers, in particular, were employed in the city.

One of the first acts of the joint meeting of the Strike Committee and Congress Executive members in Limerick had been to send a rather combative telegram to the Scottish Trade Union Congress, then meeting in Perth. It read: 'Limerick workers for nine days have been on strike against the veto placed upon their movement by your military authorities. Your servants, the army of occupation here, refuse to allow the citizens to proceed to and from their daily work, except under military permit. Limerick workers refuse to submit to this indignity and sign of subjugation. You, Scottish workers, cannot absolve yourselves from responsibility unless you take action immediately.' The following day, the Scottish Trade Union Congress responded with a unanimous resolution demanding the withdrawal of the embargo on the workers of Limerick. WB MacMahon of the Railway Clerks' Association was the Irish fraternal delegate to the TUC and he reported the decision to the Irish newspapers. Robert Allan, Secretary of the Scottish TUC, forwarded a telegram of protest to the Chief Secretary for Ireland in Dublin Castle.

This was not the only telegram or letter of protest from Britain to land on Macpherson's desk. The Executive Council of the United Operative Plumbers and Domestic Engineers Association had discussed the strike at their general office in Newcastle-on-Tyne. In an emphatic letter of protest from their Assistant General Secretary, Lachlan MacDonald, they said they were of the opinion that the circumstances in Limerick did not warrant such drastic curtailment of the citizens' rights and that there must be other means that could be adopted.

The Secretary of the Dennistoun Branch of the Independent Labour Party – a person with the Irish-sounding name of P Lavin – forwarded a resolution passed at a 'largely-attended' meeting of the Branch. They protested 'in the strongest possible way against the barbarous methods of repression resorted to by the British Government in Co. Limerick and other parts of Ireland' and they called for the immediate withdrawal from Ireland of all British troops.

Another unmistakably Irish name was on the letter of protest from the Merthyr and Dowlais Sinn Féin Club, in South Wales. Signed by J Crowley, and sent to the Home Secretary, in Whitehall, this again called for the withdrawal of troops from Ireland, and condemned 'the treatment meted out to the people of Limerick by the military authorities'. Ealing Labour Party and Trades Council unanimously adopted a resolution protesting strongly against 'the isolation and military coercion of the inhabitants of the City of Limerick' and demanding the withdrawal of troops from the city and the ending of the proclaimed area.

But if nationalist Ireland stood firmly with Limerick, the Unionist workers of North East Ulster remained aloof and suspicious. Ninety per cent of the skilled trades unionists in Ireland were employed in Belfast's factories and shipyards. The Belfast Correspondent of the '*Daily Telegraph*' reported: 'A strong line against the proposed national strike of Irish unions has been taken by organised labour in Belfast... The Limerick dispute being Sinn Féin in origin, the workers in Belfast have intimated they will be no party to the strike, and if the Irish Trade Union Congress or any other body calls for a cessation of work the order will be ignored. Local district committees of British trade unions have been warned they must not use funds for the proposed Irish strike'. This had happened previously early in 1918 during the anti-Conscription strike, when Belfast had continued working although Dublin and the South was at a standstill.

The Protestant workers of North East Ulster remained implacably opposed to Irish independence. They had long feared being subsumed into what they foresaw as a society dominated by priests and peasants. They regarded the Irish Labour Party and Trade Union Congress as little more than the industrial wing of Sinn Féin, dedicated to the establishment of Bolshevism throughout Ireland. A Unionist MP, Thomas Donald, told a meeting of electors in Belfast's Victoria Division that he could not see any difference between the people they knew as Bolshevists in Russia and those who were creating the present situation in the South of Ireland. This stance faced the trade union leadership with the impossible dilemma of trying to maintain organisational unity across the island of Ireland in the face of a diversity of economic and political interests between North and South.

Sharing a common religious outlook with their employers, in a society where many Catholics did not recognise the legitimacy or authority of the government, Protestant workers monopolised the skilled and best paid jobs and acquiesced in sectarian discrimination against

Catholics. The North's major industries depended heavily on the Imperial link for their continued prosperity and Protestant workers feared for their jobs, prosperity and privileges in an Independent Ireland pursuing protectionist trade policies. Thus, a combination of economic interest and sectarian differences kept the Protestant workers hostile to the independence movement.

The period from the end of the 1880s to 1914 failed to produce a trade union movement throughout Ireland that was united in its political as well as its industrial aims. That was so, despite the development during the period, in Britain and Ireland, of the more militant 'new unionism' and events like Jim Larkin's coalition of Protestant and Catholic workers during the great Belfast Docks Strike of 1907. Three factors combined to identify Catholic workers with Fenian nationalism. The mass mobilisation of nationalists under Parnell, and Orange resistance to Home Rule, had equated Irishness with Catholicism. The tension between the two sections of the working-class was intensified by the systematic exclusion of Catholics from skilled Ulster trades and the political radicalism of the leaders of 'new unionism' was regarded with suspicion by the Ulster's Protestant craftsmen.

The trade union organisation of previously unorganised, unskilled workers – largely Catholic – at a time of increasing political tension over the link with Britain served to divide, rather than to unite, the working-class. It became impossible to construct a labour movement that was both political and industrial and which united Protestant and Catholic, Orange and Green. It might have been possible but only if the existing separation between craft and non-craft, skilled and unskilled workers, did not also follow the sectarian gulf between Protestant and Catholic.

A united trade union movement was possible only insofar as it did not involve itself in the question of the link with Britain, in other words, by ignoring the dominant issue in Irish politics. With the exception of James Connolly, this is what the Labour leadership did in practice. Connolly, in effect, played the Green Card. He opted for a Labour movement that appealed essentially to Southerners and Catholics. This might be justified on the basis that the majority of Irish people were Catholics and the Catholic working-class may have appeared to be more promising material for social revolution than their Protestant counterparts. But Connolly's decision finally excluded the possibility of a united, political movement of all Irish workers. It meant equating and ultimately subordinating Southern Irish Labour to Irish nationalism. After Connolly's death, trade union leaders like William O'Brien and Thomas Johnson accepted this position and they did not allow events like the Limerick Soviet to threaten trade union organisational unity throughout the island of Ireland. The syndicalist orientation of Irish Labour, with its emphasis on industrial aims and means – as opposed to politics – made it all the easier for the leadership to adopt this stance.

An extensive special debate on Limerick at the Annual Congress of the Irish National Teachers' Organisation, held in University Buildings, Dublin is worth looking at in some detail for what it reveals of Northern attitudes. The National Teachers had a wide membership in all parts of the country. Their debate was spread over two days, starting on Thursday, 24 April the day the partial resumption of work was decided on in Limerick.

George O'Callaghan, a delegate from Newcastle West, in county Limerick, moved the suspension of Standing Orders to 'draw attention to the fact that several of our colleagues are unable to pursue their work at the present time.' Standing Orders were raised to allow discussion of a motion pledging support to the workers of Limerick but when it became clear that discussion on this was going to be heated, the matter was left over until the following day. O'Callaghan said that there was no question of politics involved, people of all shades of politics were united in Limerick. He appealed to the delegates to make some return for their alliance with Labour. A county Clare delegate warned that if the national teachers were capable of turning their backs on Labour, he would leave the Organisation tomorrow.

A succession of Northern delegates opposed O'Callaghan. Mr McNallis from Dungannon, county Tyrone, said they in the North could always work on Organisation matters without having a word of friction. How was it, he asked, that it was only when they met in Congress from different parts of Ireland that a jarring note was raised. Was it not evident that matters were introduced which should be left alone? McNallis continued: 'No one who had read that day's papers could have any difficulty in deciding whether this was a political matter or not. This did not begin as a Labour question. If it were purely a Labour question, there would be no difficulty about the delegates throwing in their lot with Labour, but I submit it was not purely a Labour question.' McNallis' next comments exposed how susceptible to rupture was the fragile unity of the Northern and Southern members once a 'political' issue was raised. According to the '*Irish Independent*' report, 'When it was said that this would lead to secession of branches in the North, someone said 'Small Loss!', but he would remind them there was a time when they were glad to have the men from the North to plead their cause.'

Another county Tyrone delegate, Mr Ramsay, of Cookstown, said he could not yet see that the matter was dissociated from politics. The proclamation issued in Limerick stated that they were on strike as a protest against the ban on the city – not on the ban against going to work. He placed the Organisation above everything, and knowing that this matter interfered with the Organisation, he would oppose it. Ramsay said he did not think the time had arrived when the teachers of Ireland would be convinced that this was not a political problem.

The spectre of the partition of Ireland was raised in the speech of another Northern delegate, Stanage, from Banbridge in county Down. He appealed to the teachers' Congress to think very seriously before pushing the resolution. They wanted a united Ireland, but were they going to have the first partition an educational one, and were they going to give a handle to others to put them in a peculiar position? A delegate called Judge made a similar plea not to drive a wedge between the North and the South. Had the delegates received instructions from their associations on how to vote on a question which might split the Congress and lead to the setting up of breakaway unions, he asked.

Speakers from southern counties, like Kilkenny and Tipperary, were dismissive of these arguments in their contributions. A Kilkenny delegate, Mr Frisby, appealed to the teachers to 'stick to Labour and to stick to Limerick.' If the Scottish Trade Union Congress were not afraid to call for the withdrawal of the military embargo, why should the teachers be afraid to, he asked. They had heard of partition on the subject of education in the North of Ireland, and that policy had found its most influential supporters in the ranks of their members in Belfast. Cries of 'Wrong!' greeted this remark.

Mr Mansfield, from Tipperary, was even more dismissive of the Northern anxieties and appeal for unity. 'They were all anxious for unity', Mansfield said, 'and no threat of cleavage had been made if the motion which had been brought forward by the Limerick delegates failed. Unity was very good, but if it came to a question of principle, then let them scrap unity.' He protested against the bogey of unity being brought forward to cow the majority, who were entitled on democratic grounds to rule any organised body. Let them have unity, but let principle, right and justice prevail, he declared, even if the Organisation went bang.'

In the end, a compromise resolution was carried. This referred the question of support for Limerick to the union's Central Executive Council, to await the outcome of the expected special Irish Trade Union Congress. Thus, the Northern delegates had their sensibilities respected on the day but for the Southern delegates the resolution also committed the CEC to 'act in harmony' with the decision of any Trade Union Congress.

INTO sensitivity on an issue like Limerick was understandable. As far back as 1916, in the wake of the Easter Rising, Unionist teachers had set up the Irish Protestant National Teachers' Union (IPNTU), a body that remained closely aligned to the INTO. In June 1916, the IPNTU had set up a subcommittee to 'watch Protestant teachers' interests in the so-called Irish question'. The decision was followed by a loyal toast and the singing of 'God Save the King'. Resolutions of sympathy passed by INTO branches and by the union's Central Committee in the aftermath of the Rising and the internment of its participants, led to further friction with the IPNTU. The tensions increased following the national teachers' decision, in 1917, to affiliate to what the President of the IPNTU called the 'frankly Bolshevist and Sinn Féin' Irish Labour Party and Trade Union Congress. The ILPTUC's opposition to conscription, and the decision to withdraw in favour of Sinn Féin in the 1918 General Election, led to Northern Protestant resignations from the INTO. By the INTO congress of 1919, branches in Coleraine, Lisburn, Derry and Newtownards had left the union. Later that year, on 19 July, the final breach was made when the Ulster National Teachers' Union was formed.

The sensitivity of Northern Loyalists in the trade unions on any question that smacked of nationalism or separatism was further underlined during the period of the Limerick Soviet by a controversy over a call from the Irish Trade Union Congress to suspend work on Labour Day, 1 May 1919, and to celebrate it as an unpaid holiday. The call was made in a poster, signed by the Irish TUC General Secretary, William O'Brien, and displayed in Dublin, declaring that the workers of Ireland had decided to celebrate May the First, Labour Day, as a general holiday, and that all work would be suspended that day 'to demonstrate that the Irish working class joins with the international Labour movement in demanding a democratic League of Free Nations as the necessary condition of a permanent peace based upon the self-determination of all peoples, including the people of Ireland.' For Ulster Unionists, the sting was in the tail of that resolution.

Once again, as in the case of Limerick, the attitude of the National Union of Railwaymen and their General Secretary, JH Thomas, was crucial. Irish railwaymen seemed willing to join in the stoppage. The call to stop work was supported by the Irish Railway Workers' Emergency Committee, representing the NUR, the Railway Clerks' Association, the Amalgamated Society of Engineers, the ITGWU and the railway craft unions. But, on instructions from London, the Irish Secretary of the NUR, Rimmer, issued a directive to all his branches that they were not to absent themselves from work on the first day of May without the sanction of their Executive Committee.

For the Irish TUC, William O'Brien replied in his characteristically acerbic manner. He pointed out that it was Rimmer himself, on behalf of the NUR, who had proposed a resolution at the 1917 Congress calling on them to seek to establish an International Labour Day. The resolution had been seconded by two NUR members and adopted by Congress. Now, according to O'Brien, the Irish TUC was merely acting on that resolution and therefore the attitude of Thomas, as General Secretary of the NUR, was hard to understand. He pointed out that Thomas himself had been at the International Trade Union Conference in Berne that nominated the First of May as Labour Day.

Three branches of the NUR in Cork, representing over a thousand workers, rejected Rimmer's instructions and decided to stick by their decision to stop work on May Day. The Bray Number Two Branch of the union made a similar decision, making it clear they were following the wishes of the Irish TUC in so doing. But in Derry, Loyalist workers refused to take part in a planned demonstration, believing Sinn Féin to be behind the proposed cessation of work. The 'No Surrender' band turned down an invitation from the Derry Trades and Labour Council to celebrate Labour Day. The band's reply pointed out that practically all of its members had joined the colours, while those running the Labour Day demonstration were associated in the protest against conscription. Consequently, as loyal subjects, the band declined to have anything to do with the turnout.

The Executive Committee of the Londonderry Branch of the Ulster Unionist Labour Association decided to request all their members, and all Protestant workers, male and female, not to take part in the May Day demonstration. They warned that it was 'of a revolutionary and Bolshevik nature and supported by Sinn Féin propagandists, as already stated at the opening of Dáil Éireann and that honest labour should repudiate such actions.' Believing there was a strong Sinn Féin influence at work, Loyalists were particularly aggrieved that it was proposed to assemble at the Mall Wall, close to the Derry Apprentice Boys' Memorial Hall. A similar proposal, in the past, had led to rioting.

May Day 1919 repeated the pattern of the 1918 national strike against conscription and was a harbinger of the coming partition between North and South. The call for a stoppage of work was responded to almost everywhere except Belfast and North-East Ulster and the city of Limerick. In nationalist Ireland, there were demonstrations of record sizes and the red flag was carried even in small towns. The resolutions adopted emphasised world peace, the self-determination of nations and the call for May Day to be a public holiday.

After the rigours of the fortnight long general strike, Limerick was an understandable exception. The Trades Council decided against a May Day stoppage because, they said, it would 'not be fair to stop work'. As work resumed in all Limerick factories on Monday, 28 April, the Trades Council met to decide its attitude to the proposed May Day stoppage. Some representatives of the ITGWU urged that May Day be observed, but the majority view was against another work stoppage so soon after the sacrifices made during the Soviet.

In addition, they were aware of the promise of General Griffin, the Competent Military Authority, that he would end the military restrictions in seven days' time, if there were no further disturbances, and they were not prepared to jeopardise that prospect through a confrontation on the streets on May Day. Four days after May Day, the newspapers carried reports that the proclamation of a portion of the City of Limerick as a Special Military Area, from 9 April, was withdrawn. Permits were no longer necessary and there was free access to the city.

CHAPTER TEN

<u>Why Limerick and Why April 1919?</u>

'...with the exception of Londonderry, there is perhaps no other
town in Ireland in which its history bulks so large as it does in
Limerick.'
— *'The Times', 17 March 1913*

Four main factors combined to create the conditions for the emergence of the Limerick Soviet in April 1919. They were the city's strong tradition of advanced nationalism, the influence on trade unionists and their leaders of the views advanced by the executed 1916 leader, James Connolly, the intensification of Irish separatist demands as 1918 evolved into 1919 and the Red tide that had started in Russia in 1917 and, by 1919, seemed to be sweeping unstoppably across Europe.

The Vikings founded the city and port of Limerick on the River Shannon in the Ninth Century. It became a legend in Irish history with Patrick Sarsfield's Jacobite defence of the walls in 1691 against the siege of the Orange King William. The Treaty Stone, where by tradition the subsequent Treaty of Limerick was signed, still stands as a monument near the Shannon. A *'Times'* special supplement on Ireland, published on Saint Patrick's Day 1913 caught the flavour of Limerick exactly when it said: '...with the exception of Londonderry, there is perhaps no other town in Ireland in which its history still bulks so large as it does in Limerick'

The city had a strong tradition of Fenianism, personified in the Fenian leader John Daly who was elected a Member of Parliament in the Eighteen Nineties and was Mayor from 1899 to 1901. In 1867, five thousand people marched in memory of the Manchester Martyrs, Allen, Larkin and O'Brien. With the one-time leader of the Irish National Party, Isaac Butt, as a previous MP, Limerick was also strongly imbued with the constitutional nationalist tradition. But, in Limerick, as elsewhere in Parnell's time, the dividing line between Fenianism and constitutional nationalism was often hazy.

Limerick was affected, too, by the Gaelic cultural renaissance that was emerging towards the end of the Nineteenth Century. In 1887, three years after the foundation of the Gaelic Athletic Association, a club was established in Limerick. That year, the Limerick Commercials' Club won the first ever All Ireland final in Gaelic football. In 1897, during Queen Victoria's Jubilee, the most important anti-Royalist demonstrations were in Limerick. A black flag of protest flew from John Daly's house and another was suspended across the river at Thomondgate. A branch of the Irish language revival organisation, the Gaelic League, was formed in Limerick in 1898, five years after its national foundation.

The Irish Volunteers, founded in 1913, established a Limerick branch in December of that year and at the time of the split over John Redmond's call to fight in the British Army in World War One, nearly seven thousand members followed him into the National Volunteers, while five hundred remained as Irish Volunteers. Limerick had a close connection too with the 1916 Rising. Two of those executed were born in Limerick – Edward Daly, and Con Colbert – while a third, Seán Heuston, had worked there for a number of years.

Prior to the great famines of the Eighteen Forties, Limerick had a population of over sixty thousand but starvation and emigration forced that down to less than forty thousand. Between the end of the Nineteenth Century and the Census of 1911, the population recovered slowly, to almost forty thousand people – making Limerick Ireland's fourth largest city. The city's economy was disproportionately dominated by industries engaged in food processing: Cleeve's Creamery, four large bacon curing factories and distilling. Apart from those, the only other major employers were the Limerick Clothing Factory and O'Callaghan's Tannery.

World War One brought higher prices and increased prosperity to Ireland's farmers. In turn, that meant increased wealth for the thousands of pig-buyers and cattle-dealers who acted as the middle men in the booming trade of exporting live animals to feed Britain's citizens and armed forces. Bankers' deposits and profits were boosted by farmers' savings and retailers too grew wealthy from farm spending. But the composition of Limerick's industry meant that the city derived little direct economic benefit from War work. The Clothing Factory had been getting military contracts since before the War but there were no major engineering or munitions works that would have allowed the city to really cash in on the War effort. Irish munitions works always stood in danger from extreme nationalist raids. In addition, there were the additional costs and the U Boat hazards of the sea journey to Britain. Eventually, after much local agitation, Limerick got a small share of the munitions work done in Ireland. Overall, though, there was little reason for the Government to give additional War contracts to Limerick firms, despite the frequent pleas of the city's business community.

The War also dealt a heavy blow to Limerick port. The city's geographical location, facing Westwards to the Atlantic, meant that sea journeys from there to Britain were longer and more hazardous than from ports on the East coast. Strategic and economic reasons dictated a change to ports that were nearer to Britain and faced the shorter journeys and relatively safer waters of the Irish Sea. The result was a calamitous decline in traffic through Limerick port.

The port faced other problems. In 1916, the coal importers estimated that a six hundred to seven hundred tons ship could be unloaded in Belfast in five to seven hours or in ten to twelve hours in Cork, but it took two to three days in Limerick. The employers blamed the dock labourers and their union for this state of affairs. The port was under-capitalised and unmechanised. There was no rail extension to the docks nor were there any cranes. Throughout the War years, the dockers fought a rear-guard action against the introduction of mechanisation in a vain effort to arrest a declining number of jobs. By 1917, they had reached agreement on the introduction of cranes with buckets, but when the employers tried to introduce 'grab' cranes early in 1918, these were dumped in the River Shannon.

The overall poor economic conditions in the city, even in the War years, meant daily lives of abject poverty and misery for many Limerick people. In 1916, a local priest claimed that nearly forty per cent of the population lived in one or two rooms, ten times the proportion in Belfast or five times that of Derry. Many Limerick workers faced low wages, lack of permanent jobs, emigration, ill health, poor housing and high rents.

The Limerick Trades and Labour Council was established in May 1905 – some time after similar Irish cities – to cater almost exclusively for skilled workers. Pressure to form a Council had come from the Irish TUC who had complained that Limerick had failed to manage a respectable representation even once a year at the Congress. Sometime later, a Federated Labour Council was formed to look after the interests of semi-skilled and unskilled workers. The Trades Council was dominated by men whose sole concern seemed to be the protection of their craft status and privileges. They were pre-occupied with policies on maintaining apprenticeship rules, strict ratios of journeymen to apprentices and opposition to mechanisation or other innovations that might weaken their position in the market place.

Even before the Trades Council was founded, the trade unions had been active in local politics but in a sporadic and uncoordinated way. They confined themselves largely to endorsing sympathetic election candidates. These people generally supported the unions on issues like the direct employment by Limerick Corporation of its own building workers or an insistence on the use of trade union labour in public contracts given to private employers.

Many members of the Trades Council were fairly suspicious of the new politics emanating from 'advanced' trade union elements in Dublin, particularly after the Irish TUC decision of 1912 to form an Irish Labour Party. In 1916 John Cronin, who later led the Soviet, was prepared to characterise the Dublin leadership as a 'socialist clique' and feared that 'the movement was run entirely by people who never worked at any trade or labour or were at present not following any trade or labour.'

Nevertheless, some trade union activists in Limerick had been influenced by the events of the 1913 Lock Out in Dublin, by Connolly's writings and by his part in the 1916 Rising. James Larkin, speaking at the 1914 Irish Trade Union Congress paid special tribute to the Limerick Pork Butchers who had 'sent more every week in proportion to their strength than any other union' in assisting the locked-out workers. In July 1914, an attempt to establish a branch of the Irish Transport and General Workers' Union (ITGWU) in Limerick had 'completely failed', according to a police report. However, the union finally arrived in September 1917, later than in other cities and towns.

Prior to the advent of the ITGWU there had been friendly relations between the conservative leaders of the craft trade unions and the local Catholic bishop and clergy, with the clerics keen to point the workers away from Socialism and towards 'Christian Social Reform'. Local clergy were frequently allowed or invited to intervene in trade union matters and industrial disputes. Members of the clergy attended meetings of Limerick United Trades and Labour Council and were invited to speak at their public events. When the Director of the Redemptorist Arch Confraternity of the Holy Family, Rev. Dr. Bernard Hackett, was appointed Bishop of Waterford and Lismore, LUTLC passed a motion congratulating him and another was passed expressing 'deep sorrow on the lamented death of our esteemed Bishop, Most Rev. Dr. O'Dwyer, whose loss to the labour movement cannot be replaced'.

Between 1916 and 1919 the Catholic clergy organised more than one series of lectures in a campaign to educate workers on the dangers of socialism. During one of the lectures in 1917, Timothy Smiddy, Professor of Economics at University College Cork, warned that 'the spirit of syndicalism had lately crept into labour struggles… and this matter would have to be dealt with after the war'.

The arrival of the radicalising ITGWU transformed the level of trade union organisation among workers, particularly among the unskilled, and was a catalyst for a wave of working-class militancy that swept across the city and county from 1917 to 1922 – the Limerick Soviet being its highest point. Almost every trade union was involved in industrial conflicts during that time. At a Catholic Truth Society conference in October 1917, Fr. Dwane, the Administrator of Saint Michael's Parish in Limerick, noted that 'a cyclone of revolutionary ideas was passing over the world shaking governments and thrones'.

MJ O'Connor – a skilled tradesman, from Tralee, county Kerry – arrived in Limerick as a full-time ITGWU organiser in September 1917 and began organising timber yard workers into the union. A significant breakthrough was the recruitment, within a month, of the workforce employed in Cleeve's Condensed Milk Company of Ireland. Munitions workers followed and the women workers in the Shannon Laundry and Cleeve's Condensed Milk Factory joined and won pay increases. By the end of October, local newspapers had reported that 'A very large number of workers – both men and women – have joined the Limerick branch of the ITGWU'.

Further organisational gains and wage increases followed quickly in other employments and the union lent its support to other unions and societies pursuing higher pay and better working conditions, notably in Limerick docks. Militancy continued at an elevated level throughout 1918 with ITGWU-led strikes in, for example, the docks, Spaight's Hardware in Henry Street, the forage contractors JJ Foleys, Clunes Tobacco Company, the Gas Works and O'Callaghan's Tannery. By the end of that year, there were four ITGWU branches in the city and nineteen in the county. The police estimated that the union had 3,433 members – a significant proportion of them women – in Limerick and was rivalling Sinn Féin in membership and influence.

MJ O'Connor developed a good working relationship with the Secretary of the LUTLC, Ben Dineen, and the Trades Council accepted the ITGWU No.1 Limerick Branch into affiliation in August 1918. The Trades Council began to evolve rapidly from being a localised, relatively conservative, craft-dominated body into a broadly-based, well-organised movement that would later lead the city in a time of crisis and dare to challenge the Government.

In October 1917, John (Jack) Dowling – better known in Limerick as Seán – replaced O'Connor as Limerick organiser after the latter left to take up a position as General Secretary of the Irish Automobile Drivers' and Mechanics' Union. Dowling had moved to Limerick in 1915, having been forced out of his native Cobh, county Cork, by an exclusion order made under the Defence of the Realm Act. Just before the 1916 Rising, Dowling had pleaded with James Connolly to allow him to participate, but instead, Connolly ordered him to 'Go down to the Galtees and organise workers into the union'. He followed Connolly's directive with enthusiasm. His organisational work brought him to towns in the Midlands like Tullamore and Portarlington and saw him arrested and brought to Mountjoy Prison. He was joined in Limerick by another Organiser, Seamus O'Brien. John Dowling became a pivotal figure in the Limerick Soviet and in the militant events that followed it in county Limerick and the rest of Munster.

Dowling had worked as a fitter in the naval dockyard in Haulbowline and the proximity of Cobh to the naval dockyard was probably a factor in the official thinking behind his exclusion order, since safeguarding of docks was one of the primary purposes of the Act. He was an active trade unionist and a convinced socialist from his youth. Dowling had been a member of James Connolly's Irish Socialist Republican Party and was among those who welcomed him home from his time in the United States. Together, they addressed a huge crowd in Daunt's Square, Cork, in July 1910. They toured the country together promoting the newly established Socialist Party of Ireland and the Irish Transport and General Workers' Union. As part of that recruitment drive, Connolly visited Cobh in March 1911 but was attacked with bricks, bottles and stones by a mob of conservative nationalists. Sometime later, however, a branch of the union was established.

Spurred by the example and recruitment successes of the ITGWU, the Trades Council, in February 1918, welcomed its first visit by women delegates – Mrs. P Curran, Organiser, Amalgamated Society of Tailors and Tailoresses Miss J Fowler, Organiser, the Women Workers' Federation. Ben Dinneen recorded in the Council Minute Book that 'Both ladies received a hearty welcome from delegates and spoke at some length on the necessity for better organisation among women'. A few months later, in August, the Council welcomed women delegates from the ITGWU.

While 1918 had seen greatly heightened ITGWU militancy, the union stepped up its activity even further in the early months of 1919 in both Limerick city and county. There was a veritable litany of strikes – women workers in the Model Laundry, salmon fishermen in Parteen, as well as other strikes in Kilmallock, Askeaton, Templeglantine, Newcastle West and Drombana. Other unions had become more active as well, with strikes among the asylum workers, drapers' assistants in McBirney's and coachbuilders. The increased levels of organisation and activity led to the appointment of a further ITGWU organiser, Michael O'Donoghue in February 1919.

The increased trade union activity drew a negative reaction from the Catholic clergy and from some nationalist elements. Ironically, only a week before the Soviet began, the newspaper *'Ár nÉire'* ('Our Ireland'), which was moving away from the Irish Parliamentary Party towards Sinn Féin, posed the question: 'Can any sane man advocate the handing over of, say, Limerick or Cork to the local Trades Council? A Soviet, as I understand it, is a Council of the local workers exercising political and economic power. Anyone who knows anything of the inner state of Irish Labour must realise how uneducated and narrow-minded and incompetent the workers are as yet'.

Since October 1917 another development had considerably sharpened the workers' trade union and political responses. This was the appearance of Limerick's first working-class newspaper, *'The Bottom Dog'*. On 20 October, the first issue outlined the *'Dog's'* aim: 'He believes in the truth of the old saying that 'Every dog has his day', but at the same time he must assert that the Bottom Dog's day appears to be a long way off, shrouded in the misty future. The work at hand then – hastening the day of the Bottom Dog.' The paper defined the 'Bottom Dog' as the oppressed – whether nation, class or sex. The paper strongly backed the Transport Union, saying that before its arrival the ordinary labourer had been 'down in the dust simply for the want of unity and organisation.' It insisted the 'Bottom Dog' would only come into his own when every worker, male and female, was thoroughly organised.

For the first time, the *'Bottom Dog'* brought together the forces of industrial trade unionism and radical elements among the craft unions. It was written and circulated by prominent members of Limerick United Trades and Labour Council. Ben Dineen, a baker, was the paper's editor and it could call on the services of sympathetic compositors and typographers. In November 1918, thirty-nine years old Dineen, his wife and two of his young children, succumbed to the ravages of the European-wide influenza. Up to his death, a remarkable forty-eight editions of the paper had been published, though there is evidence that the 'Dog' may have limped on for one or two more editions after the editor's death.

The editorial policy of the *'Bottom Dog'* was a curious mixture. It had an extraordinarily hazy concept of socialism, based more on practical and pragmatic opposition to bad social conditions than on any thought-out theoretical position. The paper veered frequently from advocating a syndicalist policy of taking power through industrial action to advocating the need for a socialist political party. Mixed in with this was a strong ration of nationalism, some Catholic piety, a bigoted sectarian attitude towards Protestants, some anti-Semitism and an emphasis on local Limerick issues to the virtual exclusion of earth-shaking events like the Great War or the Bolshevik Revolution.

It would be wrong to overemphasise the *'Bottom Dog's'* influence on events in Limerick. Yet its witty, tabloid-style of journalism made it popular and widely-read, even in the rural areas of the county, as the ITGWU spread its membership during 1918. Given the paper's editorial content, it could not be said to have helped develop a socialist consciousness among Limerick workers. Yet, the constant and uncompromising references to bad housing, low pay and poor working conditions must have heightened some form of radical consciousness in the city.

However, co-operation in the production of the *'Bottom Dog'* was not enough to prevent the clashes with the craft unions over 'who represents whom' that were a hallmark of the growth of the ITGWU elsewhere. In May 1918, the Delegate Board of the Mechanics' Institute tried to reduce the influence of the ITGWU and the *'Bottom Dog'* by starting a second paper, *'The Worker'*. It lacked the *'Dog's'* political and industrial bite and concentrated instead on faithful reporting of the Trades Council and its affiliates. The move could be interpreted as an attempt to reduce the influence of the *'Bottom Dog'* and the ITGWU.

Limerick Workers celebrated Labour Day for the first time ever in 1918. On Sunday, 5 May an estimated ten to fifteen thousand workers marched through the city streets in response to a call from the Trades Council. The demonstration ended with speeches from eighteen speakers standing on three platforms at the Markets' Field, where the assembled workers passed a resolution, to the sound of a trumpet. Among the speakers was Cathal O'Shannon, a senior official of the ITGWU and a close associate of James Connolly.

The first part of the resolution showed where some Limerick workers were deriving their inspiration. It read: 'That we the workers of Limerick assembled, extend fraternal greetings to the workers of all countries, paying particular attention to our Russian comrades who have waged such a magnificent struggle for their social and political emancipation.' The next section emphasised the claim for Irish independence and the right of self-determination and re-affirmed opposition to conscription. Thus, the resolution carried a socialist and republican import that presaged the attitudes later of many of the participants in the Limerick Soviet.

The resolution was drafted by the radical ITGWU Organiser, John Dowling. It was proposed by his ITGWU colleague, MJ O'Connor, and seconded by Michael Keyes, of the Railwaymen's' Union, who said Limerick had the reputation of being one of the best organised Labour centres in the country. He declared: We will no longer approach our employers as cringing slaves but as freemen and demand our rights'. The baker, Ben Dineen, Secretary of the Trades Council, said the national strike against conscription, less than a fortnight previously, had shown that 'Labour was supreme to all parties.' Limerick, he said, had been the first city in Ireland to put forth the propaganda of downing tools against conscription, a boast that was greeted with cheers. Robert O'Connor said he supposed they would be called Bolsheviks because they extended greetings to the Russian workers but Irishmen could claim that, as a small nation, they had put backbone into any part of the world they were in. Again, this comment was met with cheers.

The influence and standing of the Trades Council may also be judged from the fact that its meetings were regularly reported extensively in the local papers. A clue as to how the Council stood on the broad issue of workers taking control through a general strike may be gleaned from the minutes of a Council discussion on the revised draft constitution of the combined Irish Labour Party and Trade Union Congress, which had been circulated to affiliated bodies. The draft 1918 constitution renamed the movement to emphasise that the political and trade union elements were united in the one movement, a classical syndicalist position. It aimed to recover the nation's wealth and to win for workers, collectively, the ownership and control of the whole produce of their labour. Industry and services would be democratically managed and controlled by the whole body of workers involved, both manual and mental. In the aims and methods, it listed industrial and social organisation ahead of political. The Limerick Council agreed to the name and objects as set out and quibbled only about details of how individual membership and trade union corporate membership of the Congress-Party could be reconciled.

The stirrings of nationalism also found a response in Limerick. In 1917 and 1918 two new papers published in the city reflected this. These were the devoutly Catholic publication *'The Factionist'* and *'The Soldier Hunter'*. The first issue of the *'Soldier Hunter'* in February 1918 made it clear that it would be a weekly watch-dog against the moral corruption of the young women of Limerick by the British garrison. 'We are out to clean up the town. Social Hygiene, if you will, is our objective', the paper thundered. The paper listed many streets on the outskirts of Limerick which, it claimed, were 'dens of infamy where immorality stalks naked and unabashed.'

The *'Soldier Hunter'* realised that the clergy had been doing 'police work as well as priest's work' and this would have to be supplemented by tougher tactics. The paper carried a plaintive letter from Father Dwane, Administrator of Saint Michael's Parish, complaining about a military chaplain who had been assaulted by a Welsh Fusilier when he had sought 'to protect a girl of sixteen years of age against the lustful passion of this low clodhopper.'

Another report told of a 'khaki-clad demon' who had tried to seduce a young girl by 'offering her drugged chocolates.'

Small, local papers of this kind became a powerful weapon in the propaganda war between Sinn Féin and the Government. Early in 1917, the Intelligence Officer for the Southern Military District had commented: 'A determined effort is being made to spread extremist ideas by means of so-called newspapers, containing no current news, which circulate largely throughout the district... Papers of this kind... do an immense amount of harm among the semi-educated people who are their readers, and who notice the Government do not interfere with them or contradict their misstatements.'

But the real turning point in the development of separatist politics locally was the release of the 1916 Rising internees and the lifting of martial law on 21 January 1917. Those decisions released to Limerick, as to other parts of the country, men who had become hardened rather than embittered and who were determined to organise for a final push to freedom. Within a month, the first Sinn Féin clubs were formed in the county. In June, an estimated seven thousand people turned out to hear Michael Collins, the military and intelligence genius of the coming revolution, address a public meeting. In November, twelve thousand people welcomed home the Republican hunger strikers, much more than had received the released internees almost a year previously. Membership of Sinn Féin and the Volunteers in Limerick increased in line with the changing circumstances. At the end of June 1917, Sinn Féin had 1,661 members and the Volunteers had 943. By January 1919 there were over 4,600 Sinn Féin members and more than 2,600 Volunteers.

Early in 1918, Sinn Féin and the Trades Council became allies in an agitation to prevent the live export of pigs to Britain because of the resultant loss of processing jobs in the city. With a capacity to kill up to fifteen thousand pigs a week, the city's factories were getting only two thousand. British buyers, with good contracts to fill, were prepared to pay well over the official recommended price and live exports of pigs were booming.

The Conscription Crisis of April 1918 saw Limerick Trades Council play the same leading role locally as the Irish TUC was doing nationally. After the Government's intentions were announced, Limerick was the only Trades Council to actually call for a general strike. The call came the day after the Trades Council had led a demonstration of about ten thousand people, including Sinn Féiners and Irish Party members, against conscription. They marched behind a banner with the slogan 'Death Before Conscription' and a portrait of James Connolly. Even the banks were closed and the *'Bottom Dog'* claimed that only two shops and two workers defied the strike call.

In the 1918 Mayoral election, Alphonsus O'Mara – a convert from the Irish Parliamentary Party and Home Rule – was elected as the first Sinn Féin Mayor of Limerick, replacing the Unionist sympathiser, Sir Stephen Quin. O'Mara refused to take an Oath of Allegiance to the Crown and suggested that there might be armed opposition to conscription. Shortly after his election, the Limerick Branch of the Irish Post Office Clerks' Association held a public meeting to protest against the dismissal from his job of their Chairman, Robert Byrne, and the new Mayor shared a platform with the Trades Council to denounce what he called 'star chamber' methods.

1919 saw a strengthening of opposition to the Government and further support for separatism in Limerick. In his confidential monthly report to Dublin Castle, for January, County Inspector Yates of the RIC reported that the outward state of the city and county was peaceable but under the surface it was unsettled and uncertain. There was a strong undercurrent of discontent and disloyalty and the outlook for the future was not good. The influence of the ITGWU was spreading, according to Yates. The following month, February, after several strikes organised by the ITGWU, he was of the opinion that the union was rather overshadowing the active local Sinn Féin clubs. On Saint Patrick's Day, 1919, in Adare, county Limerick, the closeness of the two seditious forces was underlined by a joint meeting of Sinn Féin and the ITGWU addressed by a Catholic curate and a union organiser. While the police reported a static membership for the Volunteers and a small increase in Sinn Féin numbers, the number of ITGWU branches increased from fifteen to twenty-three, and membership in the city and county totalled over three thousand eight hundred.

Limerick had remained true to its history and was organised and ready to write a new chapter.

CHAPTER ELEVEN

<u>Shoulder to Shoulder</u>

'Should it come to a test in Ireland... between those who stood
for the Irish Nation and those who stood for foreign rule, the
greatest civil asset in the hand of the Irish Nation for use in
the struggle would be the control of the Irish docks, shipping,
railways and production by unions that gave sole allegiance to
Ireland.'
— *James Connolly, 'The Workers' Republic', 22 January 1916*

Dublin Castle was aware of the close link – indeed, often the overlapping of membership – between the trade unions and Sinn Féin. Through the eyes and ears of its police force, the Royal Irish Constabulary, the British administration kept a close watch on trade union activities. The monthly reports to Dublin from County Inspectors regularly listed the ITGWU among the eleven 'political' organisations monitored for their number of branches, membership and level of activity. This put the union under the same degree of suspicion and observation as organisations like Sinn Féin, the Volunteers, the Gaelic Athletic Association and the Irish language movement, the Gaelic League.

In his annual report for 1918, the Inspector General of the Royal Irish Constabulary commented that the Irish Transport and General Workers' Union represented the 'Socialist and Labour wing of the Irish revolutionary movement'. The I-G noted that in March there had been widespread political unrest, which showed no sign of abatement. Trade was good, the report noted, but the inflation caused by War prices was continuing and it was leading to Labour discontent.

The Inspector-General said Labour organisation was of comparatively recent growth but the ITGWU had spread its branches everywhere and all classes of people were enrolled in it. He recorded strikes in eighteen counties, with nearly all the strikers belonging to the labouring class and demanding wages of forty to fifty shillings a week. There were few large employers in country districts and such wages would be impossible to meet in many cases. At the same time, the I-G conceded, the enormous prices charged by the farmers and shopkeepers during the War made the demand seem less unreasonable than it looked.

In March 1919, the month preceding the Limerick Soviet, the Inspector-General sent a report marked 'Secret' and 'Urgent' to the Chief Secretary for Ireland, Ian Macpherson MP. It warned that in the prevailing discontent, if the 'extremists' decided to take Independent action, they could 'rely to a considerable extent' on the co-operation of Labour organisations and 'they would certainly find a large body of fanatical Irish volunteers through the country, ready to do their bidding. 'Ireland', the Inspector-General warned, 'is unquestionably in a highly inflammable condition, and in my opinion at no time was there more urgent necessity for the presence of an overpowering military force.'

The Castle's worries about Labour involvement in the independence movement were well-founded. James Connolly, the Commandant-General of the 1916 Rising had led the ITGWU after Big Jim Larkin's departure for the United States in 1914, in the wake of the 1913 Dublin Lockout. Apart from the practical example of his life and death, Connolly left behind a body of political writings that strongly influenced trade union aims and the methods to be used in attaining those aims. Many Labour people, apart from Connolly, had been prominent in the Rising, many more were active in Gaelic cultural bodies and activities like the Gaelic League or the Gaelic Athletic Association. Like many others, they were profoundly affected by the aftermath of the Easter Rising.

Under Connolly's influence, Irish Labour and trade unionism was strongly syndicalist in its policies and attitudes. In simple terms, syndicalism was a Socialist philosophy that stressed a close connection between workers' industrial strength – exercised through trade unions – and the political struggle for the achievement of Socialism. Syndicalism found its earliest organised expression in France, as a reaction to the failure of reformist, Socialist political leaders to make gains commensurate with their voting strength in parliament. James Connolly had been particularly influenced by this analysis during his spell in the United States where he encountered it as an organiser for the pre-eminently syndicalist trade union, the Industrial Workers of the World.

According to syndicalist theory, the workers' industrial muscle would underpin the political advances, using major strikes in pursuit of political aims. Ultimately, a general strike would paralyse the existing capitalist system and result in the workers taking over the state. The workers' industrial organisations, the trade unions, would then form the basis for governing the new commonwealth.

Connolly's unique application of syndicalism to Irish conditions was to argue that the struggle for socialism and national independence from Britain were inseparable. 'The cause of Ireland is the cause of Labour, and the cause of Labour is the cause of Ireland', he wrote. In his view, trade union power could therefore properly be harnessed in furtherance of the aim of independence. In January 1916, Connolly wrote in the newspaper '*The Workers' Republic*': 'Should it come to a test in Ireland... between those who stood for the Irish Nation and those who stood for foreign rule, the greatest civil asset in the hand of the Irish nation for use in the struggle would be the control of the Irish docks, shipping, railways and production by unions that gave sole allegiance to Ireland'. Here, clearly stated, was his synthesis of classical syndicalism and nationalism. The Irish Trade Union Congress plan for major strikes against conscription in 1918 was a clear example of the fusion of political aims with trade union organisation and methods.

Connolly saw Irish nationalism as the essential foundation for social and economic progress and the Irish revolution would have to be not nationalist merely but socialist as well. He developed close personal ties with leaders of the separatist Volunteers, like Pearse, MacDonagh, Clarke and MacDiarmada. In the '*Workers' Republic*' newspaper, he strongly advocated an insurrection and published articles on revolutionary warfare in other countries. He was severely critical of the dilatory attitude of the Volunteer leadership, something they resented greatly.

Very early in 1916 Connolly spent three days in a secret meeting with the leaders of the Irish Republican Brotherhood, being briefed on their plans for a Rising. After hearing the plans for an early insurrection, to take advantage of Britain's difficulties in the Great War, Connolly agreed to make available the forces of the workers' Citizen Army. He was appointed Commandant-General of the Dublin forces and became a member of the Brotherhood's Military Council. On Easter Monday 1916, the Council's seven members were declared to be the Provisional Government of the Irish Republic. Indeed, the proclamation of the Republic was printed in the basement of Liberty Hall, the ITGWU headquarters, under an armed guard of the Irish Citizen Army, an organisation founded during the Great Dublin Lock Out of 1913 to defend workers from police attacks.

Connolly's analysis was jealously safeguarded by his disciple and successor as General Secretary of the ITGWU, William O'Brien, notably in his Presidential address to the 1918 Trade Union Congress in Waterford. In 1918, as well, the combined Party-Congress adopted a new name – the Irish Labour Party and Trade Union Congress – and a new constitution that underlined its formal commitment, at least, to syndicalist thinking. Article 2(c) of the new constitution pledged to secure 'the democratic management and control of all industries and services by the whole body of workers, manual and mental, engaged therein... '

While the Labour 'wing' of the national movement prospered, the political element was enjoying success too. In the General Election of December 1918 to the Westminster Parliament, Labour stood to one side. Seventy-three Irish constituencies – out of one hundred and five – returned Sinn Féin Members of Parliament, committed to an independent Irish Republic. Twenty-six Unionists were returned and six members of the Irish Parliamentary, though four of those were returned as a result of a pre-election pact with Sinn Féin in some Ulster constituencies. In votes, Sinn Féin won just under half the votes cast, with more than 485,000 votes compared with slightly over 277,000 for the Irish Party.

The foundation of Sinn Féin by Arthur Griffith, in 1905, represented a development of a new kind of nationalism in Ireland. Since 1870, leaders of Irish nationalism had assumed the validity of the Act of Union of Great Britain and Ireland and had organised their strategy and tactics largely within the framework of the Westminster Parliament. Sinn Féin, instead, advocated that the elected Members for Ireland should assemble in Dublin and initiate a national programme of economic and social reform. The essence of that programme was to be Irish economic self-reliance and political self-determination – summed up in the movement's name: Sinn Féin, 'Ourselves Alone'. Instead of taking their seats in London, the Sinn Féin MPs set up a separatist Republican parliament – Dáil Éireann – in Dublin on 21 January 1919. Out of the seventy-three members elected, only twenty-six could attend the opening session – the rest were in Prison.

In the December 1918 General Election, the British electorate had endorsed a measure of Home Rule for Ireland and with that, had tried to put Irish affairs to the back of their mind. War weary as they were, the establishment of the Dáil caused barely a ripple in Britain. The '*Times*' Irish correspondent scoffed at what he termed the 'stage play at the Mansion House', where earlier that morning there had been a 'blaze of Union Jacks' at a luncheon to welcome home four hundred repatriated prisoners of war, members of the Royal Dublin Fusiliers. Few in Britain heeded the '*Daily News*' warning that it was 'very easy to laugh at the Sinn Féin Parliament, but it is not so certain that it is wise.'

The establishment of a secessionist Parliament was a sophisticated development in tactics by the independence movement. The Dáil combined the new ideas of civil resistance with the old ideal of physical rebellion. Its Address to the Free Nations of the World declared that 'a state of war existed', that could not end 'until Ireland is definitely evacuated by the armed forces of England'. This was effectively a declaration of war and it assumed more propaganda importance later, being looked to as the source of democratic backing for the armed struggle against Britain. The Democratic Programme of the First Dáil Éireann – its statement of political and economic aspirations – was Left-wing in tone, reflecting the strength of Labour's position at the time.

Prior to the first meeting of the Dáil, there were contacts between prominent Dáil members and Labour leaders with a view to drafting some sort of social programme. It is clear from the exhaustively kept diary of the Labour leader, William O'Brien, that Labour's entitlement to representation at the post-War International Labour and Socialist Conference, held at Berne in February *1919,* loomed large in the background contacts on the Democratic Programme. On New Year's Day 1919, O'Brien met Richard Mulcahy, the Dáil member who later formally proposed the adoption of the Programme and they discussed the Berne Socialist Conference. Within a fortnight, there were two other meetings of Labour and Sinn Féin leaders at which Berne and the forthcoming opening of the Dáil were discussed. At the second of these meetings, it appears the Labour leaders submitted a document and a Dáil committee was set up to draft a social programme in consultation with Labour. On the Labour side, Tom Johnson was involved in drafting and the key person on the Dáil side was Harry Boland, a regular contact between Sinn Féin and Labour. According to Sean T O'Kelly, a key organiser of the Dáil's proposed public sitting, Boland arrived on the night before the ceremonial opening with only a bundle of rough notes, received from Labour friends like Johnson and William O'Brien. The content of the notes aroused fierce controversy. Close to midnight, O'Kelly says he was given a free hand to draft the Programme as he alone wished and he worked through the night to have it ready for the following day.

O'Kelly's final draft omitted references to eliminating 'the class in society which lives upon the wealth produced by the workers of the nation but gives no useful social service in return...' Nevertheless, the Democratic Programme, in its final form, was far from being a total reflection of Sinn Féin's rather conservative economic and social thinking. It declared that the nation's sovereignty extended to all its material possessions, its soil and resources, all the wealth and wealth-producing processes. The right of private property was subordinate to the public right and, in return for willing service, every citizen had a right to an adequate share of the produce of the nation's labour. It was to be the government's first duty to provide for the physical, mental and spiritual well-being of children, 'to ensure that no child shall suffer hunger or cold from lack of food, clothing or shelter, that all shall be provided with ample means and facilities requisite for the education and training of free citizens of a free nation'.

The main purpose of adopting the Programme seems to have been to strengthen Irish Labour's hand in seeking full representation at the Berne conference. Labour could argue that although they did not hold parliamentary seats, the new separatist assembly was committed to a broadly socialist programme. In turn, as later events would prove correct, the Dáil could anticipate recognition for the Irish claim to self-determination from an important international forum. And there may have been a belief in some Sinn Féin and IRB circles that Labour should receive a tangible political reward for standing aside in the Election that, effectively, produced the first Dáil.

To an extent, Labour's eventual refusal to participate in the December 1918 General Election reflected its espousal of industrial over political or parliamentary methods of action. Ironically, Connolly, the father of Irish syndicalism, had departed from this doctrine in the spring of 1916 when he embraced the revolutionary political project of the Easter Rising. Indeed, the refusal to stand Labour candidates in the 1918 election served to reflect and reinforce the movement's predisposition towards syndicalist methods which prioritised the gaining of political through industrial strength. From beginning to end, the year 1919 saw a wave of Labour militancy wash over Ireland from North to South. Apart from the great Belfast strike of January 1919, there were strikes early in the year by building workers in Limerick, shipyard workers in Derry, asylum workers in Monaghan and strikes by farm labourers in counties Kildare, Meath and Tipperary – sometimes involving violent clashes with the police and non-union labourers.

Thus, with the formal opening of Dáil Éireann on 21 January, the year 1919 began with the lines of battle more clearly drawn than at any time previously. Home Rule was gone from the agenda, the only remaining item was a Republic. At the same time, violence was emerging more strongly as a tactic. On the day the Dáil formally met for the first time, IRA members attacked and killed two members of the RIC at Soloheadbeg, in county Tipperary. By early 1919, one of the leaders of the Soloheadbeg attack, Dan Breen, had no doubt about what form the coming struggle should take. Breen believed political campaigns, notably the General Election of 1918, had 'softened' many Republicans. 'Many had ceased to be soldiers and had become politicians. There was a danger of disintegration, a danger which had been growing since the threat of conscription disappeared a few months earlier. I was convinced that some sort of action was absolutely necessary'.

On 31 January 1919, the shooting war was given added impetus by a directive issued in the Volunteer paper, *'An tÓglach'* ('The Volunteer'). The Volunteers were reminded of the Dáil's declaration of a state of war, to last until there was a British military evacuation of Ireland. That state of war justified the Volunteers in treating the police and army as invaders. The authority of the nation was behind them, the editorial declared, embodied in the lawfully constituted authority of the Dáil. The Dáil, it said, was not just a group of 'militarists' or 'extremists' but 'the accredited representatives of the Irish people met in solemn session'. Every Volunteer, it concluded, had the legal and moral right to use 'all legitimate methods of warfare' against the army and police. From the end of January 1919, attacks on the RIC and British Army throughout the country increased in frequency and ferocity. By the end of the year, fourteen policemen and soldiers had been killed in attacks.

Dan Breen's worries reflected the concern of Michael Collins, now Adjutant General and Director of Organisation of the revived and rapidly growing Volunteers. All through 1918, Collins had complained that Sinn Féin seemed to lack 'direction' and that those who 'ought to' have been 'directing' were too 'lax' and did not spend enough time at the party's headquarters, 6 Harcourt Street in Dublin. This was despite the fact that in October 1917, the two bodies had been brought closer by the election as President of Sinn Féin of the man who was already leader of the Volunteers, Eamon de Valera.

In September 1918, *'An tÓglach'* had grimly predicted the abandonment of political methods and passive resistance. By May 1919, Collins was complaining of an intolerable position where the policy seemed to be to 'squeeze out anyone who was tainted with strong fighting ideas'. From June 1919 onwards, Collins intensified his military campaign, especially against the British detective and intelligence agencies in Dublin. By August of that year, the Dáil had passed a resolution insisting that the IRA take a formal oath of allegiance to 'the Irish Republic and the Dáil'.

The increasingly widespread sympathy with the separatist aim might never have developed to the extent that it did but for the attitude of the British Government in the years after the 1916 Rising. This has been aptly described as by the historian Charles Townshend as one of 'mild coercion – repression too weak to root out opposition but provocative enough to nurture it'. After the 1916 Rising, the changes in the British administration in Ireland were ones of personnel rather than structure. Martial law was imposed for a few months after the Rising, but in November 1916, the Commander in Chief for Ireland, General Sir John Maxwell, was recalled to Britain and replaced. The police force was split between the Dublin Metropolitan Police and, for the rest of the country, the Royal Irish Constabulary. At one time, counting military services, there were seven Independent intelligence services operating, with varying degrees of effectiveness. By 1917, the RIC was short fourteen hundred members on its establishment of over 10,700 and morale was low.

After the simultaneous enactment and suspension of the Home Rule Act in September 1914, the British government's efforts to resolve its Irish political problems were spasmodic and half-hearted. They were motivated more by the aim of eliminating any problems at Britain's backdoor and thus freeing resources for the Great War, than by any desire to respond to the increasing Irish nationalist clamour. Within weeks of the 1916 Rising, the Prime Minister, Herbert Asquith, asked his then Minister of Munitions, David Lloyd George, to initiate fresh negotiations with the leaders of Irish opinion – John Redmond for the Nationalists and Sir Edward Carson for the Ulster Unionists. Lloyd George managed to get Redmond to agree to the temporary exclusion of Ulster's six North Eastern counties from a Home Rule parliament that would govern the rest of Ireland. Pro-Unionist members of the Cabinet, fearing that all of Ulster might eventually be brought in under the proposed Dublin parliament, torpedoed this plan from within.

By May 1917, Lloyd George had become Prime Minister and he offered Redmond two alternative proposals to settle the Irish question. One was the application of the 1914 Home Rule Act but with a five-year exclusion of Loyalist Ulster. The second was an Irish Convention, representing all shades of opinion, to devise a scheme of self-government. Redmond accepted the second option and the Convention began its deliberations in July 1917. Sinn Féin's refusal to attend the Convention rendered it essentially an unrepresentative talking-shop. It sat until May 1918 and produced a report in which there was little substantial agreement between the participants.

In March 1918, Field-Marshal Viscount French was appointed Lord Lieutenant with a mandate to enforce conscription and get tougher with separatism. On May 17, the majority of Sinn Féin leaders were taken in a series of mass arrests, but this served only to increase the influence of the militarist-orientated hard-liners in Sinn Féin.

On the very last day of 1918, a strongly pro-Unionist member of the British Cabinet, Walter Long, Secretary of State for the Colonies, wrote this perceptive summary of how matters stood: 'I have watched the rise and fall of every political party in Ireland for the last forty years, and I think that the present movement is much the most difficult and dangerous of any the Government has had to deal with and for this reason. Their leaders are brave and fanatical and do not fear imprisonment or death; they are not to be influenced by private negotiations with Bishops or Priests, or captured by getting the patronage of appointments, which has been the favourite instrument of the Irish Government since 1905. Neither do they care a straw for the press. It is a fair and square fight between the Irish Government and Sinn Féin as to who is going to govern the country.'

On 10 January 1919, French was replaced as Lord Lieutenant by the Scottish born Liberal, Ian Macpherson. Macpherson favoured Home Rule for Ireland and he made some conciliatory moves initially but he was soon shocked into a stronger 'law and order' stance by the daunting challenge of the Limerick Soviet and then by the rising tide of IRA violence.

CHAPTER TWELVE

<u>Labour and Liberty</u>

'When we wanted the help of Labour against conscription, Labour gave it to us (cheers).
When we wanted the help of Labour in Berne, Labour gave it to us and got Ireland
recognised as a distinct nation (cheers). When we wanted Labour to stand down at the
election, and not divide us, but that we should stand forsworn against the enemy, Labour
fell in with us. I say Labour deserves well of the Irish people: The Labour man deserves the
best the country can give cheers).'

Eamon de Valera, Presidential Address to the Sinn Fein Ard Fheis, 7 April 1919

The years 1917 to 1919 saw Europe in a red, revolutionary turmoil. The Bolshevik October Revolution in Russia and the defeat of Germany and the Central European Powers had broken the old moulds with a vengeance. In an editorial on 7 April 1919, the *'Irish Times'* summed up the situation aptly: 'The mind of the world is still torn between war and peace.' During that month of April, Europe held its breath as the old order in Germany, in particular, reeled under a succession of Bolshevik victories. In Munich, Bavaria was declared a Soviet Republic. There were general strikes or soviets in Dusseldorf, Augsburg, Würzburg and Regensburg. Thirty-eight thousand Ruhr miners went on strike, there was a general strike in the Krupp's engineering company and the strike movement was said to be spreading. The April newspapers reported that the Red Army had occupied Sebastopol, in the Crimea, as the Bolsheviks' efforts to drive the Allies out of Russia continued to meet with success. With a Hungarian Soviet Republic already in existence, a Bavarian delegate to the Berlin Soldiers' Council could hardly be faulted for boasting: '.... Nothing could prevent a red revolution.... The whole continent of Europe would become Bolshevik.'

Further afield, the aftermath of the Great War was bringing increasing pressure to bear on the British Empire and fissures were beginning to appear in the imperial structure. In early 1919, Britain faced revolt in Egypt, Afghanistan and India. In the same edition of 15 April that reported the proclamation of Limerick and the ensuing general strike, *'The Times'* reported very grave disturbances at Amritsar, in the Punjab. An editorial laconically noted a Mr MK Gandhi figuring conspicuously in the reports and described him as a 'misguided and excitable person'.

Nearer home, the great engineering cities like Glasgow and Belfast were feeling the effects of the run-down of the war machine and there were demands to reduce the resultant unemployment and create jobs for the demobilised soldiers. The unions had negotiated a forty-seven-hour week, but in Belfast and Glasgow the workers struck for a forty-four hour week, with no reduction in wages. Belfast moved first and stayed out longer. There were twenty-six trade unions on the General Strike Committee, including representatives of workers in municipal transport and electricity. All factories, except those able to generate their own power, were closed but power to hospitals was maintained. Theatres and cinemas were closed and even the gravediggers were on strike! To move a ship in or out of the harbour or dry dock required permission from the Strike Committee. The Belfast strike involved over forty thousand workers in a loss of three quarters of a million workdays. After almost a month on strike and having endured a virtual military occupation, Belfast returned to work without a victory.

The Government called out the troops to deal with Glasgow as well. The Secretary of State for Scotland described the strike as 'a Bolshevist rising' and sixty tanks and a hundred army lorries were sent North by rail. Troops garrisoned all the major public buildings and the power stations and patrolled the streets in full battle order. Barbed wire and machine guns surrounded the City Chambers. The show of force eventually caused a drift back to work. Later on, there were major strikes in Liverpool, Southampton, Tyneside and London.

Ireland had been going through something of a revolutionary ferment during those years, too, though its place in the British Empire meant the revolution would be political in form and content as well as social and economic. Largely through the outcome of the Limerick Soviet, the year 1919 saw the resolution of the question of whether political issues could be separated from social or economic issues, and if they could, which took primacy.

During the latter part of the Nineteenth century and the first decade and a half of the Twentieth, disaffection with British rule in Ireland found expression mainly through the constitutional pressure of the Irish National Party and the extra-constitutional agitation of the Land League for land reform. Since the abortive Fenian Risings of the Eighteen Sixties, many men of the physical force tradition of Irish nationalism were forced to lick their wounds and brood over past wrongs as exiles in the United States or as convicts in Britain's distant colonies. At home, Charles Stewart Parnell's charismatic leadership and his ambivalent attitude towards the Fenians had enticed the young men towards politics. Michael Davitt's Land League campaign offered a potent blend of direct action in support of economic aims that were attractive both on an individual as well as a national level. By the outbreak of World War One, the land question had been settled by a succession of Land Acts transforming the Irish peasant from a precarious tenant of an often-distant landlord into a doughty land proprietor in his own right.

In politics, the Liberal Government's Home Rule Bill of 1912 seemed to give just the measure of self-government that was needed to satisfy the demands of Ireland's 'strong' farmers and business men. But Ulster Unionist and Conservative opposition, and the outbreak of World War One, forced the postponement until the end of hostilities of the Irish Party's most prized achievement. In June 1916, John Redmond, the leader of the Party, was forced to accept Ulster's 'temporary' exclusion from the terms of the Home Rule Act, whenever it came into force. This capitulation was extremely unpopular in Nationalist Ireland and the Irish Party began to decline in popularity. The Party's virtual demise in the General Election of 1918 was hastened by its advocacy of Irishmen fighting in the War, by the executions of the leaders of the 1916 Rising and by the death of Redmond in March 1918.

The Easter Rising of 1916 represented a new and more advanced phase in the Irish struggle for independence. The Rising came as a great shock to a Britain lulled into a false sense of security by the apparently passive acceptance of Home Rule by the great majority of Nationalists. Militarily, the insurgents did better than expected, though internal wrangling about strategy on the eve of the Rising thinned out their numbers considerably. Coming, as it did, while the Great War was not going well for Britain and her Allies, the rebellion in the second city of the Empire provoked a vehement reaction. Courts martial sentenced ninety prisoners to death and twenty-five of them were actually executed. In all, three thousand five hundred people were arrested. More than a hundred and seventy of those captured faced courts martial while over eighteen hundred were interned without trial in Britain. The execution of the leaders and the imprisonment and internment of the rank and file helped generate a growing disillusionment with British rule, with the suspended offer of Home Rule and with the moderate Irish National Party, led by John Redmond.

For over eighteen months after Easter 1916, many of the leading figures in the independence movement were out of circulation politically and the stage was, largely, left free to the trade unions. In the years immediately after 1916, the upsurge of independence sentiment found its nearest and clearest expression through the Labour movement and through associated strikes and agrarian unrest. 'By the autumn and winter of 1916, 'an Irish Trade Union Congress report noted, 'the Transport Union and Liberty Hall had begun to rise literally from their ashes... All through the country the unions had the same tale of successful organisation and successful movements to tell in 1917... and indeed the two great phenomena of 1917 in Ireland were the rapid rise of Sinn Féin, the Irish Republican Party, and the equally rapid rise to both power and popularity of the militant Labour movement.'

James Larkin had founded the Irish Transport and General Workers' Union in 1909. After initial successes in Belfast, Wexford, Dublin and other cities, the union had been almost bled to death by the Great Lock Out of 1913 in Dublin. By April 1916, it had a membership of only five thousand, mostly in Dublin. It was burdened with debts from the Lock Out and its headquarters had been destroyed in the Rising. The ITGWU Annual Report for 1918 summed up the union's progress after the Rising by saying that Easter Week

1916 had saved the union, by cancelling out the reaction from 1913 and giving birth to the links between the Labour and Nationalist movements. The report noted that the ITGWU had got the full advantage of 'a general zeal for Trade Unionism', stimulated by the economic conditions created by the War and the growth of a more self-reliant spirit in the country.

During 1918, ITGWU membership surged to almost sixty-eight thousand. That was more than double the twenty-five thousand membership of the previous year. Over the following eighteen months, the union signed up another forty thousand or so members. Many of them were farm labourers spurred on by the prospect of sharing in the benefits of the relatively high wartime levels of prosperity and employment in agriculture and by the erosion of earnings through price inflation. The wartime switch from pasture to the more labour-intensive tillage farming led to an increased demand for labourers, while at the same time, the supply of male labour was constrained by people joining the British army or working in munitions factories. The Government recognised the upward pressure on farm wages by the establishment, in 1917, of Agricultural Wages Boards. These provided a new and more effective forum where the ITGWU could satisfy its increasing membership with tangible results. In addition, the benevolent support of Sinn Féin and the Irish Party, both anxious to win Labour's favour, was a further factor in the union's tremendous growth.

The expansion of the ITGWU into many parts of rural Ireland not only brought extra membership, but gave the union an improved geographical spread and a better balance between urban and rural membership. The union mopped up many of the existing small rural labourers' societies. The traditional labourer's aspiration to independently owning a bigger plot of land was replaced by the more immediate aim of improved wages and conditions, achieved by group action – the creation of a rural working-class. In another union publication of 1918, '*Lines of Progress*', the ITGWU declared: 'The days of the local society are dead; the day of the Craft Union is passing; the day for the One Big Union has come'. These developments gave the ITGWU a dominant role in the Irish Trade Union Congress. The union was centrally strong and tightly organised and the Irish TUC's influence expanded as the Transport Union spread.

By the beginning of 1918, the overall Labour movement had doubled its membership. It was in April of that year that Labour entered the forefront of the national struggle. It took its place as an equal partner with the declining Irish Party and the resurgent Sinn Féin in the Mansion House Conference against Conscription. This position, at the centre of events, reflected Labour's greatly increased strength, influence and prestige. Early in 1918, the British Army badly needed more troops for the Western Front. On 21 March 1918, the Germans began a bombardment along a forty to fifty-mile front, with an advantage in numbers of four to one. There was a grave danger General Ludendorff's superior forces would break through, capture Paris and cut off the Allies' lifeline of the Channel ports.

The British Government turned to Ireland and conscription of the Irish as an untapped reservoir of manpower for the battlefields. Despite opposition from the entire Irish Party, conscription for Ireland was voted through at Westminster on 18 April 1918.

That same day, acting on a resolution of Dublin Corporation, the Lord Mayor of Dublin, Lawrence O'Neill, convened a conference or 'National Cabinet' at the Mansion House to 'formulate a national policy to defeat this menace' of conscription. Three representatives of the Irish Trade Union Congress and Labour Party – William O'Brien, Thomas Johnson and Michael Egan – took their places along with national figures like Eamon de Valera and Arthur Griffith for Sinn Féin and John Dillon and TM Healy for the Irish Parliamentary Party.

The Conference issued an anti-Conscription Pledge and Declaration. The pledge promised to use 'all the means that may be deemed effective' to resist compulsory military service and the declaration regarded the passing of the Conscription Bill as a declaration of war on the Irish nation. That same evening, the Catholic bishops were holding their annual meeting at Maynooth and they met a delegation from the Conference. The bishops said that conscription, forced on Ireland against its will and against the protests of its leaders, was an oppressive and inhuman law, which the Irish people had the right to resist by every means consonant with the law of God. Throughout Nationalist Ireland the pledge was signed by tens of thousands of people, often outside Catholic church gates. Despite a ban by the authorities, a substantial National Defence Fund was built up.

But Labour made its own distinctive contribution to the anti-Conscription campaign. Fifteen hundred delegates attended an Extraordinary Labour Conference in Dublin and 'amid scenes of indescribable enthusiasm' called for a general strike on 23 April 1918 in protest at the Government's proposal. The call was responded to everywhere except in the Unionist areas of North East Ulster. Railways, docks, factories, mills, theatres, cinemas, trams, public services, shipyards, newspapers, shops, even Government munitions factories, all stopped. The strike was described as 'complete and entire, an unprecedented event outside the continental countries.' It was, in fact, the first general strike in any country against measures for the more vigorous prosecution of the Great War.

The '*Irish Times*' commented that 23 April would be 'chiefly remembered as the day on which Irish Labour realised its strength'. The Irish TUC strike declaration stressed the claim to 'Independent status as a nation and the right of self-determination'. But it also contained an internationalist call to workers in other countries involved in the Great War to emulate the Irish example and 'rise against their oppressors and bring the war to an end'. The day after the strike, the Irish TUC conveyed the international message in a Manifesto to the Organised Workers of England and Wales. The Manifesto said that Irish Labour was resolutely against conscription for any war, whether imposed by a British or Irish or any other authority. The British Labour movement responded with an appeal to their Government not to apply conscription to Ireland, mainly because of the appalling consequences for both countries that would ensue.

In the Summer of 1918, the Labour members of the Anti-Conscription Conference put forward a plan for the further use of strikes in the campaign and this was adopted formally by the Conference in October 1918. The trade union plan was to swing the entire country behind the first area where the terms of the Military Service Act was imposed. If martial law was imposed and permits became necessary, special anti-Conscription organisations, based on the military areas, would be set up. The unions' 'Plan of Campaign' included the calling of a railway strike for a limited period and a general stoppage. All civil servants, including the constabulary, were to be urged to join in the downing of tools.

A trade union memorandum on the Campaign considered the possibility of calling a general strike in Dublin. It would last one week, and would be a massive demonstration of passive resistance. Food supplies would have to be maintained and it was hoped sympathetic farmers in county Dublin would help out. Inside the city, there would be a central committee to organise rationing and food distribution. The Government eventually withdrew its threat of conscription, so the trade union Plan never had to be put into action. But this planning for a general strike in Dublin bears a close resemblance to what happened later in Limerick and may be the precursor of what happened there.

By August 1918, the Press Censor was reporting that Labour had replaced Sinn Féin as the leaders in the fight against conscription. The Censor regarded the development of the Irish TUC since the month of April as the most noteworthy aspect of the previous few months. A British Cabinet report noted that Labour and Sinn Féin 'were now working together and had come to an arrangement.' Not everyone involved in the all-class Nationalist alliance against conscription was pleased at the Mansion House Conference's public endorsement of Labour's predominant role. Some senior, influential elements of Sinn Féin were unhappy because they recognised that 'direct action', such as strikes, would be outside their control and would give too much influence to the trade unions in determining the outcome of the struggle. People like Arthur Griffith, the founder of Sinn Féin, ostensibly did not want to foster any trends that might disrupt the all-class unity of the national movement, and equally, they did not foresee a dominant role for Labour in their vision of a free Ireland. In January 1919, Griffith wrote: 'The General Strike is a weapon that might injure as much as serve. It would be injudicious at present and might be injudicious at any time, unless under extreme circumstances...'

In the same month, from another perspective, an acute observer noted the growing rivalry for the pre-eminent national position between Sinn Féin and Labour. In his monthly report for January 1919, the Inspector-General of the Royal Irish Constabulary, Joseph

Aloysius Byrne, remarked that he saw Labour sooner or later becoming a formidable rival to Sinn Féin.

Towards the end of 1918, the only check to Labour's advance was its decision, under Sinn Féin persuasion and pressure, not to contest the December General Election. Sinn Féin wanted to ensure that the election in Ireland was fought on the simple issue of self-determination, uncluttered by any social issues. The original, unanimous decision of the Labour Executive was to contest a number of seats. The Waterford annual Congress, in August 1918, had called for the setting up of Labour electoral machinery in every municipal and parliamentary constituency where this was found practicable. Conscious that the new franchise laws would greatly increase the electoral register, local Labour organisations were given a four-point plan of action to maximise their vote.

The Labour-Congress decision to contest was based on three grounds: to give workers an opportunity to vote Labour, to strengthen the Irish movement's standing with the Socialist International and to prepare the way for full Labour representation in any future Irish parliament. But, in a concession to the Sinn Féin view, elected Labour members would not take their seats at Westminster unless an annual or special Congress decided otherwise. Labour in Dublin made an early decision to contest four seats. Elsewhere, there was confusion and indeed opposition to the Executive's decision – in places like Meath, Bray, Cork, Waterford and Kilkenny. At a meeting of forty-three rail workers in Kingstown, county Dublin, only six were prepared to vote Labour. The rest thought it better to have a straight fight between Sinn Féin and the Irish National Party solely on the issue of self-determination. At election rallies, Labour speakers came under increasing pressure.

Nationally, there were confidential but inconclusive negotiations between Sinn Féin and Labour to see if a compromise could be found. Some Sinn Féin leaders feared that if there was no agreement, while Labour would not win any seats, they might prevent Sinn Féin winning in up to twenty constituencies. On 1 November 1918, the Congress Executive returned to the question of the election. The Congress Treasurer, Tom Johnson, who initiated the discussion, pointed out that great changes had taken place since the first decision and said it was desirable to review the whole position in the light of the new circumstances. At a special Congress that day, Johnson argued that they had originally envisaged the election as a 'War' election, but it had now become a 'Peace' election. With the possibility of new national boundaries being drawn elsewhere, Labour in Ireland should withdraw to allow a demonstration of unity on the question of self-determination. Cathal O'Shannon, of the ITGWU, was against any change in electoral strategy. He said they would not get full representation at the Socialist International unless they had a Parliamentary Labour Party. They were cutting away one third of their numerical representation and one half of their moral strength. But, many delegates reported a determination at local level to vote Sinn Féin and the National Executive's change of policy was endorsed by ninety-six votes to twenty-three.

The desire to give Sinn Féin a 'clear run' on the issue of self-determination was obviously a major factor in Labour's decision. Equally, the national leadership could hardly impose a policy of electoral participation in the teeth of widespread local determination to support Sinn Féin. That would have led to a damaging confrontation with an increasingly confident and united Sinn Féin. In addition, because of the nature of its organisation and the looser degree of adherence of its members, Labour did not have the same organisational or electoral coherence as Sinn Féin. The latter had a highly politicised organisation and its members were strongly under the influence or control of its leaders. Labour, on the other hand, was made up of people who might well be staunch trade unionists in industrial matters but were often pledged members or supporters of Sinn Féin when it came to politics.

In the minds of some Labour leaders there was another factor – the North. It would have been relatively easy to have reached a pact with Sinn Féin on allocating the contesting of seats between them, but how would such an arrangement have been viewed by the Loyalist trade unionists of Ulster? The dilemma of trying to maintain a united trade union centre, North and South, despite the conflicting nationalist aspirations of the rank and file membership, paralysed the leadership and was at the root of its political impotence. The Irish Labour Party and Trade Union Congress maintained a fragile unity by clinging to the lowest common denominator among workers, North and South. The syndicalist concept of the 'One Big Union', one that prioritised industrial over political methods, was a safe refuge from having to take an overt stand on issues like self-determination for Ireland. The division of workers' political allegiances between unionism, constitutional nationalism and republicanism meant that – to maintain industrial unity and strength – the Party-Congress had to fudge its stance on the self-determination question.

Labour's commitment to syndicalist policies reinforced its restraint from involvement in electoral or parliamentary politics. It could be argued that the abstention decision freed attention and resources to concentrate on the industrial issues at hand. The inherent contradictions in the Labour movement between Northern and Southern workers forced it to stand aside in the 1918 General Election and the objective outcome was to sublimate the 'Parliament of Labour' to the separatist and abstentionist First Dáil.

Labour's decision not to contest the 1918 General Election is regarded by many, especially on the Left, as the starting point of the Left's subsequent historical weakness. An analysis of the electoral register for that election shows the potential there was for advance. Among many reforms, the Representation of the People Act 1918 abolished the system of plural voting which was loaded in favour of property owners. It provided a vote to men in Parliamentary elections once they were aged twenty-one and over but women were not qualified to vote until the age of thirty and over and there was an additional property-owning requirement for them. In local government elections, the franchise was extended to everyone over the age of twenty-one and there was no additional requirement for women in relation to property ownership. In Ireland, the result was a dramatic restructuring and increase in the electorate. The number of Parliamentary voters in the major cities was trebled, providing fertile ground for Labour progress.

Conscious of the international recognition it might bring, Sinn Féin and the Volunteers had to maintain close and friendly ties with Labour. In February 1919, Thomas Johnson and Cathal O'Shannon represented the Irish Trade Union Congress at the International Socialist conference in Berne called by Socialist and Labour leaders to consider the post-War situation. In a major fillip to independence sentiment, Johnson and O'Shannon succeeded in getting Ireland recognised, and seated, as a separate delegation to the conference. The Irish delegates presented a special report outlining the case for Irish independence. This was prepared in Irish, English, French and German. A further memorandum was issued in French and German sketching Irish history, reviewing the current situation and expressing working-class and Nationalist aspirations. The memorandum was intended to brief the representatives of the Labour International who were to attend the Paris Peace Conference.

At Amsterdam, in April 1919, the principles of national independence and self-determination, agreed at Berne, were applied to Ireland. A resolution, adopted unanimously, demanded that the principle of free and absolute self-determination be applied to Ireland. It affirmed the right of the Irish people to political independence and required that 'self-determination should rest on a democratic decision expressed by the free, equal, adult and secret vote of the people without any military, political or economic pressure from outside, or any reservation or restriction imposed by any government'. The International called on the Great Powers and the Peace Conference to 'make good this rightful claim of the Irish people'.

The rapid growth and negotiating successes of the trade unions, and their emphasis on industrial action over politics, intensified in 1919. In February, for example, a Special Conference was held in the Mansion House, in Dublin, to initiate a national wages and hours movement – for a forty-four hour week, a 150 per cent increase in pay and a minimum adult wage of fifty shillings a week. The conference was attended by delegates representing more than a hundred unions. Early in April, the Executive of the Irish Transport and General Workers' Union completed a two-day session reviewing the union's activity. Since the beginning of the year, there had been an increase of seventy-nine new branches, making a total of 289. Total membership was now eighty-five thousand – an increase of nine thousand in just over three months! The Executive decided on an extensive campaign of organisation and increased by five the existing complement of seventeen organisers.

The Drapers' Assistants' Association held their annual meeting in the City Hall, in Dublin, on Easter Sunday, 22 April 1919. According to newspaper reports, 'an optimistic and cheerful note pervaded the reports and speeches' and delegates were told Association membership was a thousand stronger than in the best year previously recorded. Again, underlining the growth in trade unionism, the meeting heard that sixty thousand pounds (€3.6 million) had been secured in bonuses during the previous year and one hundred and forty thousand pounds (€8.4 million) in permanent salary increases.

In his Presidential Address to the Sinn Féin Ard Fheis, held in the Mansion House in Dublin during the week beginning 7 April 1919, only a week before the declaration of the Limerick Soviet, Eamon de Valera reflected on the essential importance of Labour's role in the independence movement: 'When we wanted the help of Labour against conscription, Labour gave it to us (cheers). When we wanted the help of Labour in Berne, Labour gave it to us and got Ireland recognised as a distinct nation (cheers). When we wanted Labour to stand down at the election, and not divide us, but that we should stand forsworn against the enemy, Labour fell in with us. I say Labour deserves well of the Irish people: The Labour man deserves the best the country can give cheers).' In the end, though, it was a commitment that neither he, nor Sinn Féin, delivered on once the issue of independence had been resolved.

CHAPTER THIRTEEN

<u>Analysis and Assessment</u>

'Let them remember what the strike was. It was a protest, and the Limerick Committee emphasised the fact, against a military tyranny.'
Tom Johnson, Treasurer, Irish Labour Party and Trade Union Congress, August 1919

A good starting point for analysis and assessment of Limerick is the major debate at the Irish Labour Party and Trade Union Congress in Drogheda, in August 1919. A few months on from the ending of the strike, it provides some considered insights into how the national trade union leadership and the Limerick strikers viewed the Soviet and how it ended.

Michael O'Donnell was a member of the Soviet and a delegate to Congress from the Irish Clerical Workers' Union. He asserted that the national executive had not done everything that should have been done and he claimed that 'The Limerick strikers were let down by someone.' Subsequent speakers took opposing sides – some supporting the Executive with others being severely critical. There was criticism as well of the leaders of the British-headquartered unions who had stood back from supporting the Soviet. The pivotal role of the railwaymen was debated in some detail. Six delegates defended them, including Michael Keyes, a member of the Soviet, from the Limerick branch of the National Union of Railwaymen.

For British trade union leaders, such as the National Union of Railwaymen, one of the difficulties – or excuses – they had in dealing with Limerick was in deciding whether it was a type of ordinary industrial stoppage or some kind of 'political' (or anti-British) action. In the conventional wisdom of the British unions, political power was pursued through political parties and therefore trade unions did not involve themselves in 'political' actions. It was the 'political' nature of the Limerick strike that was seized upon by the NUR General Secretary, JH Thomas, and his executive members as their reason for withholding official sanction.

The gulf in philosophical outlook between Irish and British trade unionism was wide. An Irish nationalist's 'industrial' strike might be an Englishman's 'political' action, yet both could simply be looking at the same events from a different perspective. From the Limerick strike onwards, the British trade unions – especially the National Union of Railwaymen – were consistently cool in their attitude towards 'political' strikes in Ireland. The requests and actions of the Irish members were drowned in a welter of rulebooks, bureaucracy and procrastinating executive council decisions. As the '*New Statesman*' put it in 1920, 'a certain measure of academic approval was forthcoming but active support was lacking from the first.'

It was the British intelligentsia, rather than its workers or trade union leaders, who were most deeply opposed to the government's repressive policies in Ireland and who felt they were contrary to British traditions of public and political life. Perhaps if the trade unions there had taken direct action it would have given substance to the accusation that extremists in the British Labour movement were in alliance with the 'Sinn Féin Bolsheviks' in Ireland. In turn, that might have alienated the kind of respectable people who were active in bodies like the Peace with Ireland Council. They sympathised with Ireland's plight but did not wish to be party to a revolutionary upsurge aimed at overturning society in the British Isles.

The difference between Irish and British trade union attitudes may also be explained by the differing tactics of trade union centres in colonial or quasi-colonial countries compared with centres in metropolitan or imperialist countries. In an imperialist country, like Britain, part of the standard of living of trade unionists depended on the availability of cheap raw materials from the colonies, the restriction of colonial competition and the enforced freedom of trade for finished goods in the colonies. To that extent, there was common economic cause between the trade unions and the Empire's business interests. For many trade unionists in the old imperial states of Europe, making common cause with oppressed workers in the colonies meant, to an extent, jeopardising their own standard of living because it put their employers' profits at risk. And the Labour movements of Europe – including Britain – were far from immune from sentiments of jingoism and chauvinism where 'national' interests were concerned, as their behaviour after the outbreak of World War I had illustrated.

All of this partly explains the reluctance of the powerful British trade unions to weigh in on the side of the Limerick strikers. But there was a further compelling reason. At this time, probably over seventy per cent of Irish trade unionists were members of British-headquartered trade unions but most of that membership was concentrated in the Loyalist areas of north east Ulster. Inevitably, any words or actions that smacked of support for Irish separatism would fall foul of those members. In their desire to retain their Ulster membership, the British unions were severely constrained in how far they could go in support of actions taken by their members in the rest of Ireland.

The '*Irish Times*' noted the refusal of the British trade unions to accept that the strike had no connection with 'politics' but was merely Irish Labour's challenge to assaults on its dignity and convenience. The newspaper believed that the strike had escalated from being purely a local affair to being used as a deliberate and very ambitious attack on the whole system of Irish government. It could no longer be dissociated from the propaganda of the Irish Republicans, and the involvement of the Trade Union Congress promising to extend the strike nationally was an attempt to bring the whole nation to a social and economic standstill.

A week into the strike, the '*Irish Times*' claimed that shrewd judges detected the guiding hand of Sinn Féin in ensuring that the strike committee's functions were carried out with a thoroughness that was uncharacteristic of provincial strikes up to then. Though there was no open alliance, the newspaper conceded, there was a complete accord between the political and industrial parties. 'Defiance of British law affords them a common platform', the '*Irish Times*' declared. But, the same report said, Labour took care ostensibly to keep itself aloof from politics lest if should offend its friends in Great Britain. The paper reported seeing very few emblems of Sinn Féin, and except for the daubing of the Treaty Stone in Republican colours, there was 'no glaring display' of the tricolour. Many Sinn Féiners, apparently, had decided to stay within the proscribed area rather than apply for military permits and had even resisted the temptation to spend Easter by the seaside rather than submit to the indignity of applying.

In his memoir of the strike, the trades council treasurer, James Casey, indicates that much of the food supply for Limerick, from outside, was organised by the IRA and smuggled past the military cordon. The '*Observer*' correspondent in Ireland, the writer Captain Stephen Gwynn, saw Limerick as having been started by the 'Labour' wing of Sinn Féin but saw the ending of the strike as a defeat for the whole of Sinn Féin and a triumph for the military. Gwynn praised both the military and the Soviet for their wise and capable handling of events.

When John Cronin was asked for his reaction to the refusals of the NUR and the British TUC to lend official support, he claimed that there was 'nothing whatever political' – that is, nothing to do with nationalism – in the protest on behalf of the workers of Limerick. 'It is entirely a Labour question,' he said. 'The right to come and go without having to get military permits is involved. The attitude of the workers is completely misrepresented by and misunderstood by endeavouring to show that the situation is in any way connected with politics.'

A great deal of the propaganda, for and against the Limerick strike, therefore, was centred on this issue of whether it was a 'Labour' or a 'political' phenomenon. 'Political' in this context did not mean party politics but the political questions of Irish nationalism, Irish self-determination and Irish separatism. Often, for tactical reasons, in order to secure or maintain British Labour support, the strike's supporters stressed that it was a 'Labour' question (or in modern usage, an 'industrial relations' issue). In trying to grapple with this paradox, the Congress Treasurer, Tom Johnson, conceded that it was political, 'but only in the sense that the fight against conscription was political.'

Unwittingly, Tom Johnson put his finger on the nub of the problem for the British unions when he pointed out that Ulster Loyalist trade unionists had refused to support the anti-conscription campaign for the precise reason that they viewed it as damaging to their political and economic interests in retaining a constitutional link with Britain. If Limerick was 'political' in the same sense, there was no question of support for the strike in Loyalist Ulster. On the other hand, people like Johnson could not pursue the 'non-political' line to such an extent that they ended up alienating possible support from middle-class and farming supporters of Irish nationalism in the rest of Ireland.

James O'Connor, Secretary of Limerick United Trades and Labour Council, and a member of the Soviet, rejected any assertion that they had been let down. The official conference report continues: 'Coming from Limerick and speaking for the workers there, he declared that Limerick was not let down. [Applause] They held they made the greatest fight ever made by any united group of workers in a big city. They showed the world that the workers were able to run the city in spite of the presence of any foreign government. They held they won in Limerick [Applause] and they blamed nobody for letting them down. They fought their own fight with the help of the Executive and fought well.' O'Connor then handed in a copy of the last proclamation issued by the Strike Committee.

The Congress vice-president, Thomas Farren, mounted a robust defence of the Executive. He agreed that the strike was a 'glorious triumph' for the organised workers of Limerick but it was a mistake to have declared a strike for an indefinite period. If they had declared a strike for a week, they would have accomplished as much. On the question of declaring a national stoppage, Farren said that while the leadership had agreed that a national conference might be called, they had made it clear that if they did call a national stoppage, it would only be a demonstration for a few days as 'they realised that under the present state of affairs they were not prepared for the Revolution.'

Addressing the Drogheda conference, William O'Brien, the Congress general secretary, made a typically acerbic, but masterly, intervention in the debate. O'Brien had a long and multi-facetted career in the Labour movement; he was a close friend and confidant of James Connolly; his greatest achievements were mainly organisational but were often marked by bitter clashes with former colleagues like Big Jim Larkin and PT Daly. O'Brien set out in detail the telegrams, consultations and meetings that had been the Congress's early response to the events in Limerick. He explained the difficulties in getting the entire executive to Limerick at the earliest possible date, because of the pressure of other work on some key members. O'Brien was immediately followed by speakers from Cork and King's County (now Offaly) who accepted his explanation.

Tom Johnson gave his account of the executive's stewardship. He believed the Limerick committee were right to act quickly – without consulting the executive – if their action was to be of any effect. There were times when local people must take on themselves the responsibility for doing things and taking the consequences, and this, he asserted, was one of them. But due consideration must be given to any suggestion of an enormous extension of the local action. They could never win a strike by downing tools against the British Army, he declared. It was for them as an executive to decide whether this was the moment to act in Ireland, whether there was a probability of a response in England and Scotland. Their knowledge of those countries did not lead them to think that any big action in Ireland would have brought a responsive movement there.

'A general strike could have been legitimately called in Ireland on twelve occasions during the past two years', Johnson continued, 'but it was not a question of justification. It was a question of strategy. Were they to take the enemy's time or were they to take their own?' They knew that if the railwaymen came out the soldiers would have taken on the railways the next day. They knew that if the soldiers were put on the railways, the railways would have been blown up. They knew that would have meant armed revolt.'

'Did they as trade unionists suggest that it was for their executive to say such action should be taken at a particular time, knowing, assured as they were, that it would have resulted in armed revolt in Ireland?', he asked. There might be an occasion to decide on a down tools policy which would have the effect of calling out the armed forces of the crown, but 'Limerick was not the occasion… Let them remember what the strike was. It was a protest, and the Limerick Committee emphasised the fact, against a military tyranny.'

By implication, Johnson's speech makes it clear that the proposal of a national congress, put to the Limerick strike committee, was never really meant seriously by the Congress Executive, unless the outcome was to be a token, national stoppage as mentioned by Thomas Farren. Johnson's speech illustrates that for all the 'syndicalist' rhetoric of the Irish trade union movement they had neither the politics nor the level of organisation needed to challenge British state power in Ireland. When the section of the annual report dealing with Limerick was put to the congress it was adopted with only one vote against. That came from the delegate of King's County Trades Council, Smyth. He did not speak on the issue, so we can only speculate on his reasons for opposing.

So far as the strikers saw matters, Limerick was more concerned with making a sustained protest against intolerable conditions locally, than with being the precursor of a national challenge to the British government. From early on, the national trade union leadership made it clear that they were not prepared to offer such a challenge, at least not without the support or the blessing of Sinn Féin, the Volunteers and the Dáil. The Limerick strike was the first open challenge to British rule since the separatist Dáil was established but in the end, it proved no match for the government.

After the strike ended, there were bitter recriminations and criticism of the strike leaders in Limerick from Republican newspapers, proving how brittle had been their alliance with organised Labour in the first place. The comments showed little appreciation of the difficult organisational, let alone political, issues that would have faced the unions if they had decided to continue the strike. '*An Phoblacht*' ('The Republic') a Republican broadsheet, poured scorn on union leaders who had 'bowed the knee in shameful submission to the army of occupation'. The paper asserted that the people had been let down by 'the nincompoops who call themselves the 'Leaders of Labour' in Limerick', and the end of the strike had come as a 'death blow' to the hopes of the people. The paper's editor was Darrell Figgis, one of the main organisers of the Howth gun running in 1914, a TD in the First Dáil whose life ended mired in scandal and suicides. The real attitude of the militant Republicans to trade union action may have been betrayed in these scornful comments of Patrick O'Connor, writing in the newspaper '*An tÉireannach*' ('The Irishman'): '… a general strike is an effective weapon of defence, no doubt, but we have an even more effective weapon and we should not hesitate to use it for the sake of justice.'

The workers of Limerick were exhausted, especially financially, after the strike ended and, as part of its tacit understanding with General Griffin for the revocation of military law, the Trades Council voted not to observe Labour Day on 1 May. Some workers had received strike pay from their unions or had even been paid by employers who had Republican sympathies. But many others had received nothing and some had not been reinstated after the strike ended. It was estimated that £25,000 (€1.5 million) was needed to alleviate distress but the strike fund had closed after two weeks, holding just over £17,000. At the annual conference of the ILPTUC, some unions complained that their donations had not been registered in the fund. Other donations reported in the newspapers do not appear to have been recorded, more likely because of organisational pressures than because of any dishonesty. Nevertheless, the total amount subscribed to help Limerick, while larger than the amount recorded, still fell far short of what was needed.

In early May, the ILPTUC national executive had issued a rather perfunctory appeal for help for Limerick, in a circular asking for 'some financial assistance to be rendered to them'. When the circular was discussed at a meeting of the Dublin Trades Council on 5 May, some members of the national executive were less than enthusiastic. Thomas Farren enquired how much the executive itself had given and was told – amid laughter – by another executive member that they had 'given their moral support'. William O'Brien himself was against a council subscription, saying it should be left up to individual unions. His remarks made him extremely unpopular in Limerick. A Limerick worker wrote to the Dublin '*Saturday Post*' describing the executive's evacuation plan as the most ridiculous suggestion since 'Moses struck the rock.' He was particularly critical of their failure to go to Limerick immediately and demanded to know why the general secretary had not gone there.

The aftermath of the strike brought bitterness and division to Limerick Trades Council itself. At the best of times, there had been an uneasy relationship between the old-style craft unions and the new industrial unionism of the ITGWU. The post-strike debates allowed full scope for that latent antagonism to flourish. At national level, both the ITGWU itself and the Irish Labour Party and Trade Union Congress were wracked by a bitter rivalry between William O'Brien and PT Daly. Daly was a long-time Larkin supporter. Larkin had left Ireland for America shortly after the end of the 1913 Lockout and would not return until early in 1923. Daly had fallen out with James Connolly, O'Brien's idol, and he seemed to represent militancy and greater rank-and-file power.

These national factions had their local Limerick followers. The stance taken for or against the national executive's actions during the strike became a litmus test of where loyalties lay on the national rivalry of O'Brien and Daly. Ostensibly procedural or constitutional questions – such as the number of Limerick delegates to be sent to the Drogheda conference, became the focus of conflict between skilled and unskilled, between the ITGWU favouring a strong, centralised trade union movement and the craft unions which preferred a more local, less rigid structure.

As a carpenter himself, the council Chairman, John Cronin, was firmly opposed to the ITGWU line and did not want to oppose or embarrass the national executive. He said: 'everyone knows the facts of Limerick and the council wants no capital made out of it.' He announced that the trades council's report on the strike would not be ready before the Drogheda conference, thus avoiding the possibility that any negative comments would be seized on by delegates opposed to the leadership.

A wrangle over the delegates for Drogheda left Limerick represented by two Transport Union members (including the socialist full-time Organiser, John Dowling), with Cronin refusing to attend and failing to take up a nomination for the vice presidency of Trade Union Congress. The nomination was probably intended to honour him for his leadership of the Limerick strike but it would also neutralise him as a potential critic of the national leadership. The Drogheda conference had faced him with a dilemma. As leader of the strike, he might have wanted to criticise the national executive but, as a member of a craft union, he knew that this would play into the hands of Daly's Left faction, whom he opposed. In a closing of ranks, the radical Dowling offered to second a vote of confidence in the National Executive and the subsequent almost unanimous vote of approval of their actions over Limerick signalled a major defeat for Daly and his followers (and, by extension, for the exiled Larkin) and it was the beginning of the end of Daly's influence at the centre of the trade union movement.

Although often described as a 'soviet', to what extent were the Limerick events influenced by similar happenings in Russia and the Central European countries? Some advanced Irish Labour leaders had frequently expressed approval and support for Bolshevik Russia and the soviets. For example, on the day the Limerick strike began, at a meeting of the Socialist Party in Ireland, in Dublin, Cathal O'Shannon said that the trade unions and the agricultural workers might be made the machinery through which soviets would be established in Ireland. The SPI included among its members congress leaders like Johnson and O'Brien.

At a Sinn Féin meeting in Bray, county Wicklow, towards the end of the Soviet, the radical leader, Countess Markiewicz, said that if the American President Wilson failed, they had another solution – the Bolshevist revolution in Russia. The Countess, who fought in the 1916 Rising in Connolly's Citizen Army, said she knew Russia well and the people who had got control there were the rank-and-file, just as those listening to her were working and striving to earn a living and to help build up their country. They were building up a workers' Republic. That flame was spreading westward. If it fired France, it must fire England, and if it fired England, Ireland was free [applause]. The sort of Republic they wanted to build all over the world was the workers' Republic for which James Connolly died.

In the same week, one of Sinn Féin's most prominent leaders, Professor Eoin MacNeill, was worried about the impression militant socialist and labour activities in Ireland were making on their supporters in America. Professor MacNeill said any statements current in America that Sinn Féin was under the red flag or was Bolshevist were not made in good faith. 'We Irish,' MacNeill told the '*Chicago Daily News*', 'are neither Russian nor international. The aim of Sinn Féin is the establishment of an Independent Irish Republic in which all Irish citizens shall have a proper opportunity to live. We hold that the workers have not had that opportunity and that they must get it.' A limited number of Sinn Féiners believed in state socialism, Professor MacNeill said. The '*Chicago Daily News*' special correspondent concluded: 'The wind behind the Irish red flag is not strong.'

MacNeill might have been even more concerned had he been aware of the reports from Limerick of another Chicago correspondent, Ruth Russell of the '*Chicago Tribune*'. In her book, '*What's the matter with Ireland?*' she vividly recalled a meeting with John Cronin and the strange mixture of socialism, nationalism and Catholicism she encountered:

'All the Limerick shops I passed were blinded or shuttered. In the grey light, black lines of people moved desolately up and down, not allowed to congregate and apparently not wanting to wait in homes they were weary of. A few candles flickered in the windows. At the door of a river street house, I mounted gritty stone steps. A red-badged man opened the door part way. As soon as I told him I was an American journalist the suspicious look in his face vanished. With much cordiality he invited me upstairs. While he knocked on the door he bade me wait. On the invitation to come in, I entered a badly-lit room where workingmen sat at a long, black, scratched table. I was invited to sit down. 'Yes, this is a soviet,' said John Cronin, the carpenter who was father of the baby soviet. 'Why did we form it? Why do we pit people's rule against military rule? Of course, as workers we are against all military... You have seen how we have thrown the crank into production... The 'kept' press is killed but we have substituted our own paper.' He held up a small sheet which said in large letters 'The *Workers' Bulletin* – Issued by the Limerick Proletariat.' 'We have,' Cronin said, 'felt the sympathy of the union men in the army sent to guard us. A whole Scots regiment had to be sent home because it was letting workers go back and forth without passes.' A few of the red-badged guards came to herald the approach of the workers and then sat down outside the hall. Saint Munchin's chapel bell struck the Angelus. The red-badged guards rose and blessed themselves…'

More than any other piece written at the time, Ruth Russell's vignette probably gives the clearest insight into the nature of the strike-soviet and of the people who were involved.

They had some limited knowledge of socialist theory and certainly a fondness for its rhetoric. They felt an emotional identification with the recent stirring events in Central Europe, Bolshevik Russia and in the more distant parts of the British Empire. Some of the Limerick workers were inspired by Connolly's version of syndicalism mixed – as his was too – with Republicanism. They could call on an active trade union organisation and rely on passive and active support from middle-class, moderate nationalists. At the same time, they maintained a respectful relationship with the Catholic clergy who were more used to a position of leading than being led, in politics as well as in matters of religion. Above all the cities of Ireland, Limerick had the folk memory of earlier sieges in 1690 and 1691 that evoked comparisons with the restrictions of the military barricades and, thus, provided a rich vein of suitable rhetoric. Mixed in with all of this was an emotional and humanitarian concern for the local Republican hunger strikers, the symbolism of the death of Robert Byrne – a trade unionist and an active Republican – and the maladroit provocation of placing the city under military law.

All these ingredients went into the melting pot that produced the Limerick Soviet. In terms of socialist theory, the Limerick events met many of the criteria to be considered a 'soviet'. The workers' committee, for a time, organised and managed political and civil society within most of Limerick city – one of the hallmarks of a 'soviet'. However, there was no takeover of private property and when the coal merchants quickly asserted their property rights in the face of the strike committee's orders, the committee backed down. Essentially, the soviet's attitude to private property was pragmatic. So long as the shopkeepers were willing to act under the soviet's dictates there was no practical reason to commandeer their premises. There may also have been a view that, pending the escalation of the soviet into a general strike, it was necessary to preserve a semblance of unity across economic classes so as not to alienate actual or potential Sinn Féin support.

Few, if any, Limerick workers were either socialists or syndicalists – advocates of the general strike as a means to political power – except perhaps Connolly's old lieutenant, John Dowling, who had come to Limerick as an organiser for the ITGWU. But they belonged to a movement, one of whose founders and its leading intellectual and martyr, had imbued syndicalist influences and bequeathed them in his theoretical writings. The movement's leaders, such as Johnson or O'Brien, frequently indulged a taste for syndicalist rhetoric and the ILPTUC constitution was clearly syndicalist-orientated, with its organic unity of the Labour party and the national trade union centre and the pre-eminence of industrial aims and methods over the political.

To some extent a trade union rank-and-file subconsciously absorbs the current rhetoric of their leadership. In spontaneously reaching for the general strike as their weapon, the Limerick trade union leaders were simply responding in the pre-ordained way of members of a movement with strong syndicalist characteristics. Syndicalism was one of the dominant or reinforcing ideologies of the Irish Labour movement in the years immediately after the 1916 Rising, the other being nationalism. To that extent, it must have influenced the stance taken by the Trades Council in calling a general strike in Limerick and by the strike committee in seeking a national, general strike in support.

The Limerick workers had witnessed, too, the practical example of up to eight localised general strikes in other Irish towns that had preceded their action. The first such strike took place in Youghal, county Cork, in December 1917. The local employers' federation locked out all the unskilled workers in the town's mills, stores and workshops in response to a wage claim by the National Union of Dock Labourers. After a week, the skilled tradesmen came out in sympathy and mass pickets were placed to prevent the movement of goods. Strikers and their supporters removed horses and drays from the employers' yards and there were clashes with the RIC. After a fortnight, the strike was settled to the workers' satisfaction. In the period August 1918 to April 1919, similar localised general strikes took place in Charleville, county Cork, Ballina and Westport, county Mayo, Graiguenamanagh, county Kilkenny, Killarney, county Kerry, Boyle, county Roscommon and Thurles, county Tipperary. In Monaghan Town, a few months before the Limerick Soviet, the ITGWU Organiser and Republican Socialist, Peadar O'Donnell, led workers in a takeover of the asylum, under the red flag, and O'Donnell was appointed Governor. However, while none of these localised activities attained the degree of organisation of the Limerick strike, they were exemplars of what could be achieved by united action.

In the immediate aftermath of the Soviet, the pivotal ITGWU Organiser, John Dowling, joined the Revolutionary Socialist Party of Ireland which had been formed in Belfast in May by his political ally, the English Marxist, Jack Hedley, sometimes known as Seán O'Hagan. At one time, the party claimed to have seven ITGWU Organisers in membership. In June, Jack McGrath arrived in Limerick as an ITGWU organiser. After strikes, imprisonment and a hunger strike, Hedley eventually found his way to Limerick, apparently at the behest of the senior and respected senior ITGWU official, Thomas Kennedy. It was largely through the efforts and leadership of Dowling, McGrath and Hedley that the short to medium-term aftermath of the Soviet saw a marked increase in trade union activity and militancy in Limerick city and county.

Within a fortnight of the Soviet ending, workers in Cleeve's creameries in counties Limerick and Tipperary went on strike. The ITGWU established the Munster Council of Action to co-ordinate the strike. In Knocklong, county Limerick, the strike went on for seven weeks. In June, there was a further ITGWU strike in Clouncagh Creamery as well as in Limerick docks. The industrial struggles continued throughout the rest of 1919. In all, there were thirty-seven strikes and lockouts in Limerick that year, almost twice as many as in the previous year. They included four hundred dock labourers seeking a pay increase, as well as – for example – workers in the saddlery trade, coach makers, draper's assistants in O'Mahonys in William Street, three hundred building workers, O'Callaghan's Tannery, tailors, furniture makers, the Model Laundry, McMahons, porters, packers, and car men employed in Hassetts, PD Bourke, Spaight's, JP Evans and Newsoms, seven hundred County Council road workers, law clerks and hardware assistants. The law clerks published a newspaper called '*The Red Flag*' and set up a bureau to give free legal advice in the ITGWU office.

In the county that year, there were strikes by farm labourers in Bulgaden, O'Shaughnessy's saw mills in Newcastle West and the Abbey Tannery in Athlunkard. By the end of 1919, the ITGWU had 7,478 members in forty-two branches in Limerick and in the following year it reached the peak of its expansion in the city and county with 7,738 members in forty-five branches. During this time, industrial disputes, strikes and occupations involving ITGWU members in Limerick were probably more frequent, more sustained and more widespread than in any other city or county.

The intensification of the War of Independence in 1920 – with many significant engagements taking place in Limerick – made it more difficult to sustain trade union agitation. Nevertheless, there were strikes by gas workers, hotel workers, carters employed in O'Callaghan's Tannery, carters and yardmen at Spaight's and two separate disputes at the city's saw mills. It worth noting how workers in a number of employments went on strike more than once in the years 1918 to 1920, examples being O'Callaghan's Tannery, the docks, the furniture trade, drapery trade and Spaight's.

Starting in May 1920, a series of localised general strikes and workplace occupations took place in county Limerick, with this type of activity continuing until 1922. Under the vigilant eyes of Dowling and McGrath, with Hedley in the role of Manager, the Knocklong Soviet began on the 16 May and lasted five days. It involved the occupation of twelve other satellite creameries. It was a carefully orchestrated effort by the three syndicalist union organisers to assert workers' power and demonstrate that they were capable of managing industrial enterprises. The workers repainted the entrance door from green to red, hoisted the red flag and the green-white-and-orange tricolour over the premises and hung out the memorable sign 'We Make Butter Not Profit'. The creameries operated as normal and were handed back to Cleeve's, the owners, in exchange for a signed guarantee on wage increases and the dismissal of the much-reviled creamery manager. The success of Knocklong boosted the union's prestige and led to an influx of new members, including women workers, and sparked further episodes of militancy in the county.

These included:

Kilmallock, where farm labourers and creamery workers in a dozen locations were on sympathetic strike. Backing the farmers, the IRA arrested four strikers and three hundred workers marched through the village under a red flag demanding their release;

Castleconnell on the River Shannon, where – as part of a prolonged dispute over a pay claim – a salmon fishery was taken over for a month from the owner, Anthony Mackey, a Sinn Féin county councillor, who was regarded as exploiting the fishermen;

Bruree, Éamon de Valera's home place, where in August 1921, workers took over Cleeve's bakery and mills and replicated the actions of their comrades previously in Knocklong, erecting a sign that read 'Bruree Workers' Mills – We Make Bread Not Profits';

Broadford, in 1922, where the local absentee landlord had his land taken and declared a soviet. The land was lent to landless labourers who tilled it. The Broadford Soviet decided that £110 (€6,600) was appropriate rent for six months and the landlord had no choice but to accept it.

There were well over a hundred occupations, general strikes and 'soviets' during this revolutionary period, most of them in the province of Munster. In Ballingarry, county Tipperary, the coal mines were occupied, as well as a coach builders in Tipperary Town and a soviet operated in the town gas works for several months. It ended when Free State forces took the town and the retreating anti-Treaty forces set fire to the gas works and destroyed the municipal water supply. Elsewhere in county Tipperary, in May 1922, farm workers in Ballinacourty seized a large estate and took over the saw mills.

County Cork saw militant activity too. In February 1921, harbour employees represented by the ITGWU submitted a claim for a 'living' wage and by August they had submitted strike notice. On 2 September, a hundred and fifty harbour workers marched behind a red flag to the offices of the Harbour Commissioners and hoisted another red flag over the building. The workers imposed a blockade on the port and trade in and out began to be seriously affected. On 6 September, the ITGWU Branch Secretary, Bob Day, with two colleagues, took possession of the harbour offices for a number of hours and Day was elected as Chief Commissioner. Not long after, the dispute was settled in the workers' favour by arbitration but local Sinn Féin members were unhappy with the red flag replacing the tricolour over the harbour offices during the dispute. Day and a colleague were expelled from the Republican movement, having been 'tried' on a charge of defying the authority of the Dáil. He joined the Labour party and was elected a TD the following year. Elsewhere in Cork, in January 1922, there was an attempt to make railway employees work for more hours. They responded by seizing the railway, running it themselves and, after two days, the employers backed down. Near Mallow, workers seized the mills in Quartertown, formed a workers' council and ran production but the IRA intervened and evicted them.

In Killarney, county Kerry, workers seized a saw mills and the 'contagion' spread well beyond the province of Munster: engineers at the Drogheda Iron Foundry, in county Louth, took over the foundry for a day and proclaimed a soviet until they were removed by the RIC. The short-lived occupation was no more than a protest following an unsuccessful six weeks long strike against a wage cut. A clothing factory was taken over in Dublin and, in May 1921, the miners in Arigna, county Leitrim, occupied the mine in a successful attempt to resist a proposed pay cut. It was run as a Soviet for two months before they won an increase and handed the mine back to the owners.

The Dáil Cabinet and, later, the Free State Executive Council were extremely worried by the worker militancy because it raised class issues that they saw as having the potential to undermine the national unity needed to achieve independence. Initially somewhat sympathetic to the worker interests, the Dáil Minister for Labour, Countess Constance Markiewicz, quickly revised her attitude as the militancy escalated and threatened to brush aside the Republican campaign and its relatively more affluent supporters. In a report to the Dáil Cabinet after the soviet at Bruree, she expressed her concern that 'in some areas the workers are not willing to submit to the authority of their executive and are beginning to get out of hand'.

In October 1921, in the context of the pay dispute and workers' takeover at the Castleconnell fisheries, the Countess warned her Cabinet colleagues that 'What is to be feared in the future is small local outbreaks growing more and more frequent and violent. The immediate result of which will be destruction of property and much misery which will tend to disrupt the Republican cause.' In a speech, Markiewicz appealed 'to both workers and employers to each shoulder their share of suffering for Ireland, and to try to avoid strikes and lockouts during this coming winter by first trying to arrange their difficulties amicably by conferences under the auspices of men appointed by my Ministry.' This superficially even-handed approach was not applied in Castleconnell – perhaps because the owner was a Sinn Féin member. The Minister for Home Affairs, Austin Stack, instructed Republican police, aided by IRA Volunteers, to put the strikers 'out of Mr. Mackey's premises'. Markiewicz herself was to talk to ITGWU leaders in Liberty Hall 'with a view to having an organizer sent down to settle the dispute'.

The diversified business activities of the wealthy Cleeve's family were a particular focal point for the militant union activity during this time. The family's business empire employed about three thousand workers and it processed milk supplied by five thousand farmers. Their other interests included milling and bakeries. Thomas Cleeve had founded the Condensed Milk Company of Ireland in 1883, with headquarters at the Lansdowne plant on the banks of the Shannon in Limerick city. He was born in Canada, of English and Huguenot descent, but came to Limerick in his teens to live with relatives of his mother. In 1900, during Queen Victoria's visit to Ireland, the Lord Lieutenant made him a Knight and he was three times elected High Sheriff of Limerick. The family were unionists and had supported recruitment campaigns for the British army in World War One. Sir Thomas died suddenly in 1908 and the company passed to his son Francis.

Cleeve's had a reputation for poor working conditions and their wage levels for unskilled employees were reputed to be among the lowest in the country. The company strongly resisted trade union claims. During December 1921, the Condensed Milk Company of Ireland sought lay-offs and wage cuts of one third among its workforce in Limerick, Cork, Tipperary and Waterford, blaming a downturn in prices. The ITGWU called together delegates representing sixty-eight creameries. The workers unanimously rejected the proposed cuts.

Early in 1922, the Dáil's Department of Labour brought both sides to a meeting in Dublin and Countess Markiewicz established an arbitration procedure but their recommendations failed to resolve the dispute. Her successor as Minister for Labour, Joe McGrath, told the Dáil that the company's accounts disclosed a need for a big cut in wages to make it viable. The workers offered a temporary reduction of 10 – 12% but the company rejected this. They demanded a larger decrease, and the workers went on strike. After a time, Cleeve's retaliated by announcing the closure of all their factories from 12 May 1922, imperilling the livelihoods of thousands of farmers and throwing three thousand employees out of work.

The Workers' Council of Action called for resistance to the closure plan, including occupations of the factories if necessary. In Clonmel, the ITGWU Branch Secretary, Michael Lennon, led a workers' occupation of the factory under the red flag. In Carrick on Suir, the workers appointed the ITGWU Branch Secretary, Michael Banks, as manager of the factory and the '*Irish Times*' reported that 'Business continued under the new management, the milk being brought in on lorries by the local farmers.' The workers seized almost a hundred creameries and declared them to be soviets, including Bansha, Kilmallock, Knocklong, Bruree, Athlacca, Tankardstown, Ballingaddy and Aherlow. To prevent a seizure of the major Lansdowne plant, in Limerick city, the Free State authorities posted troops there but in Tipperary town, the local ITGWU Branch Secretary, Michael Shelly, took the keys from the manager by force and ordered him to leave the premises or be shot. At this stage of the

Civil War, Tipperary town was still under the control of the Anti-Treaty forces who took the company's side and threatened to shoot workers if they continued the occupation.

The initial co-operation shown by farmers around Carrick-on-Suir, county Tipperary, soon changed to outright opposition. Farmers there declared a boycott of the creamery until it was handed back to the owners and the supply of milk dwindled from 68,000 litres a day to a mere twenty litres. Further West along the Suir valley, farmers refused to supply milk unless the red flag was taken down from the Clonmel creamery. Elsewhere, farmers began similar boycotts and refused to supply milk, and the creamery in Caherconlish, county Limerick, was burned down after it took in milk diverted from other plants.

On 17 May 1922, the Limerick Farmers' Union formalised the boycotts by forbidding their members to supply milk under the red flag. Speaking at the farmers' meeting, the Sinn Féin chairman of Limerick County Council, Bartholomew Laffan, said that he would rather see milk spilled than supplied to the Red Flag: 'All lawful government is ignored and instead we have the cross roads legislators… We forbid our members to supply the Red Flag which is the flag of revolution and anarchy'. In Dublin, the executive committee of the Irish Farmers' Union sought full compensation for their members and pledged their full moral and physical support to the Free State government if they would 'take immediate steps to re-establish law and order'.

Liberty Hall, in Dublin, offered help to the workers by storing butter there and arranging for it to be exported to Scotland. Matters escalated in Carrick-on-Suir when farmers formed a Citizen Guard to protect their interests and farmers elsewhere began to sell their milk directly on the streets. A headline 'Bolshevism in Clonmel', appeared over an '*Irish Independent*' report that 'Cleeve's employees, mostly female, attacked and tore supplies of butter from women of the farming class at the usual Saturday market'.

For the embattled workers, strike funds were running low and they were obliged to take strike pay in butter rather than cash. They were beginning to feel severe pressure and some factories were handed back voluntarily. On 9 June 1922, the Free State Government decided that 'in the event of the present situation continuing beyond the 21st, the strikers should be ejected by troops, who would occupy the buildings until such time as a settlement should be reached'.

Not long after the Government's intervention, Cleeve's informed the Minister for Labour that they had reached an agreement on wages in Limerick and that work would shortly resume there and at thirty-four auxiliary creameries. Now, sensing complete victory, on the same day they wrote to the Secretary to the Government enquiring 'what steps the Government are taking to give us possession of our general factories at Knocklong, Tipperary, Mallow, Clonmel and Carrick-on-Suir. We think it time that the Government made some move in restoring us our property. We expect a definite reply in course of post'.

The outbreak of the Civil War at the end of that month, altered the Government's immediate focus somewhat and temporarily put on hold their plans to forcibly retake plants. The Munster 'Republic' was an anti-Treaty stronghold and had provided an environment conducive to worker militancy and factory occupations. However, as the Free State forces advanced across the province in the Summer of 1922 and towns were re-taken, they were keen to put down 'Bolshevism' and to re-assert traditional class hierarchies and structures. As the Free State took Tipperary town at the end of July, the retreating Republicans set fire to the Cleeve's plant. In August, having taken Clonmel, one of the military's first tasks was to remove the red flag from above the Cleeve's factory at Suir Island.

The dispute between Cleeve's and its workers spluttered to a conclusion through the final months of 1922 and into 1923 in some parts of Munster. The workers had suffered pay cuts, lost wages and borne job losses but the company also had sustained serious damage during the long and bitter dispute. Competitors had taken their market share and they had lost their suppliers to competitors. At the end of 1923, the company went into liquidation. It was taken over by another company and in 1927 it became part of the newly established State-sponsored Dairy Disposal Company, set up to rationalise and modernise the dairy industry by transforming privately owned creameries into farmer-owned co-operatives. On the union side, the ITGWU sacked their radical Organiser John Dowling and he returned to Cobh to resume work as a fitter.

Eventually, in 1923, after several years of intense trade union activity, faced with forceful resistance from employers and varying shades of Republicanism, the tide of militancy that had swept much of Ireland finally receded. In Waterford, a dispute in the Gas Works involved the flying of the red flag, the expulsion of the manager and the election of a workers' management committee. They ran the company efficiently and provided gas supplies to the city for a number of months until the Free State Army moved in at night, overpowered the skeleton staff and hauled down the red flag.

After Limerick, ITGWU membership continued to expand greatly in rural areas and, as well as the industrial militancy, farm labourers seized scores of big farms and major labourers' strikes occurred in counties Meath, Kildare, Wexford and Waterford – the latter, in 1923, being particularly prolonged and bitter. During the tumultuous years from 1919 to 1923 a wave of soviets, occupations and strikes rolled across Munster from Limerick to Waterford and places in between. These activities were all put down by either Free State troops or Anti-Treaty Irregulars depending on where they happened and which side was prevailing at that stage in the Civil War. In an echo of how Limerick ended and was abandoned by outside forces, these later soviets were opposed at every step by a coalition of timid national union leaders, the Catholic bishops, Republicans and Free Staters.

As Treasurer of the ITGWU, and from 1924 as General Secretary, William O'Brien saw himself not only as the custodian of the flame of James Connolly's teachings but also as defender of the tangible manifestation of those teachings, the union itself. Throughout the turbulent years from 1919 to 1923 he adroitly trod a narrow path between invoking the radical rhetoric of Connolly's teachings and conserving the fabric and existence of the union. However, towards the end of that period, the unrelenting pressure on the union's finances and membership from economic recession, employer and farmer resistance as well as from Republican and Free State suppression, forced him to choose consolidation and conservatism over militancy. His role was one of creating and maintaining a union organisation, rather than one of lead industrial struggles.

In March 1919, the ITGWU had twenty-one full-time organisers but by 1922 there were only nine. The fall in numbers reflected a steep decline in the union's membership. Following the end of the Munster soviets, having earlier fired John Dowling, O'Brien sacked the other radical union Organisers – McGrath and Hedley – thus signalling a retreat from militant trade unionism and continuing a long decline in membership and influence that did not recover until well into the 1930s, when the free market economics of the Cumann na nGaedhael Free Staters was replaced by Fianna Fáil protectionism.

In the longer term, however, as it faded from wider memory, the Limerick general strike left little mark on trade unionism or politics in Limerick, other than a contribution to trade union folklore. The strike treasurer, James Casey, became Mayor of Limerick for a short time in 1921 after British forces murdered the Sinn Féin Mayor, George Clancy, and the former Mayor Michael O'Callaghan. Casey remained a lifelong member of the Labour party and served as a city councillor for more than thirty years. The rail workers' leader, Michael Keyes, went on to be elected as a Labour Dáil Deputy and held ministerial positions in the two inter-party governments formed in 1948 and 1954. Other leaders of the strike divided on the Anglo-Irish Treaty of 1921 and drifted away from independent working-class politics. In the 1930s, Keyes and Dan Clancy spoke from platforms in support of the pro-Franco Irish Christian Front and the Trades Council itself, unanimously, sent a motion to the Papal Nuncio and the Bishop of Limerick protesting against 'the attacks on the Church in Spain'.

Apart from the Limerick strike, 1919 was the high watermark of the syndicalist influence on Irish trade unions for another reason. The Trade Union Congress of that year adopted a reorganisation plan that was to involve the establishment of ten big industrial unions, all merging into the syndicalist ideal of one big union. However, the plan was, effectively, shelved. It impinged too much on the autonomy of the existing trade unions who found it hard to overcome the divisions between craft and non-craft unions and the rapidly growing ITGWU – which saw itself as the real 'one big union' – was hardly going to cede that position to a new, untried entity. In addition, influential leaders like Tom Johnson had begun the long push towards the eventual separation of the Congress from the Labour party and the concentration on more conventional forms of organisation.

The strike had no lasting influence on the Irish Labour movement nationally nor did it become a model to be followed in later phases of the War of Independence. The annual Congress of 1919 urged trade unions to organise workers' councils in all cities and towns, but to little effect. There were, no doubt, some further general strikes: a twenty-four-hour general strike in 1920 in support of Republican hunger strikers and, in the same year, a national strike by lorry drivers and mechanics against the imposition of military permits for motor vehicles and a boycott by rail and dock workers of munitions intended for the British military. However, these actions were merely ancillary to the Republican struggle and in no way meant that Labour was challenging for leadership, as it did for a time in Limerick. The hundreds of localised general strikes, occupations of creameries and factories and seizures of estates or farms – most notably in the province of Munster – that were often known as 'soviets', were too localised and isolated to offer any concerted challenge to British rule or to the established economic and social order.

The Irish Labour Party and Trade Union Congress that faced decisions on the later soviets was substantially different to the movement that almost went to the brink of revolution in Limerick in April 1919. The Limerick experience had rendered it even more cautious. The post-1916 movement was syndicalist in organisation and rhetoric but some key leaders like Tom Johnson hankered after parliamentary means to promote their policies, while others – notably William O'Brien – applied the bulk of their energies to trade union bureaucracy and organisation. Between them, Johnson and O'Brien formed the new, full-time leadership of the Congress with Johnson's newly-formed secretariat carrying out research and drafting policy documents. The limited administrative and political abilities of others on the Congress executive gave Johnson a strong hand over policy formulation. He was a member of the Socialist Party of Ireland but in his personal politics his leanings were more towards limited trade union action rather than radical political activity. But he was a conscientious listener to the rank-and-file and tried to some extent to reflect their views. That explains why on so many occasions – the Limerick soviet being the prime example – Johnson developed the knack of sounding radical while actually restraining action. As Emmet O'Connor perceptively notes in his work '*Syndicalism in Ireland 1917–23*' 'He was particularly adept at citing radical reasons for conservative decisions'.

Despite its decline in membership from 1922 onwards, the ITGWU remained the most practical manifestation of Connolly's syndicalist legacy to the working-class. But the Labour movement's emphasis on syndicalism reflected its failure to develop and maintain a revolutionary socialist political party. In this weakness, however, lay a paradoxical strength. Syndicalism emphasised rank-and-file power and decried bureaucratic officialdom. It synthesised the sympathetic strike and respect for the picket line into formidable weapons and it offered a form of working-class democracy, based on direct workshop representation, that seemed a plausible alternative to conventional politics. In the end, though, it could not survive the traumas of Connolly's death and Larkin's absence in America, nor the cautious leadership of their successors, Johnson and O'Brien

Through his participation and death in the 1916 Rising, James Connolly had earned a place for Labour in the forefront of the struggle for Irish independence. Ironically, however, the executions removed Connolly and other socially radical Republican leaders like Eamonn Ceannt and Seán MacDiarmada from the subsequent struggles. In both the Labour and militant nationalist movements, leadership passed to the second rank – less courageous and more conservative in their political and social aims than those who had died. By participating in the Irish Free State Dáil of 1922, Labour, in effect, accepted the terms of the Anglo-Irish treaty that had provoked the bitter Civil War. Its entry into the Dáil left it free to abandon much of its syndicalist trappings and take on the parliamentary role that Johnson coveted. In so doing, it forfeited much of its rank-and-file militancy and support.

As regards the Limerick strike of April 1919, it could be argued that it was largely the lip-service paid to syndicalism by the leadership of the Irish Trade Union Congress that eventually led to the strike's demise. In the end, the soviet was basically an emotional and spontaneous protest on essentially nationalist and humanitarian grounds, rather than anything based on socialist or even trade union aims. In sporting parlance, for Labour, Limerick was a short-term honourable draw but a long-term defeat, with the subsequent struggle for national independence largely taken over by the small farming and lower middle classes. Labour intervened with the strike weapon only on occasions when it seemed that Britain had exceeded the parameters of democracy or humanitarianism. However, on each of these occasions, the Labour leadership followed the line they had set in Limerick and were careful to ensure that the protests did not escalate into a major political challenge, either to Britain or the nascent Irish Republic.

Yet, in challenging the imposition of a special military area (SMA), the Limerick workers were, unwittingly, striking at the root of Britain's power in Ireland. The theory of the SMAs was that the pressure and inconvenience caused to peaceful citizens would force them to give up members of the 'murder gangs in their midst'. Later in the Anglo-Irish War, entire counties and regions were proclaimed under the same regulations. The right to impose military restrictions, like the permit system, went to the root of British sovereignty and was crucial to their plans to hold Ireland. The denial of the right to impose such restrictions by the workers amounted to a denial of British sovereignty over Ireland. But the Limerick strike did not dissuade the British authorities from proclaiming military law on a wide scale in Ireland in the later period of the Anglo-Irish war. None of this analysis is to detract from the courage, enthusiasm and remarkable organisational qualities of the strikers, which are repeatedly commented on in contemporary reports.

For those reasons, the military and the RIC were pleased with the outcome of the confrontation. The strike had been called off at the intervention of a Sinn Féin Mayor and a Catholic bishop who was reputed to be sympathetic to Sinn Féin. Although General Griffin had made some concessions, these were strictly compatible with the continuation of the restrictions of the special military area.

The Inspector-General of the RIC in his monthly report for April 1919 enthused that the 'failure of this strike is believed to have damaged the prestige of Sinn Féin and the workers.' The chief secretary for Ireland, Ian Macpherson MP, was able to claim that the government had no hesitation in using the forces at its disposal against the strike 'when Labour attempted in Limerick to use that legitimate weapon for other than industrial means – namely for unconstitutional and political ends.' 'After the first excesses at Limerick, Belfast and Dublin', Macpherson wrote, 'things were at last becoming normal and confidence was returning to the loyal, though terrorised, people'. In its annual report for 1919, the Irish TUC dismissed Macpherson's comments as 'a lying boast'.

But the strike and its ending brought provided little long-term encouragement for Dublin Castle. Faced early on with a choice between condemning the death of Constable O'Brien or that of Robert Byrne, moderate opinion in Limerick had opted for the latter. In the end, when 'moderation' reasserted itself in Limerick, it was not directed against nationalism as such, but against the local and national trade union leadership involved in the strike. The initial widespread support, and the duration of the strike, should have warned the authorities that support for separatism had achieved and new and wider respectability. The Limerick strike was a clear warning that many elements in the civilian population were disaffected enough to provide the silent support that the Volunteers needed to launch their guerrilla war.

Despite the claims and boasts made at the ILPTUC annual conference in Drogheda, the outcome of the Limerick Soviet was limited. Mainly under clerical pressure, but also because it lacked widespread national trade union support, the strike began to fizzle out after ten days. At least the leaders adroitly turned this into an orderly, partial return to work and followed it up with a clear-cut decision some days later for a full resumption of work. In that sense, they preserved the organisation and morale of the Limerick trade unions and lessened the potential for recriminations. For three years after Easter Week 1916, rank-and-file militancy on issues like conscription had ensured that Labour maintained a place at the centre of the struggle for independence, despite the reservations of its leadership. Until the outcome of the Limerick soviet was determined, the possibility existed of Labour asserting a greater leadership role. Limerick changed that. From then on, Labour's role in the struggle for independence diminished from one of joint partnership to a subsidiary status. The outcome of the Limerick Soviet both determined and expressed Labour's subordination to 'nation' from that point onwards.

From early in 1919, violence was emerging again as a significant factor in Irish politics. The sweeping victory of Sinn Féin in the December 1918 general election and the establishment of the separatist Dáil Éireann in January 1919 were followed by an increasing level of violence. As Emil Strauss aptly commented in his book '*Irish Nationalism and British Democracy*': 'The Irish war, which began practically at the same time as the First Dáil, was to some extent a conscious assertion of leadership by the extremists.' In the heat of a violent war, a strike – even a general strike – seemed timid and ineffective by comparison. Nor would it have been a strategy that appealed to the farmers and lower middle classes who were coming to dominate the independence movement. The result of the Limerick strike suggested to many that, if political gains were to be made, sterner weapons than the strike placard would have to be used. To use a modern analogy, Labour had fulfilled its role as a booster rocket to the vehicle of mainstream nationalism. From this point onwards, whenever trade unionists played a part in the struggle, it was primarily in their capacity as individual members of the IRA, the IRB or the Dáil.

Had the Limerick general strike achieved some success against the government, the subsequent independence struggle might have been entirely different in character. Sinn Féin and the IRA would have had to pay more attention to Labour's economic demands and take account of them in any settlement with Britain. From such a position, Labour might have found greater support, and exerted greater influence, in the fledgling Irish Free State. As it was, the movement never recovered politically from an unfair perception of having remained largely on the side-lines during the War of Independence and the Civil War, and that political weakness has persisted to this day.

For Ireland and its Labour movement, the consequences of the events of April 1919 in Limerick city were profound.

Chronology of Events

1918

31 December   Party of RIC from John Street police station raid Robert Byrne's home at Town Wall Cottage.

1919

13 January   Robert Byrne, trade union activist and Adjutant of Second Battalion, Mid – Limerick Brigade, Irish Volunteers, is arrested and charged with possession of a revolver and ammunition. Remanded in custody in Limerick Prison.

14 January   Byrne starts a hunger strike in Limerick Prison.

16 January   He resumes taking food.

18 January   Byrne writes a cheerful letter to his mother.

21 January   Byrne's court martial, under DORA, begins at the New Barracks, Lord Edward Street, Limerick.

2 February   Byrne is sentenced to twelve months' imprisonment with hard labour. Within days, as senior officer in Limerick Prison, Byrne leads a campaign of disobedience in support of a claim for political status for the Republican prisoners.

8 February   A leaflet is distributed anonymously attacking forcible feeding of Republican prisoners in Limerick Prison.

14 February   Limerick United Trades and Labour Council supports the granting of political status to the prisoners and condemns their treatment.

7 March   Robert Byrne is confined to bed in the prison hospital.

12 March	A weakened Byrne is removed to Number One Ward of Limerick Workhouse, also known as the Union Infirmary.
14th March	Robert Byrne resumes taking food.
Sunday, 6 April	Robert Byrne is fatally wounded during an IRA rescue at Limerick Workhouse Hospital. He dies later that evening in John Ryan's cottage, Meelick, county Clare.
Tuesday, 8 April	At Meelick, county Clare, the inquest opens into the death of Robert Byrne. His body lies in state in Limerick's pro-Cathedral.
Wednesday, 9 April	An official communiqué warns that the government will not tolerate a military parade or assembly in military formation at Byrne's funeral. Under the Defence of the Realm Acts, Brigadier General CJ Griffin is appointed as the Competent Military Authority throughout Ireland. In a separate notice, Limerick city and part of the county is to be placed under Griffin's authority as a Special Military Area and workers and other citizens are required to obtain a military pass.
Thursday, 10 April	Thousands of Volunteers march in Robert Byrne's funeral to Mount Saint Lawrence's Cemetery in Limerick, through streets lined by military and police.
Friday, 11 April	Limerick United Trades and Labour Council describes Robert Byrne's death as 'murder' and passes a vote of condolence.
Saturday, 12 April	Workers employed at Cleeve's condensed milk factory on the Northern bank of the Shannon vote to strike against the military restrictions.
Sunday, 13 April (Palm Sunday)	Limerick United Trades and Labour Council declares a general strike against the imposition of military law on the city.

Monday, 14 April	The military restrictions requiring workers to display special passes on their way to and from work come into effect. At five o'clock in the morning, 14,000 Limerick workers begin a general strike. Gradually, the strikers tighten their control over food supplies, transport and communications.
Tuesday, 15 April	Legal representatives of Byrne's family claim his detention was illegal and his death in custody was therefore unlawful. In Dublin, executive members of the Irish Labour Party and Trade Union Congress consider the Limerick developments informally.
Wednesday 16 April	The Catholic bishop, Dr. Hallinan, and senior clergy severely criticise the military restrictions. The ILPTUC Treasurer, Tom Johnson, arrives in the city. A delegation of Limerick rail workers seeking support in Dublin receives a lukewarm reception.
Thursday, 17 April	General Griffin meets Limerick Chamber of Commerce and offers to allow employers to issue permits directly to their workers. The strikers reject this concession, despite pressure from the employers. In Dublin, after three days of meetings with representatives of the separatist Dáil Éireann, the executive of the ILPTUC decides to travel to Limerick after Easter with a secret plan to evacuate the city.
Friday, 18 April	The Sinn Féin Comhairle Cheantair – in response to an approach by the Strike Committee – issues a circular seeking gifts of foodstuffs – particularly butter, milk, eggs, potatoes and vegetables.
Saturday, 19 April	A general meeting of prominent Limerick citizens protests against the military restrictions. Young boys taunt the sentries on Sarsfield Bridge and become extremely frightened when the military draw their weapons on them.

Easter Sunday, *20 April*	About 1,000 young men and women leave the city and gather at Caherdavin Heights outside the Military Area. They later mount a mass challenge to the military sentries on Thomond bridge, at the boundary of the Special Military Area.
Easter Monday, *21 April*	The Caherdavin demonstrators breach the military cordon.
Tuesday, 22 April	Leaders of major British-headquartered unions declare their opposition to the Limerick strike.
Wednesday, 23 April	Four members of the ILPTUC executive arrive in Limerick. They immediately begin a continuous series of meetings with the local strike leaders who are under the impression that a national strike is to be called. They reject the ILPTUC alternative plan for a protest evacuation.
Thursday, 24 April	Mediation by the Catholic bishop, Dr Hallinan, and the Sinn Féin Mayor, Alphonsus O'Mara, produces a peace formula. A strike committee proclamation allows all workers who can get to their work without passing the military barricades to resume work immediately. If Limerick remains quiet for a week, General Griffin promises to lift the military restrictions.
Friday, 25 April	Most of the strikers resume work. Only those still requiring military passes remain out.
Saturday, 26 April	Some residents of Thomondgate – still cut off from work by the military barricades – block Thomond bridge in protest.
Sunday, 27 April	A strike committee proclamation calls for a full resumption of work.

Monday, 28 April　　The remaining strikers resume work. Limerick United Trades and Labour Council decides not to take part in a national May Day stoppage.

5 May　　The military restrictions on Limerick are officially ended.

Sources

Official Records

State Paper Office, Dublin Castle (incorporated into the National Archives of Ireland):

Chief Secretary's Office Registered Papers 1918–20 inclusive;

General Prisons Board Papers 1917–20 inclusive

National Archives of Ireland:

Cabinet Minutes, First Dáil Éireann, 1919

Military Archives, Dublin:

Bureau of Military History, Witness Statements, 1913–21

WS 515 Eamon Dore

WS 525 Michael Stack

WS 583 Walter Carpenter

WS 628 James Tully

WS 656 Richard O'Connell

WS 660 Thomas Leahy

WS 765 Seumas Ó Goibín (James Gubbins)

WS 883 Lieut.-Col. John M MacCarthy

WS 939 Ernest Blythe

WS 1068 Lieut.-Gen. Michael Brennan

WS 1415 Michael Hartney

WS 1420 Patrick Whelan

WS 1423 Jeremiah Cronin

WS 1700 Alphonsus J O'Halloran (also WS 910)

WS 1710 Liam Forde

WS 1730 Peadar McMahon

WS 1755 Thomas Johnson

Military Service Pensions Collection (1916 – 23):

1/D/260 Mrs. Annie Byrne, re Robert J Byrne, Capt.

F354 and 6APB13 Files associated with the above file;

CMB 106 Limerick City Branch, Cumann na mBan

DP 60, DP 7/183, 2RB 273, 2RB 686, Michael Danford

MSPC 24/SP/1727 Richard Mulcahy

MSPC 24/SP1777 Michael J Stack

MSPC 24/SP9375 Michael Brennan

MSPC 24SP9436 Peadar MacMathghamhna (McMahon)

MSPC 34/321 Thomas Leahy

MSPC 34/2414 Peadar Dunne

MSPC 34/17158 Seán Thomas Riordan

MSPC 34/5711 Patrick Dawson

MSPC 34/F4702 Cornelius McNamara

MSPC 34/8789 Walter Carpenter

MSPC 34/46345 Liam Forde

MSPC 34/59296 Michael Colivet

Public Record Office, London:

CO 903/19/5 Intelligence Notes, Chief Secretary's Office, Judicial Division

CO 904/20 United Irish League

CO 904/35 Circulars, Judicial Division, 1904 – 1919

CO/904/39 Depositions, Petitions, Judicial Proceedings 1918 – 21

CC 904/108 Inspector-General RIC, Confidential Reports on Limerick

CC 904/109 Inspector-General RIC, Confidential Reports on Limerick

CO 904/158/4 Strikes, 1918 – 19

CO 904/161/2 Press Censor's Reports Jan–Mar 1919

CO 904/161/3 Correspondence censored 1916 – 19

CO 904/161/4 Seizures of leaflets, postcards etc. 1915 – 19

CO 904/164/ Mail, correspondence 1916

CO 904/169/1 DORA Custody of Persons Awaiting Trial

CO 904/169/2 Prohibition of Meetings 1918 – 20

CO 904/169/3 Orders by Competent Military Authorities

CO 904/177/1 Attempted murder of Constables in Cork

CO 904/187/1 Withdrawals of Troops1917 – 19

CO 904/194/ 36 Byrne R

CO 904/194/37 Byrne, RJ

CO 906/18 Treatment of Internees 1918 – 19

WO 35/69/6 Publication of Seditious Articles 1916 – 20

WO/35/102/34 Defence of the Realm Regulations. Byrne Robert: – Revolver found in his bedroom, ammunition & manual field engineering found in other parts of his house

WO 35/172 Movement of Troops in Ireland 1919 – 21 (Retained by the War Office)

WO 35/173 Royal Flying Corps in Ireland 1919 – 21 (Retained by the War Office)

WO 182 Part 1/1/2 Record of Hostilities and Events 1919 – 21

Trade Union Records

Limerick United Trades and Labour Council (LUTLC) Minute Book 22 March 1918 – September 1920

Irish Labour Party and Trade Union Congress (ILPTUC) Annual Report 1919

'Ireland at Berne', Report ILPTUC 1919

National Union of Railwaymen (NUR) Executive Committee Minute Book 1919

Newspapers

The Irish Independent, 17 August 1912

The Irish Times, Jan – May 1919

The Irish Independent, Jan – May 1919; 24 August 1936

The Limerick Leader, Mar – May 1919 and 19 March 1925; 19 March 1925; 15 June 1953

Munster News and Clare Advocate, Limerick, April 1919

Weekly Observer, Newcastle West, Co. Limerick, April 1919

The Bottom Dog, Limerick, Oct 1917 – Aug 1918

The Workers' Bulletin, Limerick, April 1919

Watchdog, Limerick, November 1919

The Workers' Bulletin, Belfast, April 1919

Red Flag, Limerick, 27 November 1919

Le Matin, Paris, April – May 1919

The Cork Examiner, 28 March 1925

The Irish Press, Dublin, 21 December 1960

Newspaper Library, British Library, Colindale

Limerick Chronicle April 1919

Limerick Echo, April 1919

Limerick Weekly Echo, April 1919

The Southern Democrat, April 1919

Private Papers

Count Plunkett Papers, National Library of Ireland

Tom Johnson Papers, National Library of Ireland

O'Brien Papers, National Library of Ireland, MS 15654, Letters of Thomas Farren

Oral History

Interview: Jim Kemmy, with Michael 'Batty' Stack

Interview: Kevin O'Connor, with Charles St. George

Select Bibliography and Other Sources

https://livesofthefirstworldwar.org/lifestory/1470218 Brigadier-General Christopher Griffin

https://livesofthefirstworldwar.org/lifestory/4611413 Captain AC Ward DSO

https://irishconstabulary.com/limerick-county-t638.html The Royal Irish Constabulary Forum

Facebook: https://bit.ly/2HfAyBE The Limerick Soviet 1919

Twitter: https://bit.ly/2nZGXbQ @LimerickSoviet

Bowyer Bell, J, 'The Secret Army', London, 1972

Boyce, DG, 'Englishmen and Irish Troubles', London, 1972

Breen, John, 'A Flame in Spring – the Story of the Limerick Soviet', pageant, first performance 18 April 1989, Belltable Arts Centre, Limerick

British and Irish Communist Organisation, 'The Connolly–Walker Controversy', Belfast, 1969

Cahill, Liam, 'The Limerick Soviet: the influence of Syndicalism on the Irish Labour Movement 1916–1919', lecture to Irish Labour History Society, October 1979 and to Waterford Labour History Society, December 1981

Cahill, Liam, 'The Limerick Soviet: Sixty Years On', article, Civil Service Review, July/August 1979

Cahill, Liam, 'Brief Life of the Limerick Soviet', article, *Irish Independent*, 17 April 1979

Cahill, Liam, 'Cathair Luimní faoi smacht Choiste Stailce', article, 'Irish Press', 7 April 1979

Cahill, Liam, 'The Limerick Soviet 1919: Its Place in History and Politics', 70th Anniversary Commemorative Lecture, Limerick, 14 April 1989

Cahill, Liam, 'Forgotten Revolution, Limerick Soviet 1919', The O'Brien Press, Dublin, 1990

Cahill, Liam, 'The Limerick Soviet 1919 – 2009: Ninety Years On – A Meditation', talk, Hunt Museum, Limerick, 18 April 2009 and to Kildare Labour Party Constituency Council, April 2009

Cahill, Liam, 'A City Defies an Empire: The Limerick Soviet of 1919', Limerick Historical Society, 9 April 2018 and to Irish Humanist Association, Limerick, 9 September 2018

Campbell, Colm, 'Emergency Law in Ireland 1918 – 1925', Clarendon Press Oxford, 1994

Casey, James, 'A Limerick Challenge to British Tyranny', chapter in 'Limerick's Fighting Story', pp. 185 et seq., Anvil Books, Tralee, county Kerry, 1947.

Caulfield, Max, 'The Easter Rebellion', New York/London, 1963

Clarkson Dunsmore, J, 'Labour and Nationalism in Ireland', New York, 1926

Cody, O'Dowd, Rigney, 'The Parliament of Labour: 100 Years of the Dublin Council of Trade Unions, Dublin, 1986

Comerford, Máire, 'The First Dáil', Mercier Press, Dublin

Connolly, James, 'Socialism Made Easy', Socialist Labour Press, Dublin, 1918

Connolly, James, 'The Reconquest of Ireland', Dublin/Belfast 1968

Crosbie, Judith, 'The Era of Radicalism: Limerick's Mayors During World War One'. Pp 213 – 223, 'Remembering Limerick', Limerick Civic Trust, 1997

Cross, Brian, 'Limerick Soviet Commemorative Show', catalogue, Limerick Municipal Gallery, 24 April – 14 May 1989

Dalgleish, James M, 'The Limerick General Strike, 1919', thesis, University of Warwick, 1977

Dana, Jacqueline, 'Connolly Ain't Nothing but a Train Station in Dublin: The Expropriation of James Connolly's Revolutionary Legacy by Irish Republicanism', research study, James Connolly Society of Canada and the United States, 1998

Davies, Frank and Maddocks, Graham, 'Bloody Red Tabs: General Officer Casualties of the Great War 1914 – 18, Pen and Sword publishers, Barnsley, 2014

Dawson, Richard, 'Red Terror and Green', London, 1920

Deegan, James, 'The Limerick Soviet', paper, Irish Conference of History Students, January 1978

Donovan, TM, 'Revolution: Christian or Communist', (pamphlet), c. 1920s

Dorney, John, 'The General Strike and Irish Independence', 'The Irish Story' website, 6 June 2013, https://bit.ly/2H6mE8D

Ellis Beresford, Peter, 'A History of the Irish Working Class', London, 1972

Fanning, Ronan, 'Fatal Path, British Government and the Irish Revolution 1910 – 1922', Faber & Faber, London, 2013

Farrell, Brian, 'The Founding of Dáil Éireann', Gill and Macmillan, Dublin, 1971

Farry, Michael, 'Sligo 1914 – 21, A Chronicle of Conflict', Killoran Press, Trim, County Meath, 1992

Farry, Michael, 'The Irish Revolution 1912–23, Sligo', Dublin, 2012

Ferriter, Diarmaid, 'A Nation and not a Rabble', Profile Books, London, 2015

Finn, Mike, 'Bread Not Profits', play reading, Bell Table Arts Centre, Limerick, 14 December 2017

Fitzgibbon, Gerard, 'The Red Washed Through the Green', '*The Limerick Leader*', 10 April 2009

Fitzpatrick, David, 'Politics and Irish Life, 1913–1921: Provincial Experience of War and Revolution', Cork University Press, 1977

Fitzpatrick, David, 'Strike in Ireland 1914 – 21', pp 26 – 39, 'Saothar 6', Journal of the Irish Labour History Society, 1980

Fox, RM, 'Labour in the National Struggle', Irish Labour Party, Dublin, 1947

Framework Films, Cork (in collaboration with Limerick Council of Trade Unions), documentary, 'The Limerick Soviet', 2015

Fyfe, Hamilton, 'Keir Hardie', London, 1935

Gilmore, George, 'The Relevance of James Connolly in Ireland Today', Dublin, 1975

Goldring, Maurice, 'Connolly Reassessed', pp 50 – 53, 'Saothar 7', Journal of the Irish Labour History Society, 1981

Gordon, Cecile, 'The Military Service (1916 – 23) Pensions Collection: Evidence of a Revolution Through Ordinary Voices', pp 169 – 178, 'Saothar 41', Journal of the Irish Labour History Society, 2016

Greaves, C Desmond, 'The Life and Times of James Connolly', London, 1961

Greaves, C Desmond, 'Liam Mellows and the Irish Revolution', Lawrence and Wishart, London, 1971

Greaves, C Desmond, 'The Irish Transport and General Workers' Union: the formative years 1909–23', Gill and Macmillan, Dublin, 1982

Hamilton, Frank, 'Ben Dinneen and Days of the Bottom Dog', Address, Limerick, June 1987

Hamilton, Frank, 'The Bottom Dog: A Study in Irish Labour Journalism', essay, nd.

Hanamy, John, Strike, a play on the Limerick Soviet, first performance by Pretentious Productions, Ark Tavern, Corbally, Limerick, May Day 1989

Harvey, Trevor Gordon, 'An Army of Brigadiers, British Brigade Commanders at the Battle of Arras 1917', Ph.D. thesis, University of Birmingham

Haugh, Dominic, 'The Bottom Dog and the Bishop's Crozier': The Catholic hierarchy and the trade union movement in Limerick 1916–22, 'History Studies, Journal of the University of Limerick History Society', Vol. 7, 2006, p.1

Haugh, Dominic, 'The ITGWU in Limerick 1917 – 22', pp 27 – 42, 'Saothar 31' Journal of the Irish Labour History Society, 2006

Haugh, Dominic, 'Socialist Revolution in Ireland – A Lost Opportunity 1916 – 22', pp 7 – 19, 'Marxist Perspectives on Irish Society', ed. Micheal O'Flynn, Odette Clarke, Paul M. Hayes and Martin J. Power, Cambridge Scholars Publishing, 2011

Hehir, Niamh, 'The Limerick Soviet Revisited', lecture, Annual Seminar, Limerick Labour History Research Group

Hehir, Niamh and Morrissey, Joe, 'Ten Days that Shook Limerick', article, in Revolt of the Bottom Dog, schools history pack, Limerick Labour History Research Group, January 1989

Hepburn, AC, 'The Conflict of Nationality in Ireland', London, 1980

Hobsbawm, EJ, 'Working Classes and Nations', pp 75 – 85, 'Saothar 8', Journal of the Irish Labour History Society, 1982

Hodson, Tom, Colonel (Retd.), 'Chiefs of Staff, The Portrait Collection of the Irish Defence Forces', Irish History Press, Dublin, 2012

Holmes, Eamon, 'The Limerick Soviet 1919', BA mini-thesis, UCD, 1977

Holt, Edgar, 'Protest in Arms: the Irish Troubles 1916 – 23', New York, 1961

Hunt, RN Carew, 'The Theory and Practice of Communism', London, 1963

Inglis, Brian, 'Roger Casement', London, 1974

ITGWU (now SIPTU), 'The Limerick Soviet', supplement issued in 'Liberty', Journal of the ITGWU, Diamond Jubilee Edition, 1984

Jeffries, John, 'John Dowling – Cobh's Forgotten Revolutionary', pp 38 – 39, 'Look Left', Issue no. 23, 19 July 2017

Jupp, Peter and Magennis, Eoin, 'Crowds in Ireland c. 1720 – 1920', Macmillan Press Ltd., 2000

Keane, Thomas, 'Class, Religion and Society in Limerick City 1922 – 1939' Ph.D. (History), Mary Immaculate College, University of Limerick, 2015

Kemmy, Jim, 'The Limerick Soviet', article, '*The Irish Times*', 9 May 1969

Kemmy, Jim, 'The Limerick Soviet', series of articles, '*Limerick Socialist*', April 1972 – February 1973

Kemmy, Jim, 'The Limerick Soviet', article, 'Saothar 2', Journal of the Irish Labour History Society, 1975 – 76

Kemmy, Jim, 'Women and the Limerick Soviet', '*Limerick Socialist*', May 1979

Kemmy, Jim, 'The General Strike 1919', article, 'The Old Limerick Journal', No. 2, March 1980

Kemmy, Jim, 'The Limerick Soviet of 1919', lecture, Galway Labour History Group, June 1988

Kemmy, Jim, 'James Casey – Soviet Treasurer', pp 264 – 266, 'Remembering Limerick', Limerick Civic Trust, 1997

Kennedy, Shane 'Troops without number – Limerick Soviet: a general strike against British militarism', essay, Summer Showcase 2017, Department of History, University of Limerick

Kenny, Bob, 'The Growth of the Irish Transport and General Workers' Union: A Geographer's View', pp 78 – 85, 'Saothar 12', Journal of the Irish Labour History Society', 1987

Kenny, Brian, 'When Ireland Went Red – The Soviet Experiment 1918 – 23', Personal History Publishing, Dublin, 2017

Keogh, Dermot, 'The Rise of the Irish Working Class', Belfast, 1982

Kostick, Conor, 'Revolution in Ireland', Cork University Press, 2009 [1996]

Kostick, Conor, 'The Irish Working Class and the War of Independence', pp 18 – 28, 'Irish Marxist Review', Vol. 4, No. 14, 2015

Laffan, Michael, 'The Resurrection of Ireland, The Sinn Féin Party 1916 – 23, Cambridge University Press, 1999

Larkin, Emmet, 'James Larkin: Labour Leader', London, 1965

Lawler, Sheila, 'Britain and Ireland 1914 – 1923', Dublin, 1983

Lee, David (ed.), 'Remembering Limerick', Limerick Civic Trust, 1997

Lee, David and Toomey, Nora-Ann, 'The General Strike as a Political Weapon', pp 241 – 250, 'Remembering Limerick', Limerick Civic Trust, 1997

Lee, David, 'The Munster Soviets and the Fall of the House of Cleeve', essay in 'Made in Limerick', David Lee and Debbie Jacobs (Eds.), Volume 1, Limerick Civic Trust, 2003

Lee, Joseph, 'Irish Nationalism and Socialism: Rumpf Reconsidered', pp 59 – 64, 'Saothar 12', Journal of the Irish Labour History Society, 1987

Lenin, VI, 'Lenin on Ireland', Communist Party of Ireland, pamphlet, 1970

Limerick City Library, online index of holdings on the Limerick Soviet http://www. limerickcity.ie/Library/LocalStudies/LocalStudiesFiles/L/LimerickSoviet/

Limerick Teachers' Educational Committee, 'Limerick: A Handbook of Local History', nd

Limerick Soviet Remembered, web site, http://www.limericksovietremembered.com/

Lynch-Kearney, Frances Dr., The Potency of 'Soft Power': The Catholic Church's Influence on the Limerick Soviet of 1919', 'Scoláire Staire', January 2013, pp 14–18

Lyons, FSL, 'Charles Stewart Parnell', London, 1977

Lysaght O'Connor, DR, 'The Republic of Ireland', Cork, 1970

Lysaght O'Connor, DR, 'The story of the Limerick Soviet: the 1919 general strike against British militarism', Limerick, 1979

Lysaght O'Connor, DR, 'County Tipperary: Class Struggle and National Struggle 1916 – 24', in 'Tipperary: History and Society', Ed., William Nolan, Dublin 1985

Lysaght O'Connor, DR, 'The Rake's Progress of a Syndicalist: The Political Career of William O'Brien, Irish Labour Leader', pp 48 – 63, 'Saothar 9', Journal of the Irish Labour History Society', 1983

Lysaght O'Connor, DR, 'Of Soviets and Triple Power', Speech at the launch of the Fourth edition of 'The Story of the Limerick Soviet', April 17 2009

Macardle, Dorothy, 'The Irish Republic', London, 1968

MacCann, Sean, 'Limerick Accepts a Challenge', chapter in MacCann, Sean, 'War by the Irish', pp. 94 – 98, Anvil Books, Tralee, 1946

MacGiolla Coille, Breandán, 'Mourning the Martyrs', pp 29 – 44, 'The Old Limerick Journal', No. 22, 1987

McCarthy, Charles, 'Trade Unions in Ireland 1894 – 1960', Dublin, 1977

McCarthy, Charles, 'Labour and the 1922 General Election', pp 15 – 121, 'Saothar 7', Journal of the Irish Labour History Society, 1981

McCarthy, JM, (Ed.), 'Limerick's Fighting Story', Tralee, 1946

McCarthy, Pat, 'Waterford, The Irish Revolution 1912 – 23', Four Courts Press, Dublin, 2015

McCarthy, Pat, 'Waterford and the 1916 Rising', Waterford Commemoration 1916 Committee, 2016

McCarthy, Pat, 'The Redmonds and Waterford', Four Courts Press, Dublin, 2018

McCarthy, Terry, 'Labour v Sinn Féin', National Museum of Labour History, Labour Museum pamphlet no. 1

MacConmara, Tomás Dr., 'We had to go forward' – The Mountjoy Hunger Strike of 1917', 'The Irish Story' website, 10 December 2017, https://bit.ly/2D3AtAZ

McGee, Owen, 'The IRB, The Irish Republican Brotherhood from the Land League to Sinn Féin', Four Courts Press, Dublin, 2005

McNamara, Conor, 'An Introduction to Manuscript Sources on the Irish Citizen Army', pp 145 – 164, 'Saothar 41', Journal of the Irish Labour History Society, 2016

McNamara, Mike, 'The Limerick Soviet', Bottom Dog Publications, The Mechanics' Institute, Hartstonge Street, Limerick, n.d.

Mansergh, Nicholas, 'Ireland in the Age of Reform and Revolution', Allen and Unwin, London, 1940

Mapstone, Richard H, 'Trade Union and Government Relations: A Case Study of Influence on the Stormont Government', pp 35 – 46, 'Saothar 11', Journal of the Irish Labour History Society, 1987

Meleady, Dermot, 'John Redmond, The National Leader', Irish Academic Press, Dublin, 2014

Mitchell, Arthur, 'Labour in Irish politics, 1890 – 1930: the Irish labour movement in an age of revolution', Barnes and Noble, New York, 1974

Mitchell, David 'Ghost of a Chance: British Revolutionaries in 1919' in 'History Today', Vol. XX, No.11, November 1970

Molan, Timothy, 'The Limerick Soviet 1919', thesis, NIHE (now UL), Limerick, n.d.

Morgan, Austin and Purdie, Bob, (Eds.), 'Ireland: Divided Nation, Divided Class', London, 1980

Morgan, Austen, 'A British Labourist in Catholic Ireland', pp 54 – 61, 'Saothar 7', Journal of the Irish Labour History Society, 1981

Morgan, Austen, 'James Connolly: a political biography', Manchester University Press, 1988

Mortished, RJP, 'Trade Union Organisation in Ireland', pp 213 – 228, Journal of the Statistical and Social Inquiry Society of Ireland, Dublin, 1927

Mulcahy, General Richard, 'Chief of Staff 1919', pp 340 – 353, 'Capuchin Annual', Dublin, 1969

Murphy, William, 'Byrne, Robert ('Bobby')', The Dictionary of Irish Biography a project of the Royal Irish Academy, Cambridge University Press, ed. James McGuire and James Quinn, 2009

Murphy, William, 'Political Imprisonment and the Irish, 1912 – 1921', Oxford University Press, 2014

Nevin, Donal (Ed.), 'Trade Unions and Change in Irish Society', Cork, 1980

Newsinger, John, 'As Catholic as the Pope: James Connolly and the Catholic Church in Ireland', pp 7 – 18, 'Saothar 11', Journal of the Irish Labour History Society, 1986

O'Brien, James, 'Rare Irish Banknotes: The Limerick "Soviet" of 1919', website, 'Old Currency Exchange', https://bit.ly/2TGuDL9, 12 February 2015

O'Brien, William, (Ed. McLysaght, Edward), 'Forth the Banners Go: reminiscences of William O'Brien', Three Candles, Dublin, 1969

Ó Broin, Leon, 'Michael Collins', Dublin, 1980

O'Callaghan, John, 'Revolutionary Limerick, The Republican Campaign for Independence in Limerick, 1913 – 21', Irish Academic Press, Dublin, 2010

O'Callaghan, John, 'Limerick, The Irish Revolution 1912 – 23', Four Courts Press, Dublin, 2018

Ó Céilleachair, Ogie, musical, 'Baby Soviets', performed by students of Gaelcholáiste Luimní, Millennium Theatre, LIT, March 2018

O'Connell, Micheál, 'Remember Limerick 1919', pamphlet, Ealing & Brent Branch, London Militant Labour, April 1994

O'Connor, Emmet, 'Agrarian Unrest and the Labour Movement in County Waterford, 1917 – 23', pp 40 – 58, 'Saothar 6', Journal of the Irish Labour History Society, 1980

O'Connor, Emmet, 'An Age of Agitation', pp 64 – 71, 'Saothar 9', Journal of the Irish Labour History Society, 1983

O'Connor, Emmet, 'Syndicalism in Ireland 1917 – 23', Cork University Press, 1988

O'Connor, Emmet, 'A Labour History of Waterford', Waterford Trades Council, 1989

O'Connor, Emmet, 'Reds and the Green, Ireland, Russia and the Communist Internationals 1919 – 43', University College Dublin Press, 2004

O'Connor, Kevin, 'The Limerick Soviet', radio documentary, RTÉ, June 1974

O'Connor, Kevin, 'Permits Please', play, first performance 1989

O'Donoghue, Ciara, 'Ignorance is bliss – Cleeve's Condensed Milk Company and the Irish Revolution', essay, Summer Showcase 2017, Department of History, University of Limerick

O'Loughlin, Michael, 'Limerick 1919', poem, Atlantic Blues, Raven Arts Press, 1982

O'Malley, Ernie, 'The Singing Flame', Tralee, 1978

O'Riordan, Manus, 'James Connolly Re-Assessed: the Irish and European Connection', Aubane Historical Society, pamphlet, Millstreet, 2006

Ó Snodaigh, Aengus, 'Remembering the Past: Hospital rescue ends in tragedy', 'An Phoblacht', 9 April 1999

Paul, William, 'The Irish Crisis: Ireland and World Revolution', (pamphlet), Communist Party of Great Britain, London

Probert, Belinda, 'Marxism and the Irish Question', pp 65 – 71, 'Saothar 6', Journal of the Irish labour History Society, 1980

Queally, Nichola, 'Rebellion, Resistance and the Irish Working Class: The Case of the 'Limerick Soviet'', Cambridge Scholars Publishing, 2010

Robbins, Frank, 'Under the Starry Plough: Recollections of the Irish Citizen Army', The Academy Press, Dublin, 1977

Russell, Ruth, 'What's the Matter with Ireland?', The Devin-Adair Company, New York, 1920.

Ryan, Des, 'Shootout at the Workhouse', 'The Old Limerick Journal', Winter edition, 2010.

Ryan, WP, 'The Irish Labour Movement', Dublin, 1919

RTÉ 1 TV 'Urban Tales', short documentary, 27 February 2007

'Saothar', Journal of the Irish labour History Society, Nos. 2 – 43

Schneider, Fred D, 'Ireland and British Labour', 'The Review of Politics', University of Notre Dame, July 1978

Shaw, Francis, 'The Canon of Irish History – A Challenge', pp 115 – 53, 'Studies', Summer 1972

Strauss, Emil, 'Irish Nationalism and British Democracy', London, 1951

TG4, 'Sóivéidí na hÉireann', documentary, 2010

Townshend, Charles, 'The British Campaign in Ireland 1919 – 21', Oxford University Press, 1975

Townshend, Charles, 'Easter 1916, The Irish Rebellion', Allen Lane, London, 2005

Townshend, Charles, 'The Republic, The Fight for Irish Independence', Allen Lane, London, 2013

Walsh, Eoin Swithin, 'Kilkenny in Times of Revolution 1900 – 23', Merrion Press, Dublin, 2018

Walsh, Laurence, 'Historic Limerick: the City and its Treasures', Dublin, 1984

Yeates, Padraig, 'Irish craft workers in a time of revolution', pp 37 – 56, 'Saothar 33', Journal of the Irish Labour History Society, 2008

'Young, Derek, Ed., 'Mystery of the Limerick Soviet Notes', Irish Numismatics, No. 16, July/August 1970

Index